# SOCIAL AND CULTURAL HISTORY OF ANCIENT INDIA

## About the Author

**Prof. M.L. Bose** has been teaching in the Dibrugarh University for about thirty years and has contributed more than thirty papers in Regional and National Seminars and Journals of Repute. An Aurobindite Prof. Bose has guided many research scholars to produce Ph.D thesis. His earlier published works *Historical and Constitutional Documents of North East India*, 1979; *British Policy in the North-East Frontier Agency*, 1979; *Development of Administration in Assam*, 1985; *Social History of Assam*, 1989; *Social and Cultural History of Ancient India*, 1989, and *History of Arunachal Pradesh* were well received in the academic world.

# SOCIAL AND CULTURAL HISTORY OF ANCIENT INDIA

(Revised and Enlarged Edition)

M.L. BOSE
**Department of History**
**Dibrugarh University**
**Dibrugarh**
**Assam**

**CONCEPT PUBLISHING COMPANY, NEW DELHI - 110059**

ISBN 81-7022-598-1 (HB)

First Published 1992
Second Revised and Enlarged Edition 1998
Reprinted 2002



*Published and Printed by*
Ashok Kumar Mittal
**Concept Publishing Company**
A/15-16, Commercial Block, Mohan Garden
New Delhi-110059 (India)
*Phones:* 5648039, 5649024
*Fax:* 091–(11)–5648053
*E-mail:* publishing@conceptpub.com

*Rajumani Sharma*
*at whose solicitation writing*
*of the book was undertaken*

# Preface

The first edition of the book was exhausted within four years and as such it had become necessary to publish either a reprint or a second edition of the book, I thought it to be prudent to publish edited and enlarged edition of the book incorporating some more information and providing sanskrit rendering of the Sanskrit verses quoted in the book. Hence the enlarged and revised edition of the book.

**M.L. Bose**

# Contents


*Preface* 5

*List of Plates* 10

*Pronunciation of Sanskrit* 11

1. Introduction 13
2. Ethnic Composition and Foreign Elements in Indian History 21
3. Ancient Indian Society 32
4. Brahmachārya-Āśrama and Education in Ancient India 54
5. Gārhasthy-Āśrama, Vānaprastha and Sannyāsa 68
6. Marriage, Sex Relations and Status of Women 87
7. Spirituality, Religion and Philosophy 102
8. Language and Literature 128
9. Art 150
10. Living Conditions of the People 172
11. Conclusion 182

*Bibliography* 184

*Index* 187

# LIST OF PLATES

BETWEEN PAGES 153 - 160

1. Bhārhut (Satna-MP) Stūpa Great railing, western gate, corner pillar, top Panel, worship of Gautam's hair-lock Insc : Celebration of Lord's hair-lock in Sudharma, Assembly hall of Gods 2nd cent BC Sandstone Calcutta, Indian Museum No. 182, *Courtesy* : American Institute of Indian Studies, Vārāṇasī.

2. Sānchi (Raisen-MP) Stupa 1 Southern gateway, north side, superstructure, view from north *c* 1st BC Buff sandstone. *Courtesy* : American Institute of Indian Studies, Vārāṇasī.

3. Sānchi (Raisen-MP) Stūpa 1 General view from southeast, showing stūpa, southern gateway and temple 18 *c* 1st cent BC Brick core with stone casing and flagstone-buff stone for railings and gateways. *Courtesy*: American Institute of Indian Studies, Vārāṇasī.

4. Bhojpur (Raisen-MP) Śiva temple Garbhagṛha, doorway, doorsill, detail *c* 1050 AD Red sandstone. *Courtesy*: American Institute of Indian Studies, Vārāṇasī.

5. Bhubaneswar (Puri-Orissa) Parasuramesvara temple śikhārā from west Mid 7th cent Kalinga style Sandstone. *Courtesy* : American Institute of Indian Studies, Vārāṇasī.

6. Kumbhakonam (Thanjavur-Tamilnadu) Nāgesvarasvami temple Eastern outer gopurā, view from east *c* 13th cent Late Colanadu style Granita. *Courtesy* : American Institute of Indian Studies, Vārāṇasī.

7. Cave No. 21 (Rāmeswar) General views from south-west *c* 2nd half of 6th A.D. *Courtesy* : American Institute of Indian Studies, Vārāṇasī.

8. Ellòra (Aurangabad-Maharashtra) Cave 10, Viśvakarmā View of facade *c* first-half of 7th cent Deccan trap. *Courtesy* : American Institute of Indian Studies, Vārāṇasī.

# Pronunciation of Sanskrit

## Hints of Diacritical Marks for Pronunciation of Sanskrit Letters in English

| | | | | | |
|---|---|---|---|---|---|
| अ | stands for | a | ञ | stands for | ña |
| आ | | ā | ट | | ṭa |
| इ | | i | ठ | | ṭha |
| ई | | ī | ड | | ḍa |
| उ | | u | ढ | | ḍha |
| ऊ | | ū | ण | | ṇa |
| ऋ | | ṛ | त | | ta |
| ओ | | o | थ | | tha |
| औ | | au | द | | da |
| ं | | ṃ | ध | | dha |
| : | | ḥ | व | | va |
| ँ | | ṅ | श | | śa |
| ङ | | ṅa | ष | | sha |
| च | | cha | स | | sa |
| छ | | chha | | | |

# 1

# Introduction

It is, perhaps, necessary to put forward an apology to introduce a new title on *Social and Cultural History of Āncient India*, for over one hundred and fifty years hundreds of titles on Indian History, in all its aspects and covering regional histories of India, both on intensive and extensive scales, have been produced and are still being produced. Many of these no doubt are written, on sound historical basis, by individuals and groups of historians and institutions. Yet a new venture on the part of a modest teacher of history possibly demands an explanation.

What prompted me to undertake to write such a book is that as a teacher of Social and Economic History of Ancient India I felt embarrassed before the students for not being able to tell them the title of a sort of text-book by reading which they could form an idea as to what they ought to read from what text on social history. We usually tell them to read relevant chapters on social history provided in different volumes of *The History and Culture of Indian People Series* (edited by R.C. Majumdar and published by Bharatiya Vidya Bhavan) and the two volumes of *Comprehensive History of India*, published by Indian History Congress (Vol. II, edited by K.A. Nilakanta Sastri and Vol. III, edited by R.C. Majumdar and K.K. Dasgupta) and *The Wonder That Was India* by A.L. Basham. But these books are not only costly, voluminous and often inaccessible to the common run of students, they are also unwieldy and inadequate for the study of the society by the post-graduate students, particularly the topics like Varṇa-āśrama-Jāti, educational system and social institutions like marriage or sex relations, or the life of an individual, to mention only a few of the problems. In some books the items of information are scattered over periods on particular institutions which, for beginners, become difficult to correlate and form an idea of the total development in sequences and retrospect. Therefore, I thought of getting down all the materials available in books on social and cultural history and writing a sort of text-book for the study of social and cultural history of ancient India. Of course, the book does not lay any claim for presenting any fresh or hitherto unknown data, nor reinterpreting any established institution. What I have tried in this work is to put an account, in a proper historical perspective, of society and culture of ancient India so that its readers can get an opportunity to have a better access to original materials and gain an insight into their different aspects, particularly those which have not received elaborate treatment in the available books.

It may not be out of place if some words are said about the sources of this work apart from the well-accepted and authentic books. The picture of life of ancient India, of which we have no written history in the modern sense of the term, in its political, social, religious, literary and artistic aspects can be gleaned from various inscriptions, coins, artefacts and literary sources that have come down to us from ancient India. These sources of ancient Indian history can be conveniently divided into five categories, namely: inscriptions or epigraphic sources; coins or numismatic sources; archaeological data provided by monuments, buildings and artefacts laid bare by excavations; literary materials which include both secular and religious literature of ancient India; and foreign accounts.

Epigraphs or inscriptions issued by kings and other officials, and pious people or guilds, incised on either stones, pillars, copper-plates, images or temples, etc., provide ample data for political, social and cultural history. The decipherment of Asokan inscription by James Princep has revolutionised our knowledge of Mauryan society and culture. The Mandasore stone pillar inscription mentioning Kumaragupta I and Bandhuvarman (A.D. 436 and 473) shows how the guild activities of the Maurya period continued unabated through the political turmoils in the Classical period and throws light on their role in religious and social spheres. The Nayatakhi plate of Śilāditya I (A.D. 605) and the Valabhi grant of Dhruvasena III (A.D. 653-654) refer to the system of viṣṭi or forced labour as also a host of other inscriptions. The land grants of *Mahārāja* Pravarasena II, the Riddhapur plate of Vākāṭaka queen Prabhāvatīguptā, Khoh Copper Plate of *Mahārāja* Sarvanātha (A.D. 512) show how lands were donated for charitable purposes to pious people of various grades of society.

Similarly, the numismatic sources or coins throw important sidelight on social and cultural life of ancient India. Coins were struck in India in uniform manner from remote times for the first time by the Mauryas on an extensive scale, as evidenced by the availability of large number of silver punch marked coins. Among the foreigners, the *Kuṣāṇas* issued coins which bore the figure of the king in royal dress who struck the coin, the date of issue and also the deity worshipped by him. The Imperial Guptas continued the tradition and enlarged the currency systems. They issued gold, silver, copper and even mixed copper and silver coins which betray not only the skill of the artists and their aesthetic beauty but data on religion and culture of the Classical Age. Numismatic source provides information not only about the religious faiths and beliefs through the effigies of deities depicted on them, or about other items like polity and architecture, but also occasionally about ethnic affiliations of their issuers. For instance, a people of the Punjab called the Audumbaras, who flourished in the 5th century B.C.—2nd century A.D., have on a series of their coins the figure of the famous sage Viśvāmitra. Mythologically the birth of Viśvāmitra is attributed to an *udumbara* (fig) tree and thus this piece of evidence shows that these people had *udumbara* as their totem. Interestingly, a class of Brahmins called the Audumbaras in Gujarat now-a-days bear the Viśvāmitra-*gotra* and there are indications in the *Natural History of Pliny* that a section of the Audumbaras (mentioned there as *Odombeores*) settled in Gujarat.*

No less important are the archaeological finds. A careful examination of the extant buildings such as temples, stūpas and palaces and private dwellings, works of art like images, frescoes and host of articles used by contemporary people unearthed by the spade of the archaeologists throw fascinating glimpses into the social and cultural life of ancient India. The paintings of Ajaṇṭā, for example, acquaint us with the everyday life of the contemporary people of different stations belonging to different social strata. Here more vividly than at sāñchi we see panorama, princes in their palaces, ladies in their *harems*, labourers with their loads slung over their shoulders, beggars, peasants and ascetics, together with beasts, birds and flowers of India. The history of Indian art and religion cannot be understood properly unless they are studied in the background of various caves and temples with elaborate sculptures and paintings.

Next we have ample materials in Sanskrit, Pāli, Prākrit and Tamil literatures of India.

---

* VI. 75; See also K.K. Das Gupta, *A Tribal History of Ancient India: A Numismatic Approach*, Calcutta, 1974, pp. 39, 275.

Right from the *Ṛg Veda,* the earliest literary monument, down to the twelfth century A.D. notable regional historical works like the *Rājataraṅgiṇī* by Kalhaṇa and the dynastic chronicles like the *Ramacharita* of Sandhyākaranandī were produced. The data garnered from Sanskrit literature, one of our main sources, have been amply corroborated, supplemented and occasionally enriched by the materials culled from its sister literatures in Pāli and Prākrit.

The Vedas, though primarily religious and exegetic, give us a clear picture of the life of the Aryan people with their religion, literature and culture. Together with the Upanishads they lay the foundation of Indian religion and philosophy and social practices. The epics, particularly the *Mahābhārata,* give a total picture of Indian civilisation in all its aspects and for that it is said that what is not found in *Mahābhārata* is not to be found in *Bhārata*. The *Arthaśāstra* of Kauṭilya, primarily a work on polity, yields a mine of information relating to various aspects of the social and economic life of the Maurya period. Coming of the *Gṛhya-Sūtras, Smṛtis and Purāṇas* we get a codified picture of socio-cultural activities of the Indian people who were now united in a single society of the Hindus under a Sanskrit culture. The *Gṛhya-Sūtras* treat the numerous ceremonies applicable to the domestic life of a man and his family from birth to death. The *Dharma-Sāstras* or *Smṛtis* deal with these topics in a more analytical and systematic manner under three heads: *Āchāra* (rites), *Vyavahāra* (dealings) and *Prāyaścitta* (expiation). The important contents of them are the sources of *Dharma*, i.e., the Vedas, the *Smṛtis*, the time honoured practices of the great; the duties of the four varṇas; the various Saṁskāras or rites of men; duties of the king, e.g., taxation, ownership of properties, punishment of crimes, etc., different kinds of Śrāddhas; rules about food; duties of women and *niyoga* (levirate), sins and their expiation and penances and their conditions. The *Śrauta-Sūtras* detail the Vedic rites.

The kings of ancient India maintained official bards and chroniclers whose duty it was to record and keep up the annals of the State. The remote part of ancient Indian history is found in these works called the *Purāṇas*. The famous Sanskrit lexicon *Amarakośa* defines *Purāṇa* as a work which deals with five topics: *Sarga* or original creation of the universe from its natural cause; *Pratisarga* or dissolution and recreation of the world from its constituent elements in which it is merged at the close of each aeon; *Vaṁśa* or ancient geneologies of gods, demons and sages; *Manavantara* or fourteen cosmic cycles each of which is ruled over by a Manu, the first father of mankind; and *Vaṁśānucharita* (ancient geneologies of kings). Besides, this class of texts is replete with *ākhyānas* or tales, *upākhyānas* or anecdotes, *gāthās* or proverbial sayings current in ancient societies and sayings that had come down through ages. Originating possibly in the Vedic times, the *Purāṇas* passed into the hands of the *sūtas* or bards who used to carry this knowledge from place to place and recited in the places of assembly of sages and learned men. These were redacted in the Classical Age particularly when Brahmanism was revived. Great importance was attached to the *Purāṇas* as authoritative works on Hindu rites and ceremonies from second century A.D. onwards. Subject to corrections, whenever necessary, the *Purāṇas* provide us a faithful knowledge of ancient geography and political history of ancient dynasties together with the history of religion and culture of the ancient Hindus, Pargiter observes:

> "They *(Purāṇas)* give us history as handed down in tradition by men whose business it was to present the past."

Secular Sanskrit literature provide us ample data for the study of society and culture of India.* The Classical Sanskrit literature reflect contemporary life as widely as the murals of Ajantā caves. Kālidāsa's *Meghadutam* or Cloud Messenger gives to the cloud a guidance for its journey in which he describes the geography with its flora and fauna, and society and culture, completely and convincingly, though the main theme of the Kāvya is the charm of esotic which sublimates in the spiritual atmosphere of the temple of Māhākāla. In his *Ritusaṁhara* he unrolls the six seasons of the Hindu year. Dand in its *Dasakumaracharita* describes contemporary society, its society, festivals and culture of entire India of ancient times. The three dramas of Kālidāsa *Malavik-Agnimitram*, *Vikramarvasiyam* and *Abhijnāsa-kuntalam* throw much light on society, culture and literary developments of ancient India.

The history of the Tāmil literature goes back to hoary past; but the Tāmilians traces its beginning to 4200 B.C. The first period, however, begins with the literature of the Sangam Age which modern scholars place between 500 B.C.to A.D. 500. Its historical importance lies in the fact that it provides to us ample data of Tāmil history—of

---

* Sudraka's Mrihchhakatikam or Claycart is notable for its depiction of the city life and social conditions.

life in the town and the country side, shops and fields, temples and palaces, houses of common people, even the huts of the fishermen on coastal regions all are represented in it with rare economy of words. *Tirrukurāl* or *Kurāl* of Tiruvāllivār deals with three objectives of Tāmil life, viz. dharma, artha and kāma. The two epics *Silappādikāram* and *Manimekhali* are compared to *Rāmāyana* and *Mahābhārata* of Sanskrit literature; these throw a lot of information on the contemporary urban life and religion of the South. This Classical Tāmil literature provides evidence of blending of Aryan and Pre-Aryan as well.

The Pali works and *Jātaka* stories tell us a lot about society and culture of ancient India. Among the Pali works *Mīlindapañho (Milindapraśna)* or the conversation between the Greek king Menander and the Buddhist philosopher Nagasena is very important. It not only explains the religious doctrine of the Buddhists but supply quite a lot of data on educational and economic activities of the time. The *Jātaka* stories tell a lot of social, religious and cultural conditions of India in the pre-Christian era. Besides, the Pāli-Buddhist chronicles, like the *Dipavaṁsa* and the *Mahāvaṁsa*, are official histories of Sri Lanka composed about the fourth-fifth centuries A.D. Both the texts cast welcome light on the history of Buddhism in India and Ceylon.

The Prākrit works of the Jains also provide a lot of data on social and economic history. The canonical works are the only authentic history of Jain religion and monasticism and Jain way of life and culture. The Jain monks travelled extensively with the merchants throughout the country and wrote down about the local customs and culture. References to famine and religious festivals are available from these works.

The Classical Sanskrit literature provides ample data for the study of society and culture of India. Like the murals of Ajantā, the works of Kālidāsa and Daṇḍin reflect the contemporary geography, with its flora and fauna, and society, with its civilisation and culture, completely and convincingly.

Foreign sources of information of the ancient Indian history corroborate our evidences culled from the epigraphic numismatic, archaeological and literary sources. Some hearsay references recorded by the Greek and Roman historians, particularly the observations of Herodotus and Ktesias and the first-hand reports of the officers of the Greek army who invaded India in the train of Alexander (326 to 323 B.C.) give us their information on ancient India. These reports were later on considerably supplemented by the *Indica* of Megasthenes, the Greek ambassador sent by the Syrian emperor Selencus Nikator to the court of Chandragupta Maurya. The *Indica,* a valuable document on Maurya epoch, being lost, is not available in its entirety, but survives in the form of quotations in the writings of later classical writers like Quintus Curbius, Arrian, Phlegon, Strabo, Diodorus, etc. But the statements in the *Indica* equally suffer from some inherent defects. Of later times, two other important extant works are the *Periplus of the Erythraean Sea* written by an unknown Egyptian Greek sailor of the first century (more probably about A.D. 70-80) and *Geography* by Ptolemy composed around A.D. 140. Mention should also be made of Plny's *Natural History,* which was completed in A.D. 77.

Besides the Greeks, we have the first-hand diary records of the Chinese pilgrims who visited India purely on religious mission after the Buddha (*c.* 120 B.C. to A.D. 700). The first important Chinese monk to visit India was Fa-Hsian who entered into India about A.D. 399-400 through the north-west and after travelling many places in different parts of the country, during the reign of Chandragupta II of the Gupta dynasty, voyaged from Tamralipti (or modern Tumluk in the Midnapore district of West Bengal) via Sri Lanka and Sumatra to China in A.D. 414 His opinions very much highlight the glorious socio-economic condition of India during the Gupta period. The next two important scholarly travellers were Hiuen-Tsang and I-tsing. While the former visited India during the time of the Pushyabhūti ruler Harshavardhana (A.D. 606-647), the latter travelled the country from A.D. 671-695 and offer a portraiture on the condition of India towards the end of the 7th century A.D. More than sixty other Chinese pilgrims visited India in ancient times.

The foreign accounts provide, no doubt, first-hand and more or less impartial information collected by them during their travels. But it should be remembered that their knowledge about India was limited and in many cases they did not either understand or know the real Indian culture and state of affairs. Therefore, their reports should be accepted only after proper verification or corroboration by indigenous sources. We may mention here that Fa-Hsian who visited many parts of the Gangetic valley during the hey days of Brahmanism states that "throughout the whole country the people do not kill any living creature, do not drink intoxicating liquor, nor eat onions or garlic... . In buying and selling commodities they use *cowries*". But we know from the writings of Kālidāsa that wine drinking was a popular habit and the princes who went for hunting took meat. That there was a regular currency system in India during the Gupta period is shown by the archaeological discoveries. For instance, the observations of Megasthenes regarding Indian famine, caste system and slavery are also unacceptable in the light of the contemporary epigraphic records like the Mahāsthāngarh inscription (of the Mauryan period) and other literary sources.

Nevertheless, the accounts of the Chinese pilgrims regarding the social and economic conditions, educational institutions and religion are quite exhaustive, and from them we get a fair picture of the Buddhist vihars and universities at Nālandā, Odantapurī, Vikramśīlā, Sompur and other places.

It may very frankly be admitted that the present work is not the result of research based on the data found in the above sources alone. Rather, the write up is based on the *Foundations of Indian Culture* by Sri Aurobindo, A.L. Basham's *The Wonder That Was India*, his edited book—*A Cultural History of India*, Dr. Wm. Theodore de Bary's *Sources of Indian Tradition*, the *Cultural Heritage of India* in four volumes published by Sri Ramakrishna Mission, besides the three Bharatiya Vidya Bhavan volumes on ancient Indian History and R.C. Majumdar's book—*Ancient India*. I have also resorted to the book of Dr. S.K. Maity—*Economic History of Northern India during the Gupta Period*.

I have excluded the Indus valley civilisation from the purview of the present work not because it is unimportant and not a part of Indian civilisation but because I have written only on Historical period as my knowledge of pre-history and archaeology is very limited. History, as distinct from archaeology, is the study of the human past from written literary sources and as such the Historical period of India begins with the Aryans.

# 2

# Ethnic Composition and Foreign Elements in Indian History

The history of the origin of Man is not known for certain. It is usually believed that India had been from times immemorial peopled by immigrants.[1] But the prehistory of India, as evinced by archaeological excavations and finds thereof, suggests that civilisation had dawned in many places of the Indian subcontinent from the eastern coastal regions of Bengal and Orissa to the valley of the Indus and the Hindu-Kush in the north-west, through the Deccan Plateau to the eastern and western Ghats of South India. Traces of man before 100,000 years before Christ have been found in the Son valley and though no human remains have been found of this culture it is believed that India had primitive anthropoid types of Pithecanthropus of Java and China. The finds in the South of primitive man bear close resemblance to cave tool industries of Africa and western Europe. Paleolithic, Neolithic and Microlithic industries improving down the ages developed imperceptibly till we come across the civilisations of the Indus and the Ganga basins.[2]

K.M. Munshi writes "over five thousand years ago, aboriginal dwellers generally lived in forests; some of them, however, were slowly driven to the valleys before the pressure of more civilised immigrants".[3] Who are the people thus lived in India before the `civilised immigrants' entered into India are not known for certain. It has been asked why should India be always at the receiving end? Should not have some movements radiated out from India?[4]

We usually assume that the Indian people are an admixture of five ethnic-cultural groups—the Negroids, the Australoids, the Mongoloids, the Dravidians and the Nordic Aryans. All these are said to have come to Indian subcontinent from outside before the advent of the Islamic people from the middle east. We have not found so far any conclusive habitate used by early man, nor his skeletal remains, though the caves in Kurnool and Alicoor in South India do promise to provide some such evidence after the study and examination of these sites are completed.

The first people that came to India in pre-historic times are said to be Negrito or Negroid race in co-lith stage of their culture. They were characterised by short stature, dark skin, woolly hair and flat noses. From their original home in Africa they moved along the coast of Arabia and Iran and then across the north-western ranges came to settle in India. Their culture gradually spread over India and then passed on to the Āndāmāns and Malāy and then to the Islands of Indonesia, Philippines and New Guinea. Their survival is traced among the tribes of South India where they speak dialects of Tāmil and some traces are found in the Nāgās of Assam. But in Āndāmān islands they speak their original language. These people were later on absorbed by others who supplanted them. Sacredness attributed to trees and plants, ideas of life after death or permanence of soul are believed to have come down from the Negrito world of thought.[5]

The next race that came to live in India is said to be the Australoids who were in Neolithic stage of their culture. They are a medium-sized, long headed, snub-nosed and rather dark skinned people who are believed to have come from Palestine. These people were known in India as Nishādas, Khāsis, Nāgās, Kollas and Bhīllas in post-Christian times and characterised in India as Austrics. They spread all over India. Some of these people passed on to countries of East Asia; two main divisions of them are found there.[6] The Austro-Asiatics are a kindred of Indian-Austrics of Central India and Assam and are living in Burma, Siam, Cambodia, Cochin, China and Vietnam; the other branch known as Austronesians are the present Melanesians, Micronesians and Polynesians of Malāy. In the northern plains of India they have merged into Aryan speaking people and have lost their name and language. Ancient forms of Sāntali, Mundāri, Ho, Kurku, Gadaba, Śavara and of Khāsi dialects are said to be language of this race. The domestication of fowl, elephant, weaving of cotton, stick or hoe cultivation of rice and some plants and notion of future life later sublimated into the theory of transmigration of Soul and *Saṁsāra* are said to be contribution of these people to Indian civilisation.[7]

The third racial-cultural group of Indian society cosists of the tribes called Mongoloid who may be called Southern Mongoloids to distinguish them from the Mongolians of the North or the Great

Mongols that over-ran Turkistan, Mongolia and China and their leaders like Kublai Khan and Chenghis Khan drove the Southern Mongoloids from the places of their characterisation on the upper-waters of Yang-tse Kiang and Hwang-ho.[8] They were known in ancient India by the name *Kirāta*. These tribes in Neolithic stage of culture were habitating entire Himalayan region and their foothills as far down as Mohenjo-Daro and Rajasthan and some of them penetrated up to the Bastar district of Madhya Bharat, across the Vindhya range. They possess certain common characteristics: Yellow or yellow-brown skin, narrow or slant eyes, high cheek bones, flat nose and paucity of hair on the face. Their survivors are found all over north-eastern India. V.A. Smith observes that

> "Mongolian element in the population of northern India before and after the Christian era, I believe, is much larger than is admitted".[9]

Regarding their origin and immigration, Dr. S.K. Chatterjee wrote in *Kirāta-Jana-Kṛti* that they entered into India through the north-eastern ranges and Tibet simultaneously with the Aryan penetration into India through north-west. He had changed his view while delivering *Kamala Lectures* in Calcutta Univesity where he held that they might have come to settle in northern India before the Aryan people came to India; but regarding the route he did not change his view.[10] But it seems probable that they had followed the same route which the Aryans followed later and they had come from the Caspian Sea board to settle all over the north and central India long before the Aryan immigration.

The Neolithic people lived in caves and decorated their walls by painting the scenes of hunting and dancing. They cultivated land and grew fruits and corn. They produced fire by friction and made pottery first by hand and then by potter's wheel. They also painted and decorated their pottery. They constructed boats and went out to the sea. They buried their dead and sometimes put their deads in urns called *Dolmns* which consisted of three or more stone props in a circle supporting a massive roof of stone.[11]

The next language-cultural group that contributed to the making of Indian society is the Dravidian. They are regarded as a people of Mediterranean origin who had settled in Mesopotamia, Iraq and Iran before they came to India before 3500 B.C. Dr. S.K. Chatterjee opined that these people built up the urban culture of Mohenjo-Daro and Harappa and were living in India side by side with the Austrics and Mongoloids who were in rural stage of civilisation before the Aryan immigration.[12] Materials available for the study of early Dravidian institution are not yet sufficiently explored. An enthusiastic southern scholar has expressed the opinion that the scientific historian of India

> ". . . ought to begin his study with the basin of the Krisna, of the Cauvery, of the Vaigai, rather than with the Gangetic plain, as it has been now long, too long, the fashion."[13]

Dravidian speakers spread all over India, and were able to make their language and culture paramount throughout the whole of central India and to the south of the Vindhyan range. Place-names of Dravidian origin all over India suggest Dravidian and Austric as well as Sino-Tibetan elements.[14] But prehistoric forms of worship and many non-Aryan social practices survive in the peninsular region among the Dravidian people.[15] The most important of the non-Aryan elements of Indian civilisation is the Dravidian which constitutes not less than 50 per cent of Indian culture.

Then came the Indo-Aryans who were preceded by the Alpine people with their Nature Gods, their sacrifices, their cows and horses and their conquering zeal. They were a section of great Indo-Iranian branch of Indo-European family. The Aryans as the Indo-Europeans of India are called are believed to have left their homeland south of the Ural mountains and after their sojourns in Central Asia and Iran made way for India across the Hindu-Kush about 2000 B.C. The tribes of the Kurus, the Bharatas, the Śibis, the Madras were the some of the Aryans of the Vedic Age.[16]

The people of this Aryan family are in the main a tall, fair blond, blue eyed, straight nosed, curly haired and long headed—the Nordics. Some scholars hold that they included a shorter and round headed people among them—the Alpines—who were absorbed linguistically later by the first people. Two distinct ethnic groups thus constituted the Aryan family which provided Sanskrit language to forge composite Indian culture and civilisation.[17] The Aryans spread far and wide in the country. They opened up jungles, established large settlements and founded cities. Before the great Bharata war (*c.* 1500 B.C.), the Aryan tribes, ethnically mixed up, had already established powerful kingdoms. After the *Mahābhārata* war Bharata Yudhiṣṭhira was acclaimed as a *Chakravarti* in India.[18]

The ethnic intrusion, however, continued unabated till the entire length of ancient history. The Persians, the Greeks, the Parthians, the Scythians, the Hūṇas and the Gurjara-Pratihāras were some of the important tribes that poured into India after the great immigration of the Indo-European Aryans of Nordic and Alpine stocks and settled all over the country contributing to the building of Indian social fabric. In historic times the Persians of Aryan stock extended their sway over north-western India.[19] Some scholars hold on Avestan evidence that old Iran had obtained some hold on north-western India even before the Achaemenian period.[20] According to Herodotus, Indian possessions of Darius (*c.* 522-486 B.C.) formed the twentieth satrapy of his empire.[20A] The Persepolis inscription mentions both *Gadāra* (Gandhāra) and *Hi(n)du* (Sindhu) as provinces of the empire of Darius as also the Nakash-i-Rustam inscription.[21] The possibility of an influx of Persian population during the Persian rule over this area is just probable. A priestly class of Persians who entered into India at a later date is still known in India as *Magi-dvijas*.[22]

Macedonian king Alexander conquered north-western India in 327-325 B.C. and laid the foundation of cities of Alexandria sub-Causasum (modern Gharikar or Goian, near Kabul), Alexandria amongst the Arachosians (modern Kandhar), Bucephala and Nicaea (on the banks of the Jhelum), Sogdian Alexandria in northern Sind, etc., peopled partially by his Greek followers. The Greek element in the population of those cities remained conspicuous even after the conquest of these areas by Chandragupta Maurya.[23] Though the Aryan Brahmins denounced them as *Mlechchhas* they were honoured by the people as ṛshis.[24]

Indian literature refers to the exploits of the Bactrian Greeks who were branded as Yavana rulers. The *Yuga-Purāṇa* section of the *Gārgī-Saṁhitā* speaks of the expeditions of Sāketa near Ayodhyā in the present Faizabad district of U.P., Pañchāla (Rohilkhand in a narrow sense), Mathurā and Kusumadhvaja or Pushpapura (the same as Patliputra) by the Greek king Demetrius (*c.* 200 B.C.).[25] More than forty names of Bactrian and Indo-Greek rulers are known from their coins. They are assigned dates earlier than the establishment of the suzerainty of the Scytho-Parthians in north-western India.[26] Of these kings, Menander was the most prominent and his empire might have extended over areas comprising Kabul, Kathiawar, Rohilkhand, Kumaun and Kanauj regions. Besides, the Besnagar Garuḍa pillar inscription mentions the Greek ambassador Haliodorus who became a devotee of Vāsudeva *(Bhāgavata)* and was sent by the Greek Antialcides of north-west India to the Court of the Śuṇga king Kaśīputra Bhāgabhadra of M.P.[27]

The Scythians, known as Śakas in India, followed the Greeks and succeeded in occupying large tracts of territory in north-western India. The Chinese author, Ma-twan-lin, observes:

> "In ancient times the Hiung-nu defeated the Yuan-chi and the latter went to the west to dwell among the Ta-hia, and Yue-chi, the king of the *Sai* (The Śakas), went southward to live in Kipin. The nomenclature of the early Sakas in India shows an admixture of Scythian, Parthian and Iranian elements.[28] In India the Scythians soon adapted themselves to their new environs and began to adopt Indian names and religious beliefs. They are known to have contracted matrimonial relations with Indian families. It is, therefore, no wonder that by the time of Patanjali's *Mahābhāshya* the Śakas, like the Yavanas, were regarded as *anirvāsita* (clean) Śūdra."[29]

The Parthians had already conquered eastern Iran and adjoining parts of India under Mithradates I. Their struggle with the Scythians, in which two of their emperors lost their lives, relaxed their control over the remote provinces.[30] This led to the establishment of independent or semi-independent States of north-western India under governors of Parthian or Scythian or mixed Scytho-Parthian nationality from the first century B.C. The Chinese historian Fan-ye seems to refer to the Parthian conquest of Kabul before its occupation by the Kushāṇas about the middle of the first century A.D.[31] That even after Kushāṇa occupation of the north-west India Scytho-Parthian local rulers continued to rule, acknowledging the Kushāṇa hegemony in many places of north and west India, is borne out by inscriptions and Ptolemy's *Geography (Geographike Huphegesis)*.[32]

The Kushāṇas, a Yuch-chi-tribe of Central Asia, defeated and dispersed the Śakas or the Scytho-Parthians of Afghanistan and north-west India. They gradually penetrated down the valley of the Ganga and under the able and greatest leader Kaṇishka assumed imperial dignity. The reference to the Kushāṇas family as of Turushka or Turkish origin in the Kashmir chronicle is supported by a tradition as recorded by Alberuni.[33] According to this tradition the Hindus had kings residing in Kabul who were said to be Turks of Tibetan origin.

By the middle of the second half of the second century of the Christian era the Kushāṇa empire disintegrated. But Indian religion and social institutions assimilated these foreign tribes. The social pattern accepted as of divine origin persistently re-organised social groups; the orthodox cults, revivified by a resistance to heterodoxy, were active. In the end, social and religious tenacity developed a mighty absorbing power.[34]

The Guptas succeeded in establishing an empire comprising the whole of northern India. But before the total disintegration of their empire, the Hūṇas under Toramāṇa, over-ran north India up to Eraṇ in the Saugor district of Madhya Pradesh. His son Mihirakula became master of a vast territory. But the Hūṇas disappeared as they came, leaving their tribal population in India. "Within a few years of the death of Mihirakula, however, a new and vigorous impulse is also visible; an impulse to revive *Dharma*, to relate it to the new life, to fashion values to the new conditions, not only in the effected zones but in other parts of India as well".[35] The *Purāṇas*, some of which were redacted or newly written in the Gupta times, were the popular gospels of the new impulse. "They revived the glories of the distant past; they invested new places in the country with stimulating sanctity, weaving unity of Bharatavarsha."

The Rajputs of Rajasthan are said to be a people of Gurjar race who poured into India probably with the Hūṇas towards the close of the 5th century A.D. James Tod, the famous author of the *Annals and Antiquities of Rajasthan*, on the basis of the analysis of the analogies between the Scythians, the Rajputs and the tribes of Scandinavia concluded that the Rajputs were of Scythian origin.[36] The same theory of foreign origin of the Rajputs was established by R.G. Bhandarkar and Jackson. Their main settlements were to the west of the Aravalli hills which was known as Gurjaratrā, the earlier form of Gujarat, before it came to be known as Rajputana early in the Muslim period. When Harshavardhana founded his empire they were ruling over an independent kingdom. The ruling dynasty belonged to the Gurjara-Pratihāra clan. Prof. A.C. Banerjee in his book entitled *Aspects of Rajput State and Society* (New Delhi, 1983) states that "Gurjar population in the wide belt of territory from Peshawar in the north-west to Rohilkhand in the east, in Jammu and Kashmir, in the eastern districts of Madhya Pradesh and in Rajasthan is a good *prima facie* evidence of tribal migration from beyond the Khybar Pass".[37]

These people of Rajputana, yet of doubtful origin, claim themselves to be Hindu people of Aryan race and are stalwarts of Hinduism. They stood out as a bulwark of Hinduism during the medieval period when Islamic people and culture threatened the very existence of Hindu culture in north-west India.[38]

Foreign elements coming from different lands, which were informally and loosely drawn to Hindu ideas and Hindu way of life, were gradually made part of a growing Indian community.[39] The *Purāṇa* tradition which took time to establish itself has been a vital force in forging these diverse elements, provided, Indians a more or less consistent interpretation of their origin, past history and their present status in Indian society. Thus the *Nishādas* or Austric Kols and peoples or groups of mixed Nishāda origin, the Dāsa and Dasyu and Śūdra of Dravidian and other pre-Aryan origin, the Kirātas or other pure or mixed Mongoloid groups, and the Aryans who formed a large section of Hindu society—all these were lumped into one, within the organisation of Hindu society.[40]

The traditions were the same everywhere, and certain *Purāṇa* stories were to be found connected with various tracts of India and with diverse peoples of different origins. On the extreme north-eastern boundary of India, *Paraśurāma Kuṇḍa* is connected with the sage Bhṛgu. The same Paraśurāma is also connected with Mālābar on the south-western coast of India.[41] The Iksvākus of North India were established in the Deccan and the South, just as some Kārnātaka rulers established themselves in historical times in Mithila and Bengal.[42] The Tamil dynasties of the South claimed origin from the Pāṇḍavas of North India; the rulers of Tripura and Manipur claimed descent from the same Pāṇḍavas as Chandravaṁśia Kshatriyas.[43] Here in these *Purāṇa* traditions there is no racialism but only caste.[44]

For integrating these diverse racial elements into one single and homogeneous whole, contributions were taken over, as a matter of course, from the myths and legends of the pre-Aryan and non-Aryans in proportionate or even in greater proportion than those brought in by the Aryan people. In the old *Purāṇa* tradition there was a classification of important Kshatriya ruling houses into families of the Sun and the Moon *(Suryavaṁśa and Chandravaṁśa);* in later times foreign invaders who settled in India and became merged with the people got an almost equal status by their ruling houses being described as originating from Indra, the King of the Gods.[45] The rulers of the Ahom dynasty in Assam who established themselves in India in *c.* A.D. 1226[46] claimed to have descended from Indra; the nomadic tribes of Rajasthan, the Gurjara-Pratihāras, who are supposed to be originally from central Asia of Iranian-Turkish origin, believed to be the descendants of *Agni* or Fire God and were given the status of Kshatriyas during the first millennium A.D.[47] The immigrant Zoroastrians who introduced the new ritual of Sun worship in the early centuries by Christian era became a part of Hindu Society as *Maga* or *Śakadvīpiya* Brāhmaṇas.[48]

The modern science of history will not subscribe to the acceptance of the *Purāṇa* tradition *in toto* as truth. But this has to be understood as a factor in which these foreign elements, with their legends of caste and tribal origin, were forged for strengthening this racial and social synthesis. The truth and validity of the *Purāṇa* tradition was looked upon as something axiomatic in the consciousness of the entire Hindu people all over India and even when they are converted into other religion a good deal of these still remain in their mind.[49] It was quite effective through the centuries in establishing the conviction of the entire Hindu body-politic as being one, howsoever historical might have been its racial origins or antecedents. "Thanks to this *Purana* tradition we find that a Gorkhā or a Meithei of Mongoloid origin, a Jat and a Reddi, a Maharashtra Prabaly and an Assam Kalita and a Kashmiri Brahman considered to be a pure Aryan, a Bengali Brahman and a Brahman from Rajasthan who in language and race look upon themselves as members of a single people."[50]

The Indian people and culture are composite. The Indian people is a mixed people, in blood, in speech and in culture. Taking apart certain extreme Indian types like the pure-blooded Kashmiri Brahmans, Mongoloid Garos or Nāgās and Austric Santal or Kols, we may say that a common Indian type, a common Indian man has evolved on the soil of India.[51] This is largely due to racial and ethnic fusion which was thorough in northern India. No part of India, however, was free from this fusion. Constant streams of people from the north were going to the extreme east to the valley of the Brahmaputra across the hills to Manipur, Tripura, carrying with them Sanskrit culture. They were going to the Deccan and South India, as soldiers, adventurers, merchants, preachers and were merging themselves into the existing population. The people from the South like the Dravidians and Austrics, like some Tamil, Andhra and Kannada tribes, were also moving about the settling in northern territory of India. The result is the Indian Man.

Now we have as Indian type—a brown man, pale or dark either individually or in groups; he is not pure white as the Aryan was, or pure yellow like the Kirāta, or black like Nishāda. He is generally medium in height and of slender built, rather than very tall and muscular and in his features he is usually pleasing, if not conspicuously handsome, with an atmosphere of intelligence about him. Dressed in same kind of garb and bereft of distinguishing marks like special ways of doing hair, beard, moustache, etc., the average Indian type whether in upper classes or in the middle or lower will be ordinarily difficult to locate in a particular area.[52]

Thus India had been peopled by immigrants from times immemorial. The immigrants slowly mingled. Inter-marriage led to a free admixture of blood and prevented an impassable cleavage of cultural ideas. A vital movement in the social organisation of the country enabled one little connubial group, which did not originally form part of the Aryanised society while undergoing the necessary cultural discipline, to rise from a lower to a higher status, to the Aryanised class.[53] The racial miscegenation and hegemony of Aryan language among them, the diverse racial and ethnic groups were knit together. A mass of tradition, of mythological and historical origin, was fused to build up Itihāsa and *Purāṇas* in which every element subscribed. The Hindus and Hinduism are the results of these racial migration and fusion.[54]

## REFERENCES

1. H.D. Sankalia, *Pre-history and Proto-history in India and Pakistan*, p.1.
2. V. Smith, *Oxford History of India*, pp. 22-23.
3. R.C. Majumdar (ed.), *The Age of Imperial Unity*, p. VIII.
4. H.D. Sankalia, *op. cit.*, p.1.
5. *Ibid.*
6. *Ibid.*
7. *Ibid.*
8. M.L. Bose, *British Policy in the North-East Frontier Agency*, pp. 14-19.
9. V. Smith, *op. cit.*
10. S.K. Chatterjee, *Kamala Lectures*, p. 131.
11. *Ibid.*
12. *Ibid.*
13. V. Smith, *op. cit.*, p. 8.
14. S.K. Chatterjee, *op. cit.*, pp. 132-34.
15. *Ibid.*
16. *Ibid.*, pp. 135-37.

17. *Ibid.*
18. *Ibid.*
19. Mrs. Debala Mitra, 'Foreign Elements in Indian Population', *The Cultural Heritage of India*, Vol. II, pp. 610-26.
20. R.C. Majumdar, *Ancient India*, pp. 119-26.

20A. III. 94.

21. R.C. Majumdar, *Ancient India*, pp. 119-26.
22. R.C. Majumdar, *Ancient India*, pp. 119-26.
23. *Ibid.*
24. R.C. Majumdar (ed.), *The Age of Imperial Unity*, p. 102.
25. *Ibid.*
26. *Ibid.*
27. *Ibid.*, pp. 111-12.
28. *Ibid.*, pp. 120-35.
29. *Ibid.*
30. *Ibid.*, p. 123.
31. *Ibid.*, p. 135.
32. *Ibid.*
33. *Ibid.*, pp. 136-53.
34. *Ibid.*, p. XVIII.
35. R.C. Majumdar (ed.), *The Classical Age* (henceforth CA.) p. XX.
36. A.C. Banerjee, *Aspects of Rajput State and Society*, pp. 3-8.
37. *Ibid.*
38. *Ibid.*
39. S.K. Chatterjee, *op. cit.*, p. 138.
40. *Ibid.*
41. *Ibid.*, pp. 91-98.
42. *Ibid.*
43. *Ibid.*
44. *Ibid.*
45. *Ibid.*
46. *Ibid.*
47. *Ibid.*
48. *Ibid.*
49. *Ibid.*, p. 97.
50. *Ibid.*
51. *Ibid.*
52. *Ibid.*
53. R.C. Majumdar (ed.), CA., p. XXIV.
54. P. Thomas, *Hindu Religion, Customs and Manners*, p. 3.

# 3

# Ancient Indian Society

We have found that the Indian society consisted of diverse ethnic and linguistic elements; but they had a common basis of life, that of realistic idealism. "Indian people had evolved a basic system of individual life in the social framework to pursue the Truth and live upon the idea of Dharma long before the birth of the Buddha and Mahāvīra Jain".[1] "This was double system of the four *Varṇa* and four *Āśramas* or four graded classes of society and four successive stages of developing human life." The idea was that man fell by his nature into four types and by living in four successive stages he could attain perfection, or liberation or *Mukti* or *Moksha* or *Nirvāṇa*.[2]

There were: first and highest, the man of learning and thought and knowledge; next the man of powers and action, ruler, warrior, leader, administrator; third in the scale, the economic man, producer and wealth-getter, the merchant, artisan, cultivator, these were the twice-born who received initiation, *Brāhmaṇa*, *Kshatriya* and *Vaiśya*; last came the more undeveloped human type, not yet fit for these steps of the scale, unintellectual, without force, incapable of creation or intelligent production, the man fit for only unskilled labour and menial service, the *Śūdra*.[3] Manu emphatically asserts that there cannot exist a fifth *varṇa* though there can be some sub-divisions of a *Varṇa*.[4] The same idea is echoed in *Śrīmat Bhagavad Gītā* where the lord states:[5] चातुर्वर्ण मया सृष्टं गुणकर्म विभागश (I have created four orders on the basis of *Guṇa* and *Karma* i.e. quality and work). This recognition that men are not the same, and that there is a hierarchy of classes, each with its separate duties and distinctive ways of life was the fundamental basis of Indian society.

The Indo-Aryans had divided themselves into three classes of the Brāhmaṇas, Kshatriyas and Vaiśyas like their brethren elsewhere. This is apparent for the famous *Purusha-sūkta* of the *Ṛg Veda*, which, while referring to four *varṇas* or castes in the Aryan society, explains how the Brāhmaṇas emanated from the mouth of the Primeval Puruṣha, the Rājanyas or Kshatriyas from the breast, the Vaiśyas from the thighs and the Śūdras from the feet. But since the *Puruṣha-sūkta* occurs in the tenth-maṇḍala (believed to be a later interpolation), it has been opined that the Śudras entered into the Aryan caste system at a later date. The *Gītā*[6] stated that the qualities of the first class, of the Brāhmaṇas, are: शमो दमस्तपः शौचं क्षान्तिरार्जदमेव च ज्ञानं विज्ञानमास्तिभ्यं ब्रह्मकर्म स्वभावजम।। (Natural propensity of *Brāhman* is control over inner and outer senses, forgiveness, simplicity, persuit of knowledge and wisdom of the *sastras* and the *Brahman*). Manu echoes the same ideal when he lays down that the duty of a Brāhmaṇa is to study, to teach, to officiate in sacrifice and to take alms and receive gifts.[7] The term Brahmana, however, meant originally one who possessed the Brahma in him. A person undergoing necessary Saṁskāras became a sishṭa (refined chaste). He had studied the whole of the Vedas together with the supplementaries and other supplementary literature and had thus developed an irreproachable character, who was free from desire and whose acts were not prompted by any worldly motive. "With the holy Vedic rites the sanctifying acts which purify the body are to be done; by oblations the impurities of the seed and the uterus are wiped off; and by the rites of initiation and the austerities connected with the study of the Vedas, oblations and other sacrificial acts, the body undergoes a spiritual transformation; he becomes capable of realising and holding the Brahma in him."[8]

Usually the Brāhmaṇa lived under the patronage of a chief or king (*rājan*), on the grant of tax-free land cultivated by his pupils or hired labour or the farmers who paid taxes to him instead of the king.[9] Nāyaṇikā, wife of the Sātavāhana king Śātakarṇi I, donated a village as a gift in an Aśvamedha sacrifice in the first century B.C.[10] The Chamak plate of Pravarasena II and many other inscriptions mention that villages were donated to Brāhmaṇas.[11] These Brāhmaṇas who received land grants with the right to govern the villages in course of time became landed-gentry who held tenants, slaves on their estates and were little different from their Kshatriya or Vaiśya counterparts.[12] Buddhist sources show that there were two types of Brāhmaṇas. There were learned Brāhmaṇas who performed Vedic rites and received great respect. But there were also ordinary Brāhmaṇas who made their living by fortune-telling and magic, who were less honoured.[13] In fact, the professional Brāhmaṇas, who were later called priests, were of various types and classes. The sacrificial ritual required a number of priests with specialised duties, invokers (*hotṛ*), cantors (*udgātṛ*) and priest who performed manual operations of the ceremony (*adhvaryu*).[14]

Megasthenes divides the Brahmanas into two classes:[15] '*Brahmanes* and *Sramanes*'. He states that the life of a Brāhmaṇa was divided into two stages. In the first phase of 37 years he lives in a groove, abstains from animal food or luxuries and sexual life and acquires knowledge. In the next phase he becomes a family-holder and marries as many wives as he can manage and takes non-vegetarian food and lives a luxurious living. The other class of the Brāhmaṇas whom he calls Śramaṇas lives the life of householder and possesses no property, must have been the ascetics of all denominations who live the life of *parivrājakas*.

The different religious ceremonies and social sacraments of ancient India could not provide livelihood to all Brāhmaṇas.[16] Therefore, they had to fall back on other professions. The *Smṛti* works provide that when a person cannot earn a living by his own *varṇa* profession he may legitimately earn a living by other professions.[17] So the Brāhmaṇas could pursue trades and professions. Of course, a Brāhmaṇa is forbidden to trade in certain commodities like animals, slaves, liquor, weapons and money-lending. Generally agriculture was disfavoured, probably it inflicted injury on insects and animals.[18] Megasthenes observes that there were Brāhmaṇa physicians. Many were employed in government services, either as administrators or advisers who often turned into rulers; Chāṇakya, for example, was the prime minister of Chandragupta Maurya.[19] But the Brāhmaṇas engaged in secular professions commanded less respect than those engaged in *varṇa* profession. Chārudatta, the poor Brāhmaṇa hero of the play *Mṛchhakaṭikā*, received scurvy treatment at the hands of the court, probably because he was a Brāhmaṇa by birth only.[20]

The second class was a ruling one who were called Rājanya in the Vedic period and Kshatriya in later period. Theoretically their duty was protection of the country and the people, which included fighting in war and governing in peace. The *Gitā* says: शौर्यं तेजो धृतिदाक्ष्यं युद्धे चाप्यपलायनम्। दानमीश्वरमावश्च क्षात्रं कर्म स्वभावजम्।।[21] (Characteristics of a *Ksatriya* is prowess, dignity, fortitude, skill, presenting an undaunted front in battle, charity, lordliness, and non-attachment to worldly pleasures.) The characteristics of this class of people was prowess, dignity, fortitude, skill, presenting an undaunted front in the battle, charity and lordliness but must be a man of restraint without attachment to worldly pleasures.[22] He had to undergo the same Vedic

Saṁskāras and discipline as the Brāhmaṇa.[23] He was verily a divine representative. 'Devānāṁpiya Piyadassi' as Aśoka styled himself, the guarantor of Dharma on whose administration the world depended. To uphold Dharma the king devised a bureaucracy. "Whatever a king does for the protection of his subjects, by right of his kingly power and for the best of mankind is valid. . . . As, a husband should always be respected by his wife, a monarch should always be respected by his subjects, even though he should be a bad ruler.[24] He should shower benefits like Indra who showers rain; he should extract taxes like the Sun sucks up moisture; he is to penetrate everywhere with his spies like the wind, with *daṇḍa* he is to control all his subjects like Yama; he must punish the wicked like Varuṇa who binds the sinners with rope; he is to gladden his subjects by shining upon them as full-moon gladdens men; he is to visit criminals with his anger and destroy wicked subordinates as fire burns all; and he is to support his subjects as the earth supports all creatures."[25]

In fact, the class of Kshatriyas was of mixed origin. In the early Vedic period the Kshatriya might be of Aryan stock. Later on people of various races of foreign origin like the Greeks, Scythians, Parthians, Gurjaras and Mongolians were elevated to the ranks of Kshatriyas when they adopted Aryan way of life and performed appropriate penitential sacrifices called *Vrātyoshṭama* because they had become degraded by neglect of the Vedas and Brāhmaṇas.[26]

All the Kshatriyas were not necessarily kings; there were many who were employed in the administration and army. They had much land which might have been worked by hired labour or tenants and thus held the rank of landed-gentry or zamindars.[27] The *Arthaśāstra* of Kautilya mentions grant of lands in payment of services to the State. The Kshatriyas, however, claimed and received certain privileges. They did not always conform to orthodox way of life and could marry by capture and *svayamvara*. The rules of *Āpaddharma* applied to them also; when unable to eke living in government they took to business and crafts. Many Kshatriyas are referred to in literature as influential prosperous merchants and craftsmen.[28]

To the third category of the Vaiśya belonged the general mass of the Aryan people. They formed the economic base of the society; they were the producers and wealth-getters who upheld the social structure providing them necessities of living: कृषिगौरक्ष्यवाणिज्यं वैश्यकर्म स्वभावजम्। says the *Gītā*.[29] (*Vaisya* is prone to agriculture, cattle-rearing, and business or economic enterprise.) This class evidently originated in the ordinary peasant tribesman of the *Ṛg Veda*. They were entitled to *Saṁskāras* and Vedic studies.[30]

The Brāhmaṇic literature depicts Vaiśya as a wretched and downtrodden cultivator or petty merchant, a poor third to the Brāhmaṇas and Kshatriyas, who was of no interest to them except as a source of profit.[31] But as the political horizon began to widen, urban centres grew up, the importance of agriculture was recognised. New areas were brought under cultivation. The farmer was given all sorts of protection and due respect for his profession.[32] With the development of trade both in-land and overseas, industry, mines, forestry, commerce got much attention. Vaiśyas, sub-divided into castes, took to craft and industry which were now reorganised under the guilds.[33] By the end of the fourth century B.C. artisan and merchant guilds were an established part of the urban pattern. Guilds of merchants and craftsmen endowed gifts on monasteries or educational institutions, constructed or repaired temples, as is known from the Mandasor inscription of Kumāragupta I and Bandhuvarman wherein it is stated that a guild of silk-weavers constructed a magnificent temple of the Sun-god in the year 437-38 B.C. and repaired it again in A.D. 473-74. Guild leaders seem to have become powerful citizens.[34]

An ideal Vaiśya was not the oppressed tax-paying cattle-breeder or farmer, he was *aśitikoṭivibhava*, the man possessing eight million panas. They gradually formed a true bourgeoisie who were prosperous and influential and enjoyed the favour and confidence of the kings.[35] In *Mudrārākshasa* shows, hero Chaṇakya was anxious to enlist the support of Rakshasa for his sovereign.[36] Numerous inscriptions record great donations by wealthy Vaiśya merchants and pious farmers for charitable and religious purposes.[37]

The Aryan community was enlarged by the addition of non-Aryan people in their society. These were originally the war captives or conquered people, condemned to manual labour. He was the Śūdra—"the servant of another, to be expelled at will, to be slain at will". परिचर्यात्मकं कर्म शूद्रस्यापि स्वभावजम् says the *Gītā*.[38] (Sudra's natural quality is servitude.) They were not entitled to initiation and study of the Vedas was forbidden to them.[39] They were *eka-jāti* (meaning thereby that they had no sacramental birth but if they so desired could follow in the footsteps of the *dvijas* and do certain rites including the five daily sacrifices or *yajñas* without *mantra*.[40]

The word Śūdra is of doubtful origin. It was perhaps the name of a non-Aryan tribe which succumbed to the Aryan conquerors.[41] Nishādas, Ābhiras, Pukkasas and people of certain territories like Magadha were included in Śūdra varṇa by Manu.[42] There is every possibility that as the rigidity of Brāhmaṇa observances increased, groups which could not conform to Aryan norms and clung to old practices which were no longer respectable were relegated to the rank of the Śūdras along with the non-Aryan tribes and groups which accepted Aryan culture.[43] Persons born illegitimately, even when of high class-blood, were condemned to Śūdra class. In the Aitereya Brāhamaṇa the Andhras, Pāndavas, Śabaras, Pulindas and Mūtibas are said to be sons of Viśvāmitra. Patañjali and Manu assign to them the status of apostate Kshatriya.[44]

Śūdras were of two kinds: *aniravāsita* and *niravāsita* or excluded and non-excluded.[45] Those not excluded waited on the other three classes. They were to eat the remnants of their master's food, wear his cast-off clothing, and use his old furniture. Those excluded were virtually undistinguishable from the untouchables. The distinction was made on the basis of the customs and professions followed by them.[46]

The law-books provide very little hope to the Śūdra whose salvation lay only in the services to the upper three classes of the society and hope for re-birth in higher social class. Yet the Śūdra had a place of sorts in the Hindu fold, and was encouraged to imitate the customs of the higher classes. Though the Vedas were closed to them, the Epics and *Purāṇas* were open to them and they had a part in the devotional religion which in post-Maurya times eclipsed older Vedic religious practices.[47] Theoretically Buddhism and Jainism made no distinction of *Varṇa* in religious affairs. Śūdra kings were not unknown and mention is made of the Śūdras engaged in manufacture and commerce. By the time of the Mauryas, the Śūdras gained the status of free peasants.[48]

In the South, the *Varṇa* institutions received scanty recognition. The early Tamil literature does not mention the *Chatur-Varṇa* institution.[49] After the growth of Aryan influence by the Chola period, south Indian social structure assumed its present form. Kshatriya and Vaiśyas were rare, the whole population being divided into Brāhmaṇa and Śūdra *Varṇas*.

The four-fold division of the Brāhmaṇical society into four *Varṇas* was given a sacrosanct character by citing the *Ṛg-Vedic* hymn of the tenth maṇḍala of *Purusha-sūkta*[50] which is echoed in the *Purānas*[51] and *Smṛtis*[52] where it is stated that Brahmā created the Brāhmaṇa,

Kshatriya, Vaiśya and Śūdra out of his mouth, arms, navel and legs respectively. Birth, however, was not the sole test of *Varṇa*, though it was accepted as a gross natural indicator. The Aryans did not follow any rigid class distinction to start with. The intellectual capacity of man, the turn of his temperament, his ethical nature, his spiritual stature were equally important in selecting one's place in the *Varṇa* system. Viśvāmitra, a Kshatriya, by performance and piety, became a Brāhmaṇa and a seer (*rshi*) to boot.[53] The episode of Kavasha and Īlūsha in the Aitareya Brāhmaṇa is a further example of this social mobility.[54] Besides, non-Aryan tribes and social classes whose customs and occupations were like the Aryans of corresponding classes were called Vrātyas. Though assimilated in principle to the Śūdra they were eligible to admission into upper *Varṇa* an Brāhmaṇa, Kshatriya and Vaisya. As S.K. Chatterjee has observed "*Varṇa's* skin colour, white or yellow or brown or black, was the basis of the division of diverse types of humanity in the first period when white Aryan and brown Dāsa, yellow Kirāta and black Nishāda stood face to face with each other." But gradually economic aspect rose superior to the racial, the social to the biological.[55]

**Jati or Caste System**

A confusion arises in explaining the Hindu social system by mistranslating the terms *Varṇa* and *Jāti* as 'Caste' in English; in fact, there is clear distinction between *Jāti* and *Varṇa*.[56] It is now clear that *Varṇa* meant a class which is distinct from *Jāti* which may be translated into English as Caste.[57] The hereditary character of the *Varṇa* is clinched by the use of the word *Jāti* as synonym of *Varṇa*.[58] The term *Jāti* signifies birth. Non-Aryan tribes of various social grades were incorporated in the then Aryan society, retaining their tribal systems but largely conforming to Aryan culture and performing *Vrātyashṭoma* sacrifice were given a place in the *chatur-varṇa* system.[59] Their social behaviour and characteristics depended on their birth and the several tribes with their tribal customs of connubium and commensality crystallised into castes. Besides, the offspring of hypergamous (*anuloma*) and hypogamous marriage began to be degraded and formed distinct classes within the *Varṇa* System.[60] These sub-classes within the classes were also termed *'Jātis'*. Thus the chaṇḍālas who formed a distinct *Jāti* were believed to have descended from marriages between Śūdra male and Brāhmaṇa female.[61] The Sūtas or Charioteers were believed to have come from the marriage of Kshatriya father and Brāhmaṇa mother.[62] The Māgadhas or the bards were regarded as descendants of Vaiśya father and Kshatriya mother.[63] It is difficult to accept the view that these *Jātis* or Castes originated from *Pratiloma* marriage. Possibly these were non-Indian tribes who were segregated from the rest of the society though Manu assigned to them Śūdra-*Varṇa*. These *Jātis* hardened their class distinctions by rules of endogamy, commensality and craft-exclusiveness.[64]

The term 'caste' is derived from the Portuguese word *Casta* which means good-breed. When the Portuguese came to India they began to apply the term indiscriminately to the groups, tribes and classes in which they found the Indian society divided, irrespective of their *Verṇa* and *Jāti*.[65] The practice was adopted by the English when they undertook census operation; more than 3000 different social groups were termed as Caste in substitution of the term *Varṇa*.

The confusion of the foreigners in understanding the Indian caste systems is exemplified in the observations of Megasthenes who had lived for considerable time in the court of Chandragupta Maurya.[66] He observes that the population of India was divided into seven castes, namely, Philosophers, Husbandsmen or Herdsmen, Artisans, Military, Overseers or Spies and Councellors and Assessors. He further adds that "no one is allowed to marry out of his own caste or to exchange one's profession or trade for another or to follow more than one business." This leaves no room for doubt that Megasthenes confused caste with professions and occupations.

The first class or caste mentioned by Megasthenes is Philosophers who, he says, were divided into two classes, viz., Brāhmaṇas and Śramaṇas. The distinguished among the Brāhmaṇas whom he called *Hyloboi* lived an ascetic life in the woods, where they subsisted on leaves of trees and wild fruits, and wore garments made from the bark of the trees. Another class of them were physicians who lived in society and obtained their food, consisting of rice and barley-meal, from householders for the mere asking.[67]

This is an utter confusion. The Śramaṇas were undoubtedly the Buddhist and Jain monks who came from different *Varṇa* and *Jāti*, as were the *Hyloboi* or ascetics who were Hindu. The physicians might be a separate caste like the Vaidyas who were supposed to have been the offspring of Brāhmaṇa father and Śūdra mother. Herdsmen and Husbandsmen were definitely Vaiśyas who belonged to the same *Varṇa* but who are now divided into separate castes of peasants and milkmen.

But the Artisans, Military, Overseers and Councellors and Assessors must have come from different *Verṇas*, cannot be doubted. Chandragupta's prime minister Vishṇugupta himself was a Brāhmaṇa even though usually the administrative jobs were almost a monopoly of the Kshatriyas. It seems to be clear that what Megasthenes described was the professional sub-divisions of Indian society which were becoming, by and large, hereditary but he failed to distinguish *Varṇa* or classes which were observed by Hiuen-Tsang in the seventh century.

Dr. (Mrs.) Iravati Karve has described the caste anthropology in the following manner:

> "A clan is a group of families all tracing their descent to a distant common ancestor. Such a clan is always exogamous and has an appellation which is sometimes used as a surname by the people, who belong to that clan. . . . Exogamous unit is *gotra*.[68] Members of one *gotra* trace their descent from a mythological sage whose name is given to the *gotra*. Such exogamous clans are included in a bigger endogamous unit called popularly caste or sub-caste. So all members of the caste are related to each other by marriage or blood. The caste is inclusive of the clans which in their turn include several joint families. While the latter two groups are exogamous, the caste is endogamous.[69]
>
> Caste, however, has another aspect. Its function towards other groups is one of negative aloofness and self-preservation, but towards its own members it is almost a universe. A person is born as a member of his caste, and his life's vocation, the skill he leaves, the food he will eat and the conduct he will follow are determined by this one fact."

Without bothering about the analysis and definition of the caste it can be stated that historically speaking caste is of various origins. It is sometimes purely racial, sometimes inter-racial, largely economical, and frequently occupational and professional and occasionally religious too.

Below the Śūdras or untouchables existed groups of people who were looked upon as quite outside the pale of Aryandom. They served the society in very menial and dirty tasks. They were the untouchables who were called fifth class or *pañchama*; but the term *pañchama* was not usually accepted as if to insist that they were to be excluded from the Aryan society altogether. These were the Chaṇḍāla, Nishāda,

Kaivarta, Vena, Karavara, Pukkasa, Rathakāras, etc. Some of these were probably of non-Aryan origin but few seem to be of mixed origin.[70]

The untouchables were not allowed to live in an Aryan village or town but had to dwell in quarters outside the boundaries. No person of higher *Varṇa* was to have but distant relations with them on pain of losing his religious purity and falling to Chaṇḍāla's level.[71] In the Gupta period the Chaṇḍālas had become so strictly untouchable that they had to strike a wooden clapper on entering a town to announce their polluting approach and the practice continued to modern times in the South.[72]

The term Chaṇḍāla was applied to many groups and they followed many types of avocations. But the chief profession of the Chaṇḍāla was carrying and cremation of corpses and execution of the criminals.[73] The Pukkusas or the Paulkasas as referred to by the Buddhists were originally sweepers who took to selling of spirituous liquor.[74] Nishada was a hunter and Kaivarta was a fisherman. The Karavara lived on leather works and Vena made baskets. The Rathakāras, who were respectables in early Vedic times, fell to the status of untouchables in later times.[75]

The outcastes could not take part in religious festivals and access to temples was denied to them. They received no initiation and it was considered evil to allow them to grow numerous and powerful.[76] But it was said if an untouchable died for saving a Brāhmaṇa, women or children or cow he would secure a place in the heaven.[77] The Buddhists and the Jains preached among them and some wandering ascetics also provided initiations to them.[78]

To the class of untouchables may be placed the foreign hordes who poured into India and settled outside the pale of Aryandom. They were usually termed *mlecchas* or *yavana*. Living in India for considerable time and adopting Aryan social practices and culture, in course of time, the whole tribe was accorded a place within the *Varṇa* organisation and sometimes the badge of inferiority or the ban of untouchability was removed.[79] Such was the case with many ruling dynasties of Rajputānā.

## Family Life

The basic unit of the social structure, however, was the family. Usually it was joint family headed by senior male member of the house, usually the father. Ancient Indian family included parents, children, grand-children, uncles and descendants and other collaterals on the male-side. Besides, there might be adopted children, domestic servants, slaves, even students in Brāhmaṇa families. Like the European and Semitic family it was patriarchal and patrilineal, that is, the father was the administrator of the family and joint properties and property descended through the males.[80] Hindu tradition relates that before the time of Manu, the great law-giver, inheritance in property and succession to office succeeded to the eldest son. Manu provided for division of property among all sons.[81] The right of the father was absolute and unquestionable over his wife and children as is seen in the Epic age where father could even sell his children and wife. The Greek writers refer to the sale of slaves; the episode of king Hariśchandra and that of Nachiketā in *Kaṭha-Upanishad* show the absolute right of the father over children.[82] The same practice came down to the British times.

In property matters, rules of succession differed. There were two schools of law which have come down to the present times, viz., *Mitākshara* and *Dāyabhāga*.[83] According to the former school father or *pater-familiea* was the steward of the property. He could dispose of the property and if he died property succeeded to his sons who would divide that equally among them, the eldest son, having no special claim, could get a little consideration amounting to twentieth part of the share. The latter system provides that sons and grandsons had right in the family property even during the lifetime of the father who was very little more than a manager and trustee of the property. Only in *Mitākshara* system the wife could inherit the property in case there was no son;[84] but the other school provides that the property would pass into the hands of the collaterals.

On the death of the father the sons might be separated and set up separate households of their own, sharing the ancestral property. They usually remained united in the bond of *Śrāddha* ceremony, the rite of commemorating the dead ancestors when *piṇḍa* was offered. *Sapiṇḍas* of sons, grandsons and great-grandsons joined on the occasion to get the benefit of blessings of their ancestors.[85] In distress a member of this larger family of *sapiṇḍas* could look to others for succour and support.[86]

## Gotra and Pravara

The *Varṇa* and family were linked loosely by the two more institutions of *gotra* and *pravara*. In *Atharva Veda* where the word *gotra* first seems to appear meant a clan.[87] The meaning has been retained to some extent with a special connotation. Some Indo-European peoples such as the Romans had exogenous clans but endogenous tribes. Indian *gotra* and *pravara* institutions may be survivals of these original tribal systems with special Indian features. It is generally believed that all Brāhmaṇas have descended from the *ṛshis* or legendary seers, after whom the *gotras* were named. Religious literature generally speaks of eight such seers or *ṛshis* namely, Kaśyapa, Vaśiṣhṭha, Bhṛgu, Gautama, Bhāradvāja, Atri, Viśvāmitra and Agastya.[88] The last mentioned sage is believed to have taken Aryan culture beyond the Vindhyas and his disciples and descendants are found by and large in the South among the Dravidians. It is surmised that originally there were seven such clans or *gotras* in the North and an eighth seer was added to the list of founders of *gotras* when the Dravidians in South was Aryanised. However, these primeval *gotras* were multiplied by the addition to the list of the original sects a host of names in later times.[89] Marriage between members of same *gotra* was fobidden because they were supposed to be members of the same family.[90]

But then the *gotra* system did not remain confined to the Brāhmaṇas alone. The Kshatriyas and Vaiśyas also adopted the same *gotra* names as did the Brāhmaṇas. Of course, these *Varṇas* did not claim descent from these seers, their claim was based on the claim that these seers were their hereditary teachers and used to perform their domestic rituals.[91]

To keep the nearness to each other several families of each *gotra* added the names of their immediate-past ancestors to the *gotra* name which they recited on ceremonials. Usually three, to give such ancestral names were cited.[92] Marriage was forbidden within members of such group having *pravara* name in common; in some cases inter-marriage between members having two *pravara* names in common was forbidden.[93] Kshatriyas and Vaiśyas were also expected to follow the same practice.[94]

## Slavery

To complete the picture of social structure reference must be made to the institution of slavery which existed in India from the earliest times to the advent of the Britishers in Indian history. That it existed in some form is evident from not only indigenous sources like the Epics, *Smṛtis* but even secular Sanskrit literature, Buddhist and Jain canonical literature and even the inscriptions of ancient India establish this fact. Of course, slave markets are not mentioned in the early sources but in the early centuries of Christian era there was trade in slave-girls between India and the Roman empire in both directions.[95] The *Smṛtis* not only distinguish between different classes of slaves but lay down various rules regarding their status. There was, however, no caste of slaves.[96]

The Sanskrit word *dāsa* has been translated into English as 'slave'. The origin of the word, however, is doubtful and its use as synonym of slave is possibly not proper. The word *dāsa* meant a member of the people conquered by the Aryans.[97] Definitely in Indian history there is no evidence to prove that the entire conquered peoples or tribes were condemned into slavery, and servitude was exacted from such people, as was the case in ancient Egypt or Mesopotamia or even in the Roman empire.[98] Of course, it is quite possible that some people captured in battle were taken into slavery and they were styled as *dāsas*. The *Mahābhārata* declares that it is a law of war that the vanquished should be the victor's slave, and the captive would serve his captor until ransomed.[99] But the people who were vanquished were also designated as *dāsas*. Hence the confusion.

Whatever might have been the origin of slavery, with the progress of Indian civilisation, it was systematised as an institution and both the *Smṛtis* and the *Arthaśāstra* categorised them according to their term of servitude. *Arthaśāstra* divides the slaves into five classes:[100] *dhvajahṛta* or those who were captured in the battle; *atmavikrayin* or those who sold themselves in slavery; *udaradāsa* or one born to a master from his *dasi* or slave woman; *ahitaka* or one who could not pay for his debt; and finally *daṇḍapraṇita* or one condemned to slavery by the judgment of the court. Manu mentions seven kinds of slaves, viz., one captured in the battle, one who sells himself for food, one born in the house of a slave woman, one bought, one given, one inherited and one who is condemned by court.[101]

Of all the *Smṛti* authors Narada gives an exhaustive treatment on the institution of slavery.[102] He enumerates fifteen kinds of slavery. Those who were captured in the battle unless ransomed were slaves; those who survived the death of the master passed on to the legitimate heirs as slaves; children born to the slaves of the master were *gṛhaja* or *udaradāsa*; those who were purchased from the market were *kṛtadāsa*; slaves could be held in mortgage; a person leaving his religious order, according to Nārada, was a slave; those who could not maintain themselves could give themselves up for maintenance and they could become slaves; a debtor could become a slave to pay for his debt to his creditor, there were others who voluntarily accepted slavery either for penance or to free somebody; slaves could be had through wager, somebody having sexual relation with a female slave became temporarily a slave to the master of this female slave; one could become a slave for a stipulated period; and finally one could sell himself into slavery.

In the earlier period possibly the slaves were engaged in agricultural works but gradually slaves were engaged only in domestic works. Nārada again divided domestic works under two heads: pure and impure. The following works were to be performed by slaves only: Sweeping the gateway, the privy, the road and the place for rubbish. Massaging the secret parts of the body, cleaning the food remains, ordure and urine are the impure works to be performed by the slaves. Washing the feet of the master after his return to home was the duty of a maid-servant.

The master of the slave could let out the services of their slaves on hire; slave girls could be let out for sexual enjoyment the offspring being accepted as interest. Of course, a slave girl could not be enjoyed without proper authorisation but enjoyment without permission amounted to five to two *Paṇas* for a day.[103]

The slave did not have any right as he was not his own master. He was not that way much better than his master's chattel. The master had the right to recover his slave if he did run away or gave himself to somebody else. The master had the right to pledge him or give him up to another person. A slave could not own any property legally, for all that he earned belonged to his master.[104] A slave could not stand as a witness unless there was no other available and transaction of a slave, unless authorised duly, was invalid.[105]

Most of the slaves depended entirely upon their masters. If the master was kind they would be contented and happy with him; and they were much better than a destitute who had a precarious living. But if the master was bad the lot of the slave might be woeful. In the *Mṛchchhakaṭika* of Śūdraka we see that Sthāvaraka was beaten and put in fetters by his cruel master; of course, he was ultimately freed by the decree of new king who disgraced his master. But a female slave Madanikā was well treated by her cultured mistress who not only treated her as a friend and confidant but released her even to visit her lover.[106]

But these do not mean that a slave was without any hope of freedom. Nārada states that a slave who saves his master from imminent danger to his life becomes not only free but gets a share of his master's property as a son.[107] Yajñavalkya also approves of the freedom of a slave saving his master from death.[108] A person who gave himself up as a slave during hard times was released from bondage if he could give a pair of oxen. One enslaved for a stipulated period was freed after the expiry of that period; one who became a slave for maintenance was released on giving the said sustenance. A slave captured in war could be ransomed and slaves gained in wager could be released on giving a substitute. One enslaved for having sexual relations with a female slave was released after severing relations with female slave. Those condemned into slavery by forcible means or by the robbers were emancipated by the king as their slavery was not legal.[109]

There was a definite procedure of emancipation of the slaves. If a master desired to free his slave, the latter was asked to bring a pitcher of water on his shoulder. The pitcher was then broken by the master who sprinkled grain water and flowers on the head of the slave and muttered thrice: Thy art free. The slave was then set free with his face turned towards the east.[110]

The slave was, in fact, a subordinate member of his master's household. His maintenance was his master's responsibility, and if he died sonless it was incumbent on the master to perform funeral and rites for the welfare of his soul. A slave could be bought, sold, given away or even mortgaged and loaned but the masters had no right over the lives of their slaves, and were not allowed to abandon them in old age, as was done in many other ancient civilisations. "A man may go short himself or stint his wife and children, but never his slave, who does his dirty work for him."[111] The right of the master to punish the slave was also limited. "A wife, a son, a slave, a servant or a younger brother may, when they do wrong, be beaten with a rope or a cane, but only on the back and not on the head. If a man beats them otherwise, he should be punished as a thief."[112]

The *Arthaśāstra* lays down more humane regulations of slavery than does the *Smṛtis*. Slaves are entitled to own and inherit property, and earn money in their spare time. Slaves of upper classes cannot be forced to perform defiling duties. The chastity of the slave girl is to be protected. If a master raped his maid-slave he must set her free paying proper compensation. If, however, he begets a child on the slave-girl, both child and the girl should become free.[113] A promise by a man made in dire necessity to sell himself and his family is not a binding. Possibly these liberal regulations together with the living by the slave in the same household made Megasthenese observe "all the Indians are free and not one of them is a slave. . . the Indians do not even use aliens as slaves and much less a countryman of their own."[114]

Indian economy was never dependent on slavery as was the case with Egypt, Sumer and the Greek and even the Roman civilisations.[115] In India the labourer, farm-worker and craftsman were normally free men and the latifundia of the Roman magnate had no counterpart in India. Rhys Davis has justly remarked:

> "we have nothing of such later (Western) developments of slavery as rendered the Greek mines, the Roman latifundia or the plantdins of Christian slave owners scenes of misery and oppression. For the most part the slaves (in India) were household servants and not badly treated, and their numbers seem to have been insignificant. Of course, there are numerous references in literature to slaves being badly treated by their masters but he was definitely better off in India than most parts of the ancient world; *dāsa* was a bondsman not a chattel slave."[116]

*Varṇa-Āśrāma-dharma* or the four-fold classification of the society and the four stages in the life of an individual were devised to provide every one in society a place and fix his duty from his birth to death as God-given. *Varṇa-dharma* was meant to secure also the harmony and smooth course of social life. Duty but no right constitutes the foundation of life.[117] Successive āśramas were invented to improve the spiritual side of the life of people of all grades. People worked and lived under a sense of duty to man and God without desiring the fruits of action, the motto being: "May we have Divine protection; may we live together, with all our differences; may we not hate each other; may what we acquire in the way of the knowledge be strongly efficient in its results."[118]

## REFERENCES


1-3. Sri Aurobindo, *The Foundations of Indian Culture*, p. 111.
4. Manu, X : 4.
5. The *Gita*,. IV : 13.
6. Manu, I : 88.
7. A.L. Basham (ed.), *The Wonder That Was India*, p. 139.
8. V. Raghavan, '*Manu Samhita*', *The Cultural Heritage of India*, Vol. II, p. 346.
9. A.L. Basham, *op. cit.*, p. 140.
10-11. S.K. Maity, *The Economic Life in Northern India in the Gupta Period*, pp. 162-64.
12-14. A.L. Basham, *op. cit.*, pp. 140-42.
15. R.C. Majumdar (ed.), *The Age of Imperial Unity*, pp. 549-51.
16-20. A.L. Basham, *op. cit.*, pp 140-42.
21. The *Gita*, XVIII : 43.
22. Sri Aurobindo, *op. cit.*, p. 111.
23. A.L. Basham, *op. cit.*, pp. 142-43.
24-25. A.L. Basham (ed.), *A Cultural History of India*, p. 132.
26. Manu, X : 44.
27. A.L. Basham, *op. cit.*, p 143.
28. *Ibid.*
29. The *Gita*, XVIII : 44.
30. A.L. Basham, *op. cit.*, p. 143.
31. *Ibid.*
32-33. R. Thapar, *Asoka and the Decline of the Mauryas*, pp. 61-73.
34. S.K. Maity, *op. cit.*, p. 204.
35-37. A.L. Basham, *op. cit.*, pp. 143-44.
38. The *Gita*, XVIII : 44.
39. A.L. Basham, *op. cit.*, pp. 144-45.
40. V. Raghavan, *op. cit.*, p. 346.
41-42. A.L. Basham, *op. cit.*, p. 144.
43. R.S. Sharma, *Sudras in Ancient India*, pp. 8-41.
44. D.C. Sircar, *Society and Administration of India*, p. 102.
45-46. A.L. Basham, *op. cit.*, pp. 144-45.
47-48. R. Thapar, *op. cit.*, p. 23.
49. A.L. Basham, *op. cit.*, p. 139.
50-52. Wm. T. de Bary (compiled), *Sources of Indian Tradition*, p. 219.
53. A.L. Basham, *op. cit.*, p. 147.
54. J.R. Basu, 'Recognition of merit in caste system in Ancient India', *The Journal of the Ganganath Jha Research Institute*, Vol. III, 1970.
55. S.K. Chatterjee *op. cit.*, pp. 162-63.
56. A.L. Basham, *op. cit.*, p. 36.
57. R. Choudhary, *Vrātyas in Ancient India*, p. 74.
58-59. D.C. Sircar, *op. cit.*, pp. 103-04.
60-64. A.L. Basham, *op. cit.*, pp. 148-52.
65. J.P. Hutton, *Caste in India*, p. 112.
66. R.C. Majumdar (ed.), *The Age of Imperial Unity*, pp. 549-50.
67. *Ibid.*
68. I. Karve, 'The Indian Social Organization—An Anthropological Study', *The Cultural Heritage of India*, Vol. II, pp. 544-45.

69. *Ibid.*
70-75. A.L. Basham, *op. cit.*, pp. 145-46.
76. *Ibid.*
77. *Ibid.*
78. *Ibid.*
79. *Ibid.*, p. 147.
80-86. *Ibid.*, pp. 156-59.
87-94. *Ibid.*
95-100. *Ibid.*, pp. 153-54.
101-102. S.K. Maity, *op. cit.*, pp. 186-91.
103-110. *Ibid.*
111. A.L. Basham, *op. cit.*, p. 153.
112. Manu, VIII : 299 f.
113. S.K. Maity, *op. cit.*
114. R.C. Majumdar (ed.), *op. cit.*
115. A.L. Basham, *op. cit.*, p. 154.
116. R.C. Majumdar (ed.), *op. cit.*, p 571.
117. T.R. Venkataramana Sastri, "The Smrtis — their outlook and character", *The Cultural Heritage of India*, Vol. II, pp. 333-34.
118. *Ibid.*

*APPENDIX*

## SOCIAL CHANGE
## BETWEEN C. 500 B.C. — A.D. 500

Indian traditional culture from an early stage siezed upon a double idea for its own guidance which it threw into a basic system of individual life in the social frame. This was the double system of the four *varnas* and four *āsramas* four graded classes of society and four stages of a developing human life. The economic order of society was cast in the form and gradation of the four types, viz. *Brahmana*, *Ksatriya, Vaisya*, and *Sudra*.[1] The *Brāhmana* class was called upon to give the community its priests, thinkers, men of letters, legislators, scholars, religious leaders and guides. The *Ksatriya* class gave it its kings, warriors, governors and administrators. The *Vaisya* order supplied it with its producers, agriculturists, craftsmen, artisans, merchants and traders. The *Sudra* class ministered to its need of menials and servants.[2] But it should be remembered that birth was not the sole test of *varṇa* and at no time adherence to this economic rule was quite absolute. The intellectual pursuit of the man, the turn of his temperament, his spiritual stature were the important factors determining his position in society.[3]

After the invasion of Alexander, the political canvas was torn asunder and the Imperial Mauryas succeeded in establishing an empire which covered almost the entire territory of the Indian sub-continent. With a break through the Sungas and Kanvas the Kusanas again raised by the Imperial standard which after a brief interludge found a solid footing during the rule of the Imperial Guptas. The tradition continued till the end of the reign of Harsabardhana in the 7th century A. D. With the expansion of political horizon during this period of imperial unity the outlook of society was broadened and a catholic attitude to life made the society cosmopolitan. The foreign hordes like the Bactrians. Greeks, Kusanas, Sakas, Hunas were absorbed in the social fabric mostly by inter-racial marriages and appropriated into different *varnas* and professions.[4] Non-Aryan tribes of various social grades were incorporated in the Aryan society retaining their tribal systems but largely conforming to Aryan culture and performing *vrastyashtama* sacrifice. Their social behaviour and characteristics depended on their birth and the several tribes with their tribal customs connubium and commensality crystallised into castes. Besides, the offsprings of hypogenous and hypogemous marriages began to be designated as distinct castes as well.

Thus the basic system of individual life in the social frame underwent change. No longer the individual conformed to the ideal of *varna-āsrama*. People began to take up professions which suited them and proved lucrative at the same time. Going for *vānaprastha* or *sannyasa* was not considered necessary for *moksa* or liberation.[5] It was then ordained that by following *svadharma* i.e. following one's own profession according his propensity one could attain salvation. The *Gita* echoed the same ideals—*svae svae karmani avirata svamsidhi lavate nara*, i.e. by following one's own profession one can attain *moksa*.[6] Education which was so long limited to the twice born Brahmacharis and provided by the Guru in the hermitage was opened to people of all *Varna* and caste — it was imparted in centres or schools run by teachers who now charged fees.[7] Students lived in their own houses or hostels run by themselves. Students were not necessarily bachelors. The Buddhist and Jain monasteries turned into colleges and universities where not only theology but secular subjects were also taught by regular staff of teachers who were paid for their services. Mode of aquiring knowledge was not *sravana, manana*, and *nidhidhayasana* but attending to lectures and reading books of the libraries.[8]

Over this period the religious orthodoxy and social bigotry made room for liberal religious practices and created breach in the social frame. The growth of gnostic and non-theistic religions like Buddhism and Jainism dealt a death blow to the *varnaasrama* institutions. The ritualistic sacrifices of the Brahmanical religion and the supremacy and domianance of the *Brahmana*, were at stake. Buddhism and Jainism not only cast-off the sacrificial ritualisms of the Vedic religion but attempted to overthrow the caste and class distinctions of the Brahmanic society. In the face of this challenge the Hindus offered devotionalism in which God was presented to masses in theistic form of *Krishna* or *Visnu* or *Visnu* or *Mahadeva*, ready and anxious to deliver the devotees who would approach them personally without any intermediary.[9] Buddhists now offered *Mahayanism* in which *Bodhisvattas* could help the followers attaining *nirvana*.

These politico-religious developments together with foreign immigration fostered intercaste (*inter-varṇa* marriages both *Anuloma* and *Pratiloma* type) and interracial marriages offsprings of which in turn created new castes. Sylvain Levi writes : [Seleurcus] concluded a matrimonial alliance with him [Chandragupta] which no doubt introduced a Greek princess into the Maurya *harem* . . . . Bindusara married a Greek princess whose son was Asoka.[10] Rudra-Sena, a scion of the orthodox *Brahmana* family married Prabhabati Gupta, a princess of the Imperial Gupta family which was a Vaisya origin.[11] The Kadanbas who were *Brahmanas* married their daughters in the Gupta family.[12] The Ikshaku rulers who were orthodox *Brahmanas* had no objection for accepting a bride from the Saka family of Ujjain as had been done by the Satavahanas in an earlier period. Later *Smṛtis* recognised (hypogamy) *Pratiloma* marriage which was tabooed by the earlier *Smṛties*.[13] In fact it was by this inter-racial marriage by which the foreigners were absorbed in Hindu society.

This liberal religious social changes ushered in an era of religious toleration. Asoka commonly believed to be a Buddhist styled himself as "*Devanam* Pyja Piya Dassi Raja Asoka".[14] The *yavana* Haliodorous became not only a convert to Vaisnavism but erected a Garuda-Dhvaja before the Visnu temple of Besnagar. Kharavela provided grants to all religious sects like Asoka.[15] Even pious ordinary people donated money for the religious mendicants who did not conform to the religion of the donee, Nathśarmā and Rāmi, (*Brāhmanas*) donated lands for the maintenance and Jain Arhats.[16]

Social change paved the way for professional mobility. Governance and administrative jobs which was a preserve of the Ksatriyas were opened to people of other *varnas* and the foreigners. The origin of the Mauryas is still a controversial issue. But it seems quite sure that they did not belong to the *Ksatriya varna*. The Sungas who overthrew the Maurya dynasty were Brahmanas and the Kanvas were also not *Ksatriyas*[17] The Kuśanas, Sakas and Hunas were Central Asian tribes and the Imperial Guptas were of *Vaisya* origin. The Vākatakas and the Kadambas were *Brāhmanas,* exchanged sacrificial ladle for the sword.[18]

In both *Jātaks* and *Suttas* the *Brāhmanas* are found pursuing tillage, cowherding. goat keeping, trade. hunting, woodworks or carpentry, weaving caravan-guarding, archery, carriage driving, and snake charming and no reflection was passed on them for doing so.[19] The president of the oil-mongers of Indore is expressedly described as a *Ksatriya* in a fifth century record. *Ksatriya* carried on commercial and industrial pursuits.[20] Yajñavalkya permits the Sudras to become agriculturists, artisans and traders and some of them took to military services and rose to the position of captains and generals.[21] There was horizontal mobility in arts and crafts which is also confirmed by epigraphical records.[22]

Cut-off from the rest of Asian continent by the Himalayas, with its extensions to the east and west and surrounded by the seas on three sides, the people of India had developed a culture which holds a unique place in the world. Indian society and culture did not succumb to the foreign hordes, instead the immigrants were absorbed within the Hindu society. Education, marriage, family life made necessary adjustments to cope with the demand over centuries. Hindu religion, spirituality and philosophy continued to hold the imagination of Indian people and attracted the foreigners. The caste system had replaced the *Varna* system professional mobility expelled the concept of *varna* avocation. But an air of liberalism and catholicity and vitality ran through the socio-economic and cultural life of the people. Society of India established certain norms and ideals which with necessary adjustments made India great as a nation and civilisation.

## REFERENCES


1. Wm T.D. Bary — *Sources of Indian Tradition*, p. 210.
2. Sri Aurobindo — *The Foundation of Indian Culture*, (1972) p. 111.
3. *Ibid.*
4. R. C. Majumdar *et al* — *Vakataka Gupta Age*, p. 343.
5. M.L. Bose, *Social and Cultural History of Ancient India*, pp. 52-65.
6. *The Gita*, XVII, 45 p.
7. R.C. Majumdar *et al. The Age of Imperial Unity*, pp. 591-94.
8. M.L. Bose, *op. cit.*
9. R.C. Majumda *et al.*, *Vakataka Gupta Age*, pp. 342-365.
10. *Ibid.*
11. *Ibid.*
12. *Ibid.*
13. *Ibid.*
14. R. Thapar, *Asoka and the Decline of the Mauryas*, p. 226.
15. R.C. Majumdar, *The Age of Imperial Unity*, p. 213.
16. S.K. Maily, *Economic Life in Northern India during the Gupta period*, pp. 39-67.
17. R.C. Majumdar *et al. Vakataka Gupta Age*, p. 343.
18. *Ibid.*
19. Rapson, *Combridge History*, Vol. I, p. 181.
20. R.C. Majumdar *et al. Vakataka Gupta Age*, pp. 342-43.
21. *Ibid.*
22. *Ibid.*

# 4

# Brahmachārya-Āśrama and Education in Ancient India

The aim of Indian education in ancient times was the training of the mind as an instrument of knowledge by *śravaṇa*; *manana* and *nididhyāsana* and *brahmachārya*; it did not furnish the mind with the furniture of objective knowledge.[1] It was believed that an individual was an *ādhāra* which could be vitalised by the cosmic energy pervading the world and pouring itself into every name and form, the cloud, the plant, the insect, the animal or man. When the *ādhāra* was prepared to bear the inrush, and impact of this energy, the cosmic energy poured into it and its evolution was completed, and the man became *siddha*, the fulfilled or perfected soul.[2] His education was completed. The same was the aim of the Buddhist education in India. The monks or students of the monasteries had to follow strict rules and regulations to develop their physical and moral excellence; then by self-exertion, intuition and meditation brought about a success in spiritual life.[3]

People in ancient India were preoccupied with idea of spiritual attainment. Man was never allowed to lose sight of the use of life as a discipline for spiritual perfection and passage to the Infinite.[4] As such one had to acquire knowledge and prepare for life under a teacher or *guru*. The selection of the teacher was a matter of great importance, for, if a teacher himself lacked in knowledge and virtue, he could not shape the life of his students. Therefore, a Brāhmaṇa, who was well-read, of good family, of good character and purified by penance, should have been selected as a *guru*.[5] Students might go to Kshatriya or even Vaiśya teacher after studying under a Brāhmaṇa teacher for further instruction or if they did not get any suitable Brāhmana teacher.[6] Manu, however, mentions two classes of teachers, viz., *Upādhyāya* who taught only a portion of the Veda or Vedānga; and *Āchārya* who taught the Veda with *Kalpasūtra* and *Upanishad* without fee, besides the *guru*.[7]

The period of education began with initiation or *Upanayana*. The *Upanayana* ceremony, as explained in the *Atharva Veda*, took three days, during which the teacher held the pupil with him for three days to impart to him a new birth whence the pupil emerged as a *dvija* or twice-born.[8] The kernel of the ceremony was the investing of the boy, clad in the garments of an ascetic and with a staff in his hand, with the sacred thread (*yajñopavīta*) which hung over his right shoulder and under his left arm. It was a cord of three threads each of nine twisted strands made of cotton, hemp or wool for Brāhmaṇa, Kshatriya and Vaiśya respectively.[9] His first birth he owed to his parents who gave him only the physical body, his second birth was spiritual, it unfolded his mind and soul.[10] Originally *Upanayana* meant the taking charge, thus, of a student for spiritual education, but gradually in the Sūtra period its mystic significance increased and overshadowed the aim. In course of time it took the form of a ritual and the undertaking of the vow became the chief object, and education but secondary.[11]

*Upanayana* was to take place in proper time. The age of the initiate was as much important as was the season. A Brāhmaṇa was to be initiated at the age of eight, a Kshatriya at eleven and a Vaiśya at twelve. The last permitted age of *Upanayana* for Brāhmaṇa was sixteen, of a Kshatriya twenty-two, of a Vaiśya twenty-four.[12] If pupil was not initiated within the limit set forth, he became a *Vrātya* or fallen which could be atoned only by the performance of *Vrātya-shṭoma*.[13] The age of *Upanayana* varied according to spiritual and temporal attainment each pupil was expected to develop. If a Brāhmaṇa was to develop special eminence in the sacred knowledge, he was to be initiated at the age of five from the date of conception. A Kshatriya was to be initiated at the age of six if he was intended to be famous; and a Vaiśya boy was to be initiated at the age of eight if he would aim at wealth. The *Upanayana* was further to be performed in season specified for each class.[14] A Brāhmaṇa was to be initiated in the spring, a Rajanya or Kshatriya was to be given initiation in the summer, a Vaiśya in the autumn and a *Rathakāra* (Chariot-maker) in the rainy season.[15] The choice of the season seems to have a relation to temperament of the particular class or *Varṇa*.

The sacrament of *Upanayana* marked the dawn of a new life, it was his second or spiritual birth, his birth from his parents being only a physical birth. After *Upanayana* he is called a *dvija* or twice-born. The pupil who was initiated thus was *upanīta*, one who was introduced to a life of perfect discipline of *Brahmcharya*. The initiated was still a minor but he had taken the status of an Aryan and now it was his duty to master the lore of the Aryans to prepare himself for the future life by maintenance of celibacy.[16] The following injunction was put before him :

> "A student art thou; drink water; do thy work; do not sleep during day-time; keep silence; be obedient to the teacher; study the Vedas; fetch alms morning and evening; morning and evening put fuels into the fire; observe *Brahmcharya* for twelve years or till the Vedas are learned."[17]

The Brahmachari was given a *kaupīna* or a loin-cloth to cover the private parts of his body; a *mekhalā* or girdle to support the *kaupīna*; a *yajñopavīta* or sacred-thread; an *ajina* or skin and a *daṇda* or staff.[18] The colour of the *kaupīna* was according to *Varṇa*, e.g. for Brāhmaṇa reddish-yellow; for Kshatriya light-red; for Vaiśya yellow.[19] As for the girdle, that of the Brāhmaṇa should be made of *muñja*-grass, that of a Kshatriya a bow-string, and that of a Vaiśya woollen. As for the staff, that of a Brāhmaṇa should be of *Palāśa* wood; that of Kshatriya of *Udumbara*; and that of Vaiśya of *Vilva* wood.[20] The length of the staff and the material used for making the *upavīta* varied also according to the *Varṇa* of the *upanīta*.[21]

The object of education being the building up of the future man his growing physical, mental and spiritual constitution was taken into consideration in prescribing the code of life.[22] He was allowed to eat as much as he liked twice a day but without any intermediate refreshment and avoiding luxurious food like meat, honey, etc. He was to take bath twice a day in cold water without scrubbing or cleaning, he was to sleep on the bare ground and avoid contact with women. The object of the regulations seems to preclude possibility of exciting sexual desire and loss of chastity.[23]

The din and bustle of life distracted the attention of the pupils from education and, therefore, the seats of learning or Āśramas were situated within the sylvian surroundings on a stream or within a forest away from habitations. The *Rāmāyaṇa* depicts the hermitage of the sage Bharadvāja of Prayāga and in the *Mahābhārata* we read the account of the hermitage of Saunaka in Naimisha and that of Kaṇva on the bank of the Mālinī. A typical hermitage is represented in Bāṇa's *Harshacharita* in the depth of Vindhya forest as late as the seventh century.[24]

A fullfledged hermitage or Āśrama for education consisted of the following departments:

(i) *Agni-sthāna*, a common prayer hall for all for the worship of Fire-God;
(ii) *Brahma-sthāna* or college of divinity or Vedic studies;
(iii) *Vishnu-sthāna* or college of Rajaniti or political science consisting of Rājanīti, Arthanīti and Vārtā;
(iv) *Mahendra-sthāna* or military centre;
(v) *Vivasvata-sthāna* or department of astronomy;
(vi) *Garuḍa-sthāna* or department of Botany; and
(vii) *Kartikeya-sthāna* or department of military organisation.[25] One or more teachers were attached to each *Sthāna*.

The *Milindapāño* gives an elaborate account of the courses of study.[26] The Brāhmaṇas studied the four Vedas with their auxiliaries: astronomy, astrology, materialistic philosophy and the sciences of omens. A Kshatriya or prince learnt the arts of managing horses, elephants and chariots, of writing of accounts and of waging wars. The Vaiśyas and Śūdras learnt the arts of husbandry, merchandise and the care of the cattle. In other words the Brahmaṇas were expected to learn all the known branches of literature and sciences while the Kshatriyas and Vaiśyas were to specialise in their respective occupational duties. Therefore, the *Arthaśāstra* of Kautilya provides for a special course of training for the Kshatriyas. It states: After tonsure ceremony and before reaching the age of seven, a Kshatriya child was to learn the alphabets and accounts: after *upanayana* ceremony he was to study the four sciences—*Trayī*—the Vedas with their auxiliaries, *aniviksiki* or three schools of philosophy, *vārtā* or economics and *daṇḍanīti* or jurisprudence. After the completion of his studies and marriage in his sixteenth year he had to go through daily routine of receiving lessons in the art of war and in *itihāsa*, which included *Purāṇa*, *itivṛtta*, *ākhyāyikā*, *udāharaṇa*, *dharmaśāstra* and *arthaśāstra*.[27]

The method of acquiring knowledge was *śravaṇa*, *manana* and *nididhyāsana* or listening to the discourse of the teacher, meditation on the meaning thus heard and concentration or meditation on the Truth.[28] Knowledge was imparted in the form of *mantra* and *sūtra*, maximum of meaning was compressed within minimum of words of which crowning example was the *Praṇava* or *Aum* which contained within itself world of meaning. The teacher was the walking library and source of knowledge which he transmitted to his pupils orally—*guruparamparā*. The teacher would instruct the students seated on the ground about him by role and students would repeat the verse until these were mastered. *Śabda* or word uttered by the teacher had its own potency and value apart from its sense and its intrinsic and innate implications; its rhythms, its vibrations had to be realised. *Śadba* was considered to be Brahma itself. The receiving of this knowledge as it was uttered by the teacher was to be followed by the process of its assimilation by *manana*, deliberation or reflection on the topic taught. But such reflection resulted only in a mere intellectual apprehension of the meaning of the text imparted by the teacher to his pupils. Therefore, the third step in the process of learning was *nididhyasana* or meditation leading to the realisation of the Truth after its intellectual apprehension and reasoned conviction by the pupils themselves.[29]

The usual term of the session was from *Śrāvaṇa* (July-August) to *Paush* (December-January) about one hundred and fifty days.[30] There were thirty holidays — *Ashṭamis* (eighth lunar day) *chaturdaśīs* (fourteenth day) and *Purṇimās* (full-moon) and *Amāvasyās* (new moon). Sometimes *Pratipadās* (days after the new and full-moon) were holidays; with occasional breaks in-between, about a hundred days were devoted to the study. Of such academic years, twelve were allotted for the study of one Veda.[31] If anybody wanted to read all the four Vedas, he took forty-eight years. Students usually learnt one or more Vedas as was the tradition in his family. Those who read two Vedas were titled *Dvivedin*, who read three was given the title of *Trivedin* and one who learnt all the four was known as *Chaturvedin*.[32]

### Teacher-Student Relation

In early Vedic times the students did not pay any tuition fees to his teachers but rendered physical service and shared his alms with his teacher.[33] He collected fuel for the sacrificial fire, tended the cattle of the *Guru* and cultivated the land of the *Guru*; if he had any. The pupil, besides, did personal service like massaging and anointing the body of his *Guru*. At the completion of education the pupil, after taking bath, offered a little fee to his *Guru* before leaving the hermitage for his home.[34] As the teacher was in *loco parentis* he did not usually inflict punishment on his students. In case of serious dereliction he might chastise him or use a light cane or rope to punish him.[35]

**Advanced Seats of Learning**

Students becoming *Snātaka* usually went home and after marrying settled down to the life of a *Gṛhastha*. But there might be pupils who would prefer to continue as students throughout their life, dedicated to the persuit of learning. They wandered about the country as *parivrājakas*. The Upanishads called them '*charakas*' who were the diffusers of knowledge.[36] Uddālaka Āruṇi after finishing education went to Ṛshi Śaunaka for further instruction. Besides, there were advanced centres of learning known as *parishads*. The most famous *parishads* were *Pañchāla parishad* which was patronised by the philosopher king of the country Pravāhana Jaivāli who daily drove out of his palace to attend its sittings, and that of Mithila where many celebrities like Uddālaka Āruṇi, Aśvala and Gārgi and Vāchaknavī gathered around Janaka, the philosopher king.[37]

These higher centres of learning gave a new turn to the education system. Sometimes hundreds of students gathered in the cities which acquired renown for their learned teachers and achieved a reputation comparable to that of the Universities of mediaeval Europe.[38] Chief among these were Vārāṇasī and Takshaśīlā which attained fame in the time of the Buddha; later around the beginning of the Christian era. Kāñchi acquired a similar reputation in the South.[39] We read of an establishment at Varāṇasī with 500 Brāhmaṇa students and a number of teachers all of whom were maintained by charitable donations.[40] Varānasī was also noted for its school of music under an expert who was the chief of his kind in all India.[41]

But the Jātaka stories show that Takshaśīlā was then most prominent centre of learning to which students flocked from distant parts of India. Takshaśīlā offered courses of study in the Vedas and crafts—it had special schools of law, medicine and military science.[42] It also offered courses of study in elephant-lore, hunting, animals' cries, archery and the like. There is an interesting story of a Brāhmaṇa boy named Jotipala, a native of Benares, whose king sent him at his expense to Takshaśīlā for education in archery. When he finished his education and wanted to return home, his teacher presented him with his own sword, a bow and arrow, a coat of mail and a diamond and asked him to take his place as the head of a school of 500 pupils, to be trained by him, as he was himself old and about to retire.[43]

By this time education had become a little catholic. There were both public schools and community schools. Schools kept a cock to serve a clock or alarm bell to rouse students early from their bed. Students of all castes were admitted into schools by some and other admitted Brāhmaṇas, Kshatriyas and sons of magnates and magnificos and even sons of ordinary merchants, tailors and fishermen.[44] But, Chaṇḍālas were not accepted by any teacher.[45] Rich students paid fees, which ran as high as 1,000 pieces of money, sometimes in advance. The majority of the students, however, were poor and rendered services to their teachers in lieu of fees.[46] There were also day-scholars along with the resident pupils in the schools of those days. Some such students were married and were householder. Prince Junha of Vārāṇasī lived in a rented house in Takshaśilā for education.[47]

Along with the academic education there developed a system of vocational and technical training. Some light is thrown upon the training of the craftsmen by the *Smṛtis* of Nārada onwards and their commentaries and digests. Vocational and professional training was provided by master craftsmen and professional experts in respective fields in their workshops and homes.[48] When trainees or apprentices were accepted, an agreement on both sides was entered into, the breach of which was punishable. When an apprentice was accepted, he was provided with shelter, food and treated as a son. Carefully and gradually training in the craft and its technique was imparted to the trainee. The preceptor refusing to give him training or compelling him to do works other than his craft or art was liable to punishment but the apprentice deserting his teacher without valid reason was liable to corporal punishment and compulsory repatriation. According to the Venetian traveller, Marco Polo, the boys of tradesmen of the Pāṇḍya kingdom were given a pocket money at the age of thirteen by their fathers and asked to eke their livelihood by independent trade.[49] *Divyāvadāna* refers to the training of the sons of the rich merchants in the art of writing, arithmetic, coins, debts and deposits, examination of gems and residences, elephants and horses, young men and women and so on.[50]

The condition of medical education at the time of the rise of Buddhism illustrated by the narrative of the career of Jīvaka is found in a Pāli canonical work.[51] Born as the son of courtesan at Rājagṛha and brought up by prince Abhaya of Magadha, he was sent to study medicine under a world-renown teacher at Takshaśilā. There he stayed for seven years and he completed his training by passing a difficult practical test in the knowledge of medicinal plants. His subsequent career is said to have been exceptionally brilliant, as he rose to the position of court physician of Bimbisāra, king of Magadha, and established a country-wide practice in medicine and surgery.[52]

The student, we learnt from the same narrative, had to apprentice himself to a teacher of the profession on payment of his fee in advance or else on the condition of offering personal service.[53] *Śuśrūta-Saṁhitā*, a well-known surgical-work written in the early centuries of the Christian era, gives the following account of training.[54] The preceptor admitted his student by performing a special *upanayana* ceremony. At the ceremony the pupil solemnly undertook in the presence of the sacred fire to observe a number of rules relating to physical purity and moral probity, and to obey his preceptor, the teacher on his part agreed with equal solemnity not to behave towards his pupil otherwise than teaching him properly. The pupil, it was emphatically stressed, should acquire proficiency both in theory and practice, failing either of which he would be in a position to the bird clipped off one of its wings.

Most significant development in institutional learning, however, emerged out of the Buddhist monasteries. The Buddhist monks used to stay in a house called *āvāsa* during the rainy season. There they utilised their time in academic discussions.[55] The newly admitted monks were required to place themselves under a teacher after making formal application and receiving his consent.[56] The teacher was called *āchārya* or *upādhyaya*, the former being regarded in context with the *Smṛtis* as a deputy of the latter. The relation between the teacher and the student followed the pattern of the *Smṛti* scheme.[57] The pupil was to serve the teacher at his bath, toilet and meals and on his begging tours and nurse him during his illness.[58] The teacher on his part was to give a complete instruction to his pupils, to supply their necessities, to nurse them during their illness and so on and so forth. The method of instruction was the usual way of oral instruction by delivering lectures and answering questions.[59] The pupils were required to observe strict rules about food, clothing, equipment, shelter based upon the *Smṛti* scheme of duties of the Vedic students. The Buddhist monasteries built up self-sufficient colonies, growing their own food by agriculture and dairy farming in its own grounds which came into their possession as gifts.[60] There was need of organisation and machinery in this system. The collective monastic life in vihāras gave scope for individual life of study and meditation in the cells provided to the monks under personal direction of his teacher.[61]

Thus the Buddhist monasteries developed gradually an intellectual culture surcharged with the spirit of questioning, scrutinising and debating. Purely canonical and exegetic at the beginning, they drew into their purview in later times the results of metaphysical speculations of other systems of thought and religions as well. Two Chinese records, viz., Yuan Chwang's *Si-Yu-Ki* and I-tsing's *Nan-hai-Chi-Kuei-nai-fa-chuan* threw much light on these practices. We gather from these that a few monasteries developed under the patronage of the enlightened Gupta emperors (*c.* A.D. 320-550) developed into large-scale seats of learning which were resorted to by teachers and learners.[62] In practices and observances of communal life, their monastic character was maintained, as also the traditional and monkish atmosphere. But fully equipped with usual educational paraphernalia—professors, students, graded courses and syllabi academic regulation, lecture halls, libraries and even system of examination—they were universities in the modern sense of the term.[63]

## Nālandā

Among these monasteries the *mahāvihāra* of Nālandā in Magadha attained highest distinction because of the magnificence of its establishment and intellectual and moral eminence of its allumni. Its establishment was the work of a succession of six sovereigns, says Yuan-Chwang.[64] The tradition of the local people during the time of Chinese pilgrim was that to the south of the *vihāra* there was a mango garden in the middle of which there was a pond. In the pond lived a Nāga called Nālandā after which the monastery was named by Śakrāditya who built it in obeisance to the Buddha after the latter's *parinirvāṇa*.[65]

The establishment was surrounded by a brick wall which enclosed the entire *vihāra*. One gate opened to the great college, from which were separated eight other halls, standing in the middle (of the samghovana). "All the outside courts, in which are the priests' chambers, are of four stages. The stages have dragon projections and coloured caves, the pearl red pillars, covered and ornamented, the richly adorned bakestrades and roof covered with tiles that reflect the light in a thousand shades, these things add to the beauty of the scene."[66] Besides, the *vihāra* maintained gardens of mango and flowers and ponds of lotus flowers of different kinds.

Nālandā maintained a splendid and well-equipped library. Tibetan sources tell us that there were three huge buildings named practically

Ratnasāgara, Ratnadadhi and Ratnarañjaka for housing books.[67] Of these Ratnasāgara housed texts of *Prajñāpāramitā* Śāstras and Tantricism. This was the most rich library from which the foreign scholars could get authoritative texts. Yuan Chwang took 124 copies of Mahāyāna texts and others amounting to 520 fasient. I-tsing took away 400 copies of the Buddhist Sanskrit works from this library. Inscriptions refer to Sumatran scholars copying manuscripts at Nālandā.[68]

Nālandā University was supported by the revenue of 100 villages and donations by many patrons like Harsha. Two hundred householders of the village, day-by-day, supplied "several hundred *picules* of rice and several hundred *catties* in weight of butter and milk to the university."[69] The students could devote to their study without bothering for clothes, bedding, food and medical care, for they got everything without any payment. Yuan Chwang writes that 10,000 students resided in the university.[70]

The Nālandā inscription of Malada refers to it as an abode of erudite men famous for their knowledge of the sacred lore (*āgama*) and the arts (*kalā*), as testified by Yuan Chwang.[71] Within the university they arranged 100 pupils for preaching and the students attended these discourses without any break, even for a minute.[72] Such was the fame of the great centre of learning that students from far and wide came to it for admission. A monk-scholar conducted pre-admission test which was so strict that two to three out of ten succeeded in getting admission there.[73] The university was a centre of higher education and advanced studies; only such students who possessed necessary qualifications were admitted to its post-graduate course.

There seems to be three grades of teachers in the university, besides the Vice-Chancellor of Nālandā as we find it in present day Indian universities. Yuan Chwang observes:

> "There are 100 men who can explain twenty collections of Sutras and Śāstras; 500 men who can explain thirty collections, and perhaps ten men, including the Master of the Law, who can explain fifty collections. Śīlbhadra alone has studied and understood the whole number."[74]

During the declining years of Nālandā in the middle of the seventh century two other universities became famous in eastern India. These are Odantapura, somewhere between the borders of Bengal and Bihar, where illustrious Indian missionary of Buddhism in Tibet, Dīpaṅkara Śrījñāna, deified by the Tibetans as *Atīśa*, received his education, and Vikramaśīlā, where Dīpaṅkara after completing his education was posted as *Āchārya* or head of the institution.[75] The site of Vikramaśīlā has been located at Sultanganj in Bihar.[76] The Tibetans hold that it was situated on the right bank of the Ganga on a bluff-hill. This university was a centre of Tantricism and had a magnificent establishment with six noble gates each of which was guarded by a university officer called the guardian scholar of the gate. There were 108 temples and six colleges, besides 108 schools, all of which were maintained by the State. Out of 108 temples, 53 were meant for esoteric practices and 54 for general use.[77] Although it was a seat specially of Tantricism other topics like grammar, logic, philosophy, etc., were also taught. It had a great attraction for Tibetan scholars who translated Prajñā and Tantra and very many Buddhist Sanskrit works into Tibetan.[78]

In the west, the city of Valabhi or Valabhipura in Kathiawār developed as a great centre of Hinayāna Buddhism.[79] A number of inscriptions of the Maitraka kings ranging from 5th to 8th centuries A.D. refer to educational and religious activities of their kingdom. The first building of this monastic college was raised by Princess Duddā, the daughter of the sister of king Dhruvasena I. Other buildings of this university were the Abhyantarika-*vihāra* of venerable Mimma and the Bappapada-*vihāra* of Bhadanta Sthiramati. Dhruvabhata, son-in-law of emperor Harsha, was the greatest patron of this university.[80]

Yuan Chwang found about a hundred monastic buildings in Valabhi and the strength of the students amounted to six thousands.[81] Names of the three important scholars who received their higher education at Valabhi University are Jayasena, a native of Saurāshṭra, Guṇamati and Sthiramati—all three lived in or around the Nālandā *mahāvihāra* later.[82] I-tsing observes that Valabhi, like Nālandā, imparted education on secular subjects as well. The fame of the university is mentioned in the *Kathāsaritsāgara* of Somadeva. It is mentioned in this work that a Brāhmaṇa of the Gangetic plain, Vasudatta, sent his son to Valabhi for higher education at the age of sixteen.[83] It is interesting to note that the Brāhmaṇa of *Antarvedī* (of the Gangetic doab) sent his son to Kathiawar, instead of sending him to Vārāṇasī or Nālandā which would have been nearer to his home. It is also known from the epigraphic sources that Valabhi University had a rich library financed by the royal treasury and magnificence of the local people.[84]

A complete and most authentic account of the courses of studies during this period has come down to us from the pen of the illustrious Chinese pilgrims I-tsing and Yuan Chwang. According to Yuan Chwang, the children after mastering a short primer called the *Twelve Chapters* or the *Siddha composition* which consisted of alphabets and combinations of vowels and nouns were trained in five sciences, namely, grammar, the science of arts and crafts, medicine, the science of reasoning and the science of the internal.[85] The curriculum of studies, according to I-tsing, comprised in graded sequence of Pāṇini's grammar consisting of 1000 slokas with the commentaries, logic and metaphysics, in addition to which the Sūtras and the Śāstras were prescribed for monks.[86] The parallel list of subjects studied at Nālandā monastery comprised, according to Yuan Chwang, not only the works of all the eighteen Buddhist schools but also the Vedas, logic, grammar, medicine, the *Atharvavidyā*, the *Sāṁkhya*, and so forth.[87]

I-tsing observes that monastic schools had, besides the novices, two classes of lay pupils.[88] One class called *Mānavas* (children) chiefly read the Buddhist scriptures with the intention of receiving initiation in future, while the Brahmachāris read the secular books alone without any intention of becoming monks. Unlike the novices who were maintained by the common fund of the *saṁgha* the lay pupils had to provide for their own expenses.[89] I-tsing says that the children began the work called *Siddha-composition* in their sixth year and mastered it in six months. In the eighth year they took up Pāṇini's Sūtras and the *Dhātupāṭha* which they completed in eight months time. In their tenth year they began and finished within three years the three *Khilas*, namely, (i) the *ashṭadhātu* dealing with cases and numbers of nouns, as well as the tenses and ending of verbs, (ii) the *moṇḍa* (or Muṇḍa) and (iii) the *uṇādi* dealing with the verbal contexts. In his fifteenth year the young student began the *Kāśikāvṛtti* on Pāṇini's grammars which he finished in five years time. For the complete mastery of grammar four other works were studied by monks and laymen alike. These were: (i) the *Chūrnī* (otherwise called *Mahābhāshya* of Patañjali, (ii) Bhartṛhari's commentary on the *Churṇī*, (iii) his *Vākyapadīya* and (iv) his unidentified work called the *Peina*. After studying the *Kāśikavṛtti*, I-tsing continues, the students learnt the *hetuvidyā* (logic), the *abhidharma* (metaphysics) and so forth while the monks learnt in addition all the *Vinaya* works as well as the Sūtras and the Śāstras.[90]

The universities thus turned out not only Buddhist doctors but statesmen, administrators and economists who could get jobs in government establishments and academics. Records of Valabhi state that "to try the sharpness of their (students-alumni) learning, they preceded to the king's court to lay down before it the sharp weapon of their abilities; there they present their schemes and show their political talents seeking to be appointed in the practical government."[91]

The universal character of the educational institutions are well attested by Bāṇa's *Harshacharita* (7th century A.D.). In a passage it is observed that the king saw[92] "Buddhists from various provinces, Jains in white robes, mendicants, ascetics, followers of Kapila, *Lokāyatikas* (materialists), followers of *Kaṇāda* (of the atomic school), followers of the Upanishads, students of legal institutions, students of the *Purāṇas*, adepts in sacrifices, adepts in grammar, followers of Pāñcharātra and others, besides all diligently following their own tenets, pondering, urging objections, raising doubts, resolving them, expounding etymologies and disputing, discussing and explaining moot points. Can there be a more thought-provoking and suggestive description of a true university with no exclusions and many preferences ?

**REFERENCES**


1. R.K. Mookerjee, "Ancient Indian Education", *The Cultural Heritage of India*, Vol. II, p. 64.
2. *Ibid.*, p. 640.
3. *Ibid.*, p. 648.
4. Sri Aurobindo, *op. cit.*
5. T.R. Venkataramana Sastri, *op. cit.*, p. 331.
6. *Ibid.*
7. *Manu*, II : 140-42.
8. R.K. Mookerjee, *op. cit.*, p. 641.
9. *Ibid.*
10. *Ibid.*
11. *Ibid.*
12. *Manu* II: 36-38.
13. *Ibid.*
14. *Ibid.*
15. R.B. Pandey, "The Hindu Sacraments (*Saṁskāras*)", *The Cultural Heritage of India*, Vol. II, p. 402.
16. Wm. T. de Bary, *op. cit.*, p. 402.
17. *Ibid.*, p. 230.

18-21. *Manu*, II: 41-46.

22-23. T.R. Venkataramana Sastri, *op. cit.*, pp. 330-31.

24. R.K. Mookerjee, *op. cit.*, p. 649.
25. R.C. Majumdar (ed.), *The Age of Imperial Unity*, p. 589.
26. R.K. Mookerjee, *op. cit.*, p. 648.
27. *Ibid.*
28. *Ibid.* p. 642.
29. *Ibid.*
30. T.R. Venkataramana Sastri, *op. cit.*, p. 331.
31. *Ibid.*
32. *Ibid.*
33. R.K. Mookerjee, *op. cit.*, p. 647.
34. *Ibid.*
35. T.R. Venkataramana Sastri, *op. cit.*, p. 330.
36. R.C. Majumdar (ed.), *op. cit.*, p. 586.
37. *Ibid.*
38. R.C. Majumdar, *op. cit.*, p. 452.
39. A.L. Basham, *op. cit.*, p. 165.
40. R.C. Majumdar (ed.), *op. cit.*, pp. 591-94.
41. *Ibid.*
42. *Ibid.*
43. *Ibid.*
44. *Ibid.*
45. *Ibid.*
46. *Ibid.*
47. *Ibid.*
48. R.K. Mookerjee, *op. cit.*, pp. 650-52.
49. *Ibid.*
50. *Ibid.*
51. *Ibid.*, pp. 650-54.
52. *Ibid.*
53. *Ibid.*

54-57. *Ibid.*

58. *Ibid*, pp. 647-49.
59. *Ibid.*
60. *Ibid.*
61. L. Joshi, *Studies in the Buddhistic Culture of India*, pp. 122-32.
62. S. Datta, "Monasticism in India", *The Cultural Heritage of India*, Vol. II. pp. 589-90.
63. *Ibid.*
64. R.K. Mookerji, *op. cit.*, p. 652.
65. S. Beal, *The Life of Hiuen-Tsiang*, pp. 110-12.
66. *Ibid.*
67. L. Joshi, *op. cit.*, pp. 135-37.
68. *Ibid.*
69. S. Beal, *op. cit.*, pp. 112-13.
70. *Ibid.*

71-74. *Ibid.*

75. R.K. Mookerjee, *op. cit.*

76-78. L. Joshi, *op. cit.*, pp. 139-40.

79-84. *Ibid.*, pp. 137-38.

85-90. R.C. Majumdar (ed.), *The Classical Age*, pp. 586-88.

91. L. Joshi, *op. cit.*
92. C.P. Ramaswami Aiyar, "Some Aspects of Social and Political Education in India", *The Cultural Heritage of India*, Vol. I, p. 494.

# 5

## Gārhasthy-Āśrama, Vānaprastha and Sannyāsa

The Gṛhastha is given the following commandments when he becomes a *Snātaka* by his *Guru* or teacher: "Speak the truth, walk the way of thy duty, neglect not the study of the Veda. When thou hast brought to thy Master the wealth that he desires thou shalt not cut short the long thread of thy race; thou shalt not be negligent of truth; thou shalt not be negligent of the duty; thou shalt not be negligent of welfare; thou shalt not be negligent towards thy increase and thy thriving; thou shalt not be negligent of the study and teaching of Veda."

"Thou shalt not be negligent of they works unto the Gods or thy works unto the father. Let thy father be unto thee as thy God and thy mother as thy Goddess whom thou adorest. Serve the Master as a God, the stranger, within thy dwelling. The works that are without blame before the people thou shalt do these with deligence and no others. The deeds we have done that are good righteous, thou shalt practise those as a religion and no others."

"Whosoever are better and nobler than we among the Brāhmaṇas thou shalt refresh with a seat to honour them. Thou shalt give with faith and reverence; without faith thou shalt not give. Thou shalt give with shame, thou shalt give with fear; thou shalt give with fellow-feeling."

"Moreover if thou doubtest of thy course or of thy action then to whatsoever Brāhmaṇas be there who are careful thinkers, devout, not moved by others, lovers of virtue, not severe or cruel, even as they are towards these, so be thou."

"This is the law and the teaching. These are the commandments. In such wise shalt thou practise religion, yea, verily, in such wise do ever religiously."[1]

The ideal *Gṛhastha* receiving these commandments possibly

agreed with the declaration of Triśanku: "I am He that moves the Tree of the Universe and my glory is like the shoulders of a high mountain. I am lofty and pure like sweet nectar in the strong, I am the shining riches of the world, I am the deep thinker, the deathless one who decayest not from the beginning."[2]

A *Snātaka* who professed such lofty was held in high esteem by the people. He conducted himself decently like an educated man—he "assumes a dignified demeaner", as Gobhila puts it.[3] He was honoured everywhere—he was reverentially welcomed when he visited a house—"a great being indeed is a Snātaka", says Āśvalāyana:[4] "On the road every one makes way for him; it is said that even the king, meeting him, showed respect and yielded him precedents". Any father would like to give him his daughter in marriage.

The *Snātaka* became a *Gṛhastha* setting up sacrificial fire in his house after his marriage. The sacrificial fire had its origin in marriage sacrament. When the married man carried his wife home in a chariot (*vi-vāh*), the nuptial fire was carried in the carriage and set up in his house as his domestic fire. It had to be kept up till he retired from his domestic life and went to *vānaprastha*. From it his wife lighted the kitchen-fire; in this fire an *agnihotṛ* offered oblations everyday morning and evening, with his wife.[5]

The aim of the life of a *Gṛhastha* was the attainment of '*purushārtha*' by pursuing *Dharma*, *Artha*, *Kāma* and *Moksha*.[6] *Dharma* means righteousness, duty and virtue. When a man sought to gain something by following his own avocation it is *Artha*. When it is love or pleasure in life it is *Kāma*. Finally, when one renounced all his activities in order to devote oneself to religious and spiritual activities with a view to liberate oneself from the worldly life it is *Moksha*. These four are called '*chatur-varga*' or the tetrad of life. Hinduism does not hold up monasticism or eremitism as a common ideal for all; it considers rather that the strains and trials of life or household management, family-life and social obligations are a useful discipline contributing to the preparation of man for the final life or retirement and spiritual endeavour.[7] The Vedas hold that there is but one *āśrama* that of the householder.[8]

The meaning of the word *Dharma* is derived from the root *dhṛ* to sustain; in other words the implications of *Dharma* is the law which sustains the world, human society and the individuals.[9] *Dharma* takes the place of the Vedic ideal of *Ṛta*, the principle of cosmic *ethical* interdependence. Though *Dharma* generally refers to religiously ordained duty in some places it means simply morality, right conduct, or the rules of conduct of people.[10] In the Upanishadic mysticism and quitism *Dharma* is classified into two aspects—the one relating to *pravṛtti* and the other to retirement from life (*nivṛtti*). Gradually *nivṛtti* itself became a separate end of life under the name of *moksha* or liberation or *nirvāṇa*. *Dharma* now stood for ritual activities and ethical conduct like righteousness, virtue, justice, propriety, morality, beneficence and non-violence, and so on.[11]

*Dharma*, however, is not divorced from life. As the great epic *Mahābhārata* puts it ". . . from *Dharma* material gains and pleasure follow; then why is not *Dharma* pursued? Neither for the sake of pleasure, nor out of fear or avarice, no, not even for the sake of one's life should one give up *Dharma*; *Dharma* stands alone for all time; pleasure and pain are transitory."[12] *Dharma* is the foundation of the whole Universe. "That from which result material gain and spiritual good is *Dharma*", says *Vaiśeshika Sūtra*.[13] "*Dharma* when violated verily destroys us; *Dharma*, when preserved, preserves us: therefore, *Dharma* should not be violated, lest the violated *Dharma* destroy us," ordains *Manusmṛti*.[14] In fact, *Dharma* is a way of life; it was conceived as the only mode of individual and social life at all times and in all places.[15]

The *Gṛhastha* was the economic support of the entire social structure composed of the four *āśramas*. All *āśramas* followed to rest in him; he was the refuse and the breath of life for those in other stages of life.[16] Therefore he should earn money by following his *Varṇa-āśrama* and *svadharma*.[17] He must earn that by honourable means by following irreproachable occupation. He should not hoard wealth; he should be ready to share with others whatever he had earned.[18]

At birth an individual was charged with liabilities to gods, to *ṛshis*, to fathers; further the society provided him succour and support. Therefore, he was indebted to and obligated to all around and above him.[19] Getting freed from all these debts and obligations one could go for liberation and *moksha*. "Debtless in this world, debtless in the other, debtless in the third world may we be; what worlds there are, traversed by the gods and traversed by the fathers, may we abide debtless on all those paths," says the *Atharva Veda*.[20]

Debt to the gods could be repaid by religious sacrifices and prayers. The gods were worshipped through *home* and rituals. Gods contribute to the welfare of the people by rain and other boons. It was considered necessary to recognise their debt and offer a share of whatever one possessed in his possession.[21] Debt to the *Ṛshis* could be repaid by living a virtuous life necessary for the maintenance of personal purity and study and teaching the Vedas. All study was considered to be a sacrifice since it increased knowledge beneficial for the society.[22] Debt to the dead ancestors could be repaid by marrying a pure girl and mating with her on permitted days to beget offsprings and rearing them up for keeping up the line of succession and provision for *tarpaṇa* to the dead ancestors.[23] This could be further extended to comprehend the rites and ceremonies like *śrāddhas* which involve the giving of foods, clothing and presents to the Brahmaṇas.[24]

The debt to the society and the world at large had to be repaid and obligation fulfilled by performing sacrifices daily and occasionally. A *Gṛhastha* was supposed to perform vaiśyadeva sacrifice or *Bhūtayajña* which consisted of in feeding or offering *bali* to the beings visible and invisible around us; *Nṛ-yajña* or the entertainment of guests; *pitryajña* or offering *tarpana* to dead ancestors; *Deva-yajña* or oblation to fire for gods; *Brhma-yajña* related to the maintenance of learning. Together these constituted *pañcha-mahā-yajñas*.[25] A householder committed sins for using five paraphernalia of his house, namely, furnace, pestle, pitcher, udukhal and sweeper; he was absolved of these sins by performing the above five sacrifices. It is said that a *Gṛhastha* performing the sacrifices and feeding those dependant on him should eat the remnants with his wife; he who cooks for himself alone eats sin, not food.[26]

Besides the daily round of sacrifices, a *Gṛhastha* was supposed to perform from time to time seven kinds of *pāka-yajñas*, or small sacrifices, seven kinds of *Havir-yajñas*, seven kinds of *Soma-yajñas*, *Rāja-sūya*, *Aśvamedha* and even *Purushamedha* sacrifices, according to his capacity. Seven kinds of *Pāka-yajñas* or small sacrifices are the *Ashṭkas*, the *Śrāvaṇī*, the *Āgrahāyanī*, the *Chaitrī*, the *Āśvayujī*, the *Pārvaṇa* and the *Śrāddha*.[27]

The *Ashtaka* sacrifices were offered on the eighth day of the dark halves of the four months from Kartika to Māgha. The *Śrāvaṇī* was offered on the full-moon day of Śrāvaṇa, the *Āgrahāyanī*, on the fourteenth day of the full-moon day of the Agrahāyaṇa, the *Chaitrī* on the full-moon day of Chaitra and the *Āśvayujī* on the full-moon day of the month of *Āśvina*. *Pārvaṇa* was offered on the new and full-moon days. The *Śrāddha* was offered to the manes on the new-moon days every month as funeral offering.[28]

The *Havir-yañjas* as well as the *Soma-yajñas* were more highly developed rituals and are treated in details in the *Śrauta-sūtras*.[29] The essential point in both in the kindling of at least three sacred fires, to which offerings of cakes, grains, milk, honey, etc., were made. In the case of *Soma-yajña*, the additional offering of *Soma*, of course, forms an essential part, and most of them were characterised by killing of animals.[30] There was another important distinction between these and the other rituals which have been described in the *Gṛhya-sūtras*.[31] In these *Śrauta*-rituals, the priests play the most prominent part, whereas in the *Gṛhya*-rituals the essential duties are performed by the householder himself.[32]

The seven kinds of *Havir-yajñas* are the *Āgnyādheya*, the *Agnihotra*, the *Darśa-paurṇamāsas*, the *Āgrayaṇa*, the *Chāturmāsya*, *Nirūḍhapaśubadha* and the *Śautrāmaṇi*.[33] The establishment of the sacred fires in the house three or more in number was the bounden duty of every householder. These fire-places served the purposes of temples where God was worshipped. an Agnihotṛ was supposed to offer oblation in the three sacred fires daily. The *Darśā-paurṇamāsas* were *yajnas* of the full and new moon. In *Āgrayaṇa* oblation of the first fruit of the harvest was offered. The *Chaturmasya-yajñas* were performed at the beginning of each of the three seasons. The *Nirūḍhapaśubadha* was an animal-sacrifice performed separately. The essence of *Śautrāmaṇi* is the offering of *surā* (wine) to the *Aśvinīs* and Sarasvati. It was usually an epilogue to *Soma-yajñas*, its object being to cure persons who might have drunk too much *Soma*.[34]

The seven kinds of *Soma-yajñas* are the *Agnishṭoma* or *Jyotiragnishṭoma*, the *Atyagnishṭoma*, the *Ukthya*, the *Shoḍaśin*, the *Vājapeya*, the *Atirātra* and the *Āptoryama*.[35] All these were more or less different forms of the *Agnishṭoma* and varied only in details.[36]

The actual ceremony of the *Agnishtoma* lasted for only one day in which *soma* was pressed thrice, in the morning, in the midday and in the evening, and cattle was offered to *Agni*. But the ceremony was preceded by a long period of *dikshā* or consecration, sometimes extended for a year, during which the sacrificer and his wife lived as austere life in two adjacent huts, built for the purpose.[37] One of the most interesting features of this ceremony was the purchase of the *soma* plant, which was brought on a cart and solemnly received as a guest.[38]

There were many other sacrifices, besides these, which a householder might perform from time to time, but four of them deserve special mention.[39] The first is the *Vrātyashṭoma*. It consisted of four rites, by means of which persons outside the pale of Brāhmanic-fold were admitted into the orthodox society. The existence of this sacrifice conclusively proves that the Hindu society in the old days was not so right as at present, and opened its doors to all persons.[40]

The *Rājasūya* was a ceremony for the consecration of a king. It spread over a period covering two years. The details are given in *Śatapatha Brāhmaṇa*. The principal ceremony was preceded by a long period, extending to a year, in which the various preliminary rites were celebrated. The principal officers of the State took part in the ceremony, and the king, in his State-dress, received from the priest a bow and arrow, and declared himself king. He performed various acts symbolising his conquests in all directions, and was then anointed by a priest a kinsman, a kshatriya and a vaiśya.[41]

In the *Aśvamedha* ceremony, a horse, duly consecrated and protected by warriors, was let loose, along with 100 other horses, to move about at its own free will as a challenge to other kings. Then, for about a year, the king, accompanied by his queen, with the maids-in-waiting and high officials, performed daily sacrifices, in course of which the legends of the king's ancestors were recited. After the year was over, the horse was brought back, and the king was consecrated. The horse was anointed by the queen, and various ceremonies were gone through. It was then killed and its flesh roasted.[42]

There can be no doubt that both the *Rājasūya* and *Aśvamedha* ceremonies could only be performed by powerful sovereigns, and were usually regarded as a visible symbol of their supremacy over other kings. In order to emphasise this aspect, the subordinate kings were sometimes made to perform menial services in these sacrifices, particularly in the *Rājasūya*.[43]

More efficacious than the *Aśvamedha*, but far more dreadful, was the *Purushamedha*, in which a human being was sacrificed instead of a horse. The ceremonies performed were very similar in the two cases. As the horse was let loose for about a year, the human victim was allowed to enjoy himself for the same period, during which all his wishes were satisfied. The queen behaved with the human victim exactly as she did with the horse in the *Aśvamedha* sacrifice.[44]

For every-day life *Yajñavalkya Smṛti* lays down the following commandments to the *Gṛhastha*:[45]

"Having risen before the dawn the householder should ponder over what is good for the self. He should not, as far as possible, neglect his duties in respect of the three ends of man, namely, virtue, material gain and pleasure, at their proper times.

"Having attended to the bodily calls, having performed the purificatory rites and after having first washed the teeth, a twice-born man should offer the morning prayer.

"Having offered oblation to the sacred fire, becoming spiritually composed, he should murmur the sacred verses addressed to the Sun-God. He should also learn the meaning of the Vedas and various science.

"He should then go to his lord for securing the means of maintenance and progress. Thereafter having bathed he should worship the gods and also offer oblations of water to the manes.

"He should study according to his capacity the three Vedas, the *Atharva Veda*, the *Purāṇas*, together with *Itihasas*, as also the lore, relating to the knowledge of the self, with a view to accomplishing successfully the sacrifices of muttering prayers (*japa-yajña*).

"Offering of the food oblations (*bali*), offering with the utterance `*svāhā*', performance of Vedic sacrifices, study of the sacred texts and honouring of the guests—these constitute the five daily sacrifices dedicated, respectively, to the spirits, the manes, the gods, the Brāhmaṇas and men.

"He should offer the food oblations to the spirits (by throwing it in the air) out of the remnant of the food offered to the gods. He should also cast food on the ground for dogs, untouchables and crows.

"Food as also water should be offered by the householder to the manes and men, day after day. He should continuously carry on his study. He should never cook for himself only.

"Children, married daughter living in the father's house, old relatives, pregnant women, sick persons and girls as also guests and servants,—only after feeding these should the householder and his wife eat the food that has remained. . . .

"Learning, religious performance, aged family relations and wealth—on account of these and in the order mentioned are men honoured in society. By means of these, if possessed in profusion, even a Śūdra deserves respect in old age."

The routine of daily round provided in the *Manusmṛti* does not differ substantially from that provided in the *Yajñavlkya Smṛti*.[46]

Life of the householder as depicted so far is full of duties but there was much beauty in it as well. The Hindu scheme of life assigned to *kāma* or pleasure or enjoyment its due importance in developing well-rounded personality of the *Gṛhastha*. Constantly reminding him of his duties as also of higher nature of the Ultimate Reality, Hindu code of conduct provided for due enjoyment of the man. The claim of sense satisfaction was not ignored, it was given its just importance.[47] "Man, who could live normally up to hundred years, must apportion his time and take to virtue, material gain and pleasure in such a way that these are mutually integrated and do not harm each other," says Vātshāyana.[48] *Manusmṛti* lays down similar commandments: "Some say that *dharma* and material gain are good, others say that pleasure and material gain are good, still others say that *dharma* alone or pleasure alone is good, but the correct position is that the three should co-exist without harming each other."[49] "In fact love chastened by suffering was held even by poets and dramatists as capable of effecting a lasting spiritual union."[50] Sri Aurobindo says :

> "Indian thought recognised that the normal life of a man has to be passed through with a conscious endeavour to fulfil its purpose; its power must be developed with knowledge; its forms must be pursued, interpreted and fathomed; its values must be worked out, possessed and lived; its enjoyments must be fully taken on their own level. Only afterwards one could go on to self-existence or supra-existence."[51]

For the purpose of enjoyment or pleasure *Kāma-sūtra* was developed on scientific basis systematically in exhaustive detail. The best work on the subject is Vātsyāyanas *Kāma-sūtra* or aphorism on love which states that gods and sages promulgated this science of material gain and pleasure along with the sacred law.[52] *Kāma-sūtra*, however, provides for the pleasures of an ideal cultural man whom it designates as *Nāgaraka*. Such a person, in contrast to the ideal householder who might live in rural setting, is wealthy, enjoys the good things of life, has a cultured taste and moves in most refined social and artistic circles. He is expected to be educated in sixty-four *Kalās*, a term equated with *śilpa* or art of *vidyā* or science. These arts include dancing, singing, acting, flower arranging, gambling, legerdemain, distillation of spirituous liquors, sewing and embroidery work, first-aid, metallurgy, chemistry, cooking, posture, duelling, gymnastics, horology, dyeing, architecture and engineering, mineralogy, calliography, swimming, leather-works, archery, driving horses and elephants, composition and solution of riddles and puzzles, nursing and rearing of children, and so on and so forth.[53]

But the Indian *Kāma-śāstra* did not hold the idea that enjoyment was an end in itself. The enjoyment or pleasure though momentary leads oneself to self-realisation and thus provides an insight into supreme beautitude or a momentary glimpse of the supreme bliss. Whole artistic creation was surcharged with an aesthetic spirit and transported one enjoying *rasa* beyond the mundane world. Art, architecture, sculpture, painting, music, dance and even literary creations, viz., poetry, drama and painting—all were primarily intended to give a taste of the supreme bliss or beautitude or melody.[54]

Notwithstanding the fact the life style of Vātsyāyanas *Kāma-sūtra* presents before us, the pleasures and pastimes of a cultured town's man, *Nāgaraka*, are varied and comprehensive. Let Vātsyāyana speak for himself.[55]

> "After acquisition of learning, a person should with the help of the material sources obtained by him through gifts from others personal gain, commerce or service, marry and set up a home and then follow the ways of the man of taste and culture (*nāgaraka*).
>
> "He may make his abode, in accordance with the profession chosen by him, in a city, in a commercial centre, or a town; any of these he chooses should be inhabited by good people.
>
> "There he should make for himself a house, with water nearby, having a garden, provided with square apartments for different activities and having two retiring rooms.
>
> "In the retiring room in the forepart of the house there shall be fine couch, with two pillows, pliant at the centre, having pure white sheets; there shall be by its side another couch of lesser height (for lying down); at the head there shall be wicker-seat (for doing his prayers) and a platform for the sandal paste left over after the night's use, a garland, a box of waxes and scents, peeling of pomegranate fruit (a small decorant) and betel-leaves, a spittoon on the ground, a lute hanging on a bracket on the wall, a painting board and a box of colours, some books and

garlands of kuruntaka flowers, not far away on the floor, different kinds of seats, a dice board; outside the room, cages of the birds kept for playing with; and at a remote end (outside), things for private use.

"In the garden, a swing, well covered and under the shade of a tree, as also an earthen dais strewn with the falling flowers of the garden. Such is to be the layout of his residence.

"He must get up early in the morning, answer the calls of nature, wash his teeth, smear his body with just a little fragrant paste, inhale fragrant smoke, wear some flower, just give the lips a rub with wax and red juice, look at his face in the mirror, chew betel-leaves along with some mouth decorants and then attend to his works.

"Every day he must bathe; every second day have a massage; every third day, apply phenaka to the legs; every fourth day have a partial shave and clipping of the nails; every fifth day or tenth day a more complete shave; he must frequently wipe off the perspiration of the armpit; have his food in the forenoon and afternoon.

"After eating (in the forenoon) comes playing with parrots and myna-birds and making them talk; and indulging in cock and ram fights and in other artistic activities; also attending to the works he has with his friends and companions. Then have a little nap. In the forenoon still he dresses and goes out for social calls and for enjoyment of company of others. In the evening he enjoys music and dance. At the end of it, in his own apartments, decorated and fragrant with smoke, he awaits, along with his companions, his beloved who has given him an engagement or else sends her a message and himself goes out to meet her . . . such is the daily routine.

"He should arrange excursions in parties for attending festivals, saloons for enjoying literature and art drinking parties, excursion to parks, and group games. Once a fortnight or a month, on the day sacred to the deities, the actors and dancers attached to the temple of Saraswati (goddess of learning) gather and present shows (for the cultured citizens of the place); or visiting actors and musicians from other places present their programmes in the Saraswati temple."

The different modes of acquiring wealth of the Brāhmaṇa,

Kshatriya, Vaiśya and Śūdra were acceptance of gifts, personal earning, agriculture, trade and commerce and service to upper three classes, respectively.[56] Vātsyāyana writes any person acquiring wealth by either of these means can set up a residence in *Nāgara* and thus may start the life of a *Nāgaraka* or man of taste and refinement. It can be surmised from this fact that enjoyment of the pleasures of the city life was not confined to any class or *Varṇa*.[57] *Mṛchchhakaṭika* gives similar impression.[58] Chārudatta, a Brāhmaṇa, having come to a *Nagara* set up a residence which compares favourably with the plan provided in the *Kāma-sūtra*. In the inner portion of the house lives his first wife, married according to *śāstric* injunction, while he himself spends the day with his servants, companions and lover in the outer part of the house, with attached garden. The drawing room is furnished with slender furniture but he has musical instruments like *mṛdanga* (drum), *dardūra* (flute), *vīṇa* (a lute), *vaṁśa* (reed-pipe), and even manuscripts. He wears perfumed garments and goes out to join musical concert parties in the evening. He meets his mistress outside the city in a garden. The works of the greatest Sanskrit poet Kālidāsa bear ample testimony to the rich and variegated town life of ancient India.

**Saṁskāras**

It has already been noticed that Hinduism as an organised religion provides for a comprehensive scheme for purification, elevation and enlightenment of man through *karma*, *upāsanā* and *jñāna*. *Saṁskāras* or sacraments form an important part of *karma*. A man born and left to himself is a mass of elements—crude and brutal—and slightly removed from his fellow beings in the forest. Therefore, *saṁskāras* were provided to develop of the character of the individual by consciously moulding it and to integrate his personality with the society, in which he was born, by constant care, cultivation and refinement.[59] As such they embrace the whole course of man's life, from his conception in the mother's womb up to his death, or rather beyond it as several rites relate to the departed soul.

The word *Saṁskāra* is derived from the Sanskrit root *kr* with the prefix *saṁ* and suffix *ghañ*.[60] But it is used in different senses.[61] In classical Sanskrit literature, *saṁskāra* has the sense of education, cultivation, training, refinement, perfection, etc. The different systems of Hindu philosophy, of course, employ the term to denote different meanings. In English, the Sanskrit word *saṁskāra* is nearest to sacrament which is defined in *Oxford Dictionary* as "Religious ceremony or act regarded as outward and visible sign of inward spiritual grace."[62]

The first systematic description of the *saṁskāras* is found in the *Gṛhya-sūtras*. Beginning with *vivāha* or marriage, they end in *samāvartana* or graduation. Majority of them omit *antyeshti* or funeral, perhaps because of inauspiciousness attached to the dead body. The works of Parāśara, Aśvalāyana and Baudhāyana, of course, have sections dealing with it.[63] The number of *saṁskāras*, however, fluctuates between 12 and 18. In course of time 16 have become the classic numbers, consisting of the following:[64]

(i) *garbhādhāna* or conception;
(ii) *puṁsāvana* or engendering of male issues;
(iii) *sīmantonnayana* or parting of hair;
(iv) *jātakarmaṇa* or natal rites;
(v) *nāmakaraṇa* or naming the child;
(vi) *niṣkramaṇa* or first outing of the child;
(vii) *annaprāśana* or first rice taking;
(viii) *chūḍākaraṇa* or tonsuring;
(ix) *karṇavedhana* or piercing of ear;
(x) *vidyārambha* or learning the alphabets;
(xi) *upanayana* or giving the sacred-thread;
(xii) *vedārambha* or beginning of the study of the Vedas;
(xiii) *keśānta* or cutting of hair;
(xiv) *samāvartana* or graduation;
(xv) *vivāha* or marriage;
(xvi) *antyeshṭi* or funeral.

According to the nature of the *saṁskāras*, they may be divided into five categories, namely,[65] (i) pre-natal, (ii) post-natal or childhood, (iii) educational, (iv) manhood and (v) post-mortem. The life of a man does not start with his birth; it goes back to his parents union. The married couple approached each other in proper time in an attitude of religious serenity for the sake of progeny. The putting of the seed by the male in the womb in such an attitude is *garbhādhana*. The next is *puṁsāvana* performed in third or fourth month of constellation, particularly in *tishya-nakshatra* to ensure the birth of a male issue. The last pre-natal *saṁskāra* is *simantonnayana* in which the hair of the pregnant mother is ceremoniously parted. The performance of these with rules to be followed ensured the health of the pregnant mother and the child in the wombs.[66]

The second phase of the life begins with the birth of the child. The birth of the child is regarded as the fruition of the conjugal life and birth of a male child, which ensures continuation of the family, is celebrated in all felicity and pomp. The first post-natal *saṁskāra* is *jatakarma* in which first item is *medtayanana* when the child is fed ghee and honey with a gold spoon. The next item is *ayushya* to ensure longevity, when prayer to *ṛshis*, *pitri*, *agni* and *soma* are offered. Third is for *sakti* or strength when the father speaks to the child for becoming a worthy person and congratulates his wife. Then the umbilical cord is severed. The next *saṁskāra* of the childhood is *nāmakaraṇa*, which is performed on tenth or twelfth day of birth after a god who is regarded as protector or whose blessings with a consonant with a semivowel in it and with long vowel or with *visarga* at the end. The name of girl contains an uneven number of syllables and ended in a, and in *taddhita*. It is suggested that the name of a girl should be easy to pronounce, not harsh to hear, clear in meaning, charming to pronounce, not inauspicious, ending in a long vowel and containing blessings. Four-fold naming is suggested: according to the deity or the month, after the family deity, and finally according to calling.[67]

The taking out of the child first timeout of the house to show him the world is known as *Nishkramaṇa*. The child is taken out to a square area cleaned with cow-dung where grains are scattered by a nurse and the father of the child make the child look at the sun. *Annaprāśana* followed in the sixth month when on an auspicious day cereal food with ghee, honey, milk is given in the mouth of the child. *Chuḍākaraṇa* is performed in the third year to ensure long life and beauty and *karṇavedha* between first and the fourth year for protection and decoration.[68]

Educational and marriage sacraments have been dealt with in separate chapters. With *Antyeshṭi saṁskāras* this section is concluded. It is said though *saṁskāras* after birth one conquers the earth, and through *saṁskāras* after death the other world. The eagerness for an easy and peaceful passage from the world of mortals to that of the immortals cremation and in special cases burial and water burial were resorted to. Beginning with predisposal ceremony like the distribution of alms and offering of oblations, they ended with *Śrāddha* and *sapiṇḍakaraṇa*.[69]

*Saṁskāras* express the beliefs, sentiments and the knowledge of the Hindus about the nature of the Universe, human life and man's relation to superhuman powers.[70] They believe that they are surrounded by super-human influences—good and evil. To remove the evil influence, the unfavourable powers are propitiated and beneficial ones are invited to help develop the personality.[71] *Saṁskāra* also express their joy, felicitations and even sorrows at every stage of one's life. Further it is believed that a man is born as a *Sūdra*: he becomes a twice-born (*dviya*) by the performances of *saṁskāras*. Acquiring the Vedic knowledge made him a 'vipra' or inspired person, and finally by attainment he becomes a Brāhmaṇa.[72]

**Penance**

The word *prāyaśchitta* in English means penance. It is defined as an act or means of removing sins.[73] In every day life man is subjected to so many influences and from time to time he might commit acts, knowingly or unknowingly, which are not approved by the *Śastra*. Indian sages assumed this concept and formulated an elaborate scheme for perfection of the conduct (*āchāra* and *vyavahāra*) of man.[74] He was supposed to perform *prāyaśchitta* for *ātmaśuddhi* or self-purification. Non-performance of *prāyaśchitta*, it was believed, condemned the sinners to hells, animal-life and human afflictions.[75]

In the Vedic texts references to penances are given in many places. There is a story that Indra, the king of gods, threw some heretic ascetics unto the wild-dogs which amounted to *Brahma-hatyā* or killing of Brāhmaṇas. He ran to Prajāpati who prescribed to him *upahayya* or penance for single day.[76]

There are, however, differences of opinion regarding the efficacy of *prāyaśchitta*, i.e., to expiate sins.[77] Some, following Gautama, hold that sin can be expiated; others state that sin, under no circumstance, can be expiated; sitll a third school hold that though sin cannot be expiated, non-performance of penance creates extra sin. Penances, however, are generally regarded, following *Purāṇas*, as means of expiating sins.[78]

Associated with sinful acts committed in this life is the theory of *Karma-vipāka* or ripening of anti-natal acts.[79] This is based on the belief of transmigration. It was usually believed that all diseases of the human body were the result of sinful acts committed in the previous life.[80]

There seems to be no agreement between the authorities on the classification of the sins; but broadly they are divided into two classes; namely, *mahāpātakas* and *upapātakas*.[81] The former constitutes killing of a Brāhmaṇa, drinking of wine, stealing and adultery with *Guru's* wife, while the list of *upapātakas* is a long one which vary from author to author.

There is also wide divergence among the sages in the matter of formulating exact means of expiation of the various sins. Generally law of penance was administered by an assembly (*parishad*) of learned in the Vedas, *Mīmāṁsa* and *Dharma-śāstra*.[82] The mode of *prāyaśchitta* ranged from recital of the Vedas. Suicide for *mahāpātakas*, twelve years; vow or life long vow, *kṛchhra* or taking a fast, *Chāndrāyaṇa* or regulation of food by the phases of the moon or gifts of various kinds.[83] Two well-known virtues of *yama* and *niyama* are also mentioned by Yajñavalkya for penance.[84]

Penance was supposed to expiate one's sin by making it public and thereby making one feel ashamed of it and refrain from doing it again. "A sinner gets purified of his sin by making it public, by repentence and by sacred study. As the sinner goes about telling people of the wrong committed by him, the sin falls away from him, even as a slough from a snake. To the extent his own mind derides him from having committed the sin, to that extent his body becomes rid of that sin. By repentence, by the resolve that he will not repeat that the sinner is purified. For any act which leaves no peace of mind, one shall submit oneself to voluntary austerity till one gains mental peace."[85] Thus penance meant a real mental transformation.

**Importance of the Gārhasthy-āśrama**

The *Gṛhastha's* struggle was considered to be the hardest, placed as he was in an environment ordinarily unfavourable to spiritual growth. Manu observes :

> "The duties of this order, which cannot be practised by men with weak organs of sense, must be carefully observed by him who desires imperishable bliss in heaven and constant happiness in this life."[86]

As the greater part of the *Dharmas* ordained by the *śāstras* including the sacrifices was to be performed with a wife, as the *brahmachārin* and *sannyāsins* had to live with the help of the *Gṛihastha* and his wife and as all his life with all duties to gods, sages and fellow-beings, this order of life has always been eulogised in the *Smṛtis*.[87] Control of passions, a well-balanced mind, discrimination and renunciation, these make one the knower of the truth. *Gṛhastha-āśrama* is the field of *karma-yajña* and it is here one can strike a balance between *pravṛtti* and *nivṛtti* and by disciplining and gradually sublimating oneself one can proceed towards spiritual goal.[88] *Śrīmad-Bhāgavat* enjoins: "Always must he remember that the ideal good is not enjoyment but the attainment of knowledge in this life and of everlasting happiness hereafter. As travellers meet by chance on the way, so does a man meet wife, children, relatives and friends; let him, therefore, be in the world and yet separate from it.[89]

**Vānaprastha**

The ultimate end of man was the attainment of *moksha* or salvation, a culmination of the first-three stages of life. For that the more serious person was advised to go for *vānaprastha* and *sannyāsa* successively. But before going for *vānaprastha* a person must discharge his duties and debts as a householder and then with a properly disciplined mind, mature and free from sins and attachments go for these *āśramas*. Manu says that it is only after discharging three debts that one should direct one's mind towards *moksha*; to do otherwise is sinful.[90] When rinkles and grey hair appear on a person, and a grandson has appeared in the house, it is time for a householder to retire; he should leave the village and go to the forest; he may leave his wife under the care of his son or he may take her with him, but in the latter case he should live the life of continence and abstinence from sense-enjoyment.[91] He should not shave and would perform the rites like an *Agnihotri* but would otherwise live the life of a recluse subsisting on roots, fruits and water, dressing in barks of tree and engaged in the study of the scriptures; composed, friendly towards all the compassonate, giving but never receiving anything from anybody.[92] He engages himself in severe austerities. In the summer he should sit exposed to the heat of five fires, in the rainy season he should live under the sky: in the winter he should wear wet clothes, and so he should gradually augment his hardships.[93]

## Yati or Sannyāsa

In the next stage one passed on to the stage of *āśrama*, that of *Yati* or *Sannyāsa* or *Parivrājaka* to attain the Truth which is identified with *moksha* by Manu.[94] He takes the sacrificial fire and moves out of his habitation and goes on moving till his body falls, not staying in one place more than a day except during the rainy season, leaving his wife behind.[95] Practising control of the breath and contemplation he should see the course of the self through high and low births, through the regions of hell and heaven, through the pains and pleasures of life.[96] The *Sannyāsi* should shave his hair and beard, put a brown-red garment as emblem of the order, subsist on alms, sleep on the ground as does the *vānaprasthi*.[97] On death he was supposed to become one with god and freed from the cycle of births and deaths.[98]

Indian people tried to understand the fundamental meaning and purpose of life; they discovered that life was a continued pilgrimage to the infinite and the eternal. They made this discovery the essential basis of everyday life. The *āśramas* were devised as the four life-stages with graduated course of duties to lead the individuals, step by step, towards realisation of the spiritual ideas. "The whole life should be passed in a series of gradually intensifying ascetic stages, through which a man, more and more purified from all earthly attachments, should become fitted for his *ashṭa* (home)."[99]

## REFERENCES

1. *Taittriya Upanishad*: XI.
2. *Ibid.*, X: English renderings have been taken from Sri Aurobindo's book entitled, *The Upanishads*, pp. 324-26.
3. H.C. Chakladar in *The Cultural Heritage of India*, Vol. II, p. 571.
4. *Ibid.*
5. *Ibid.*, p. 572.
6. S.K. Chatterjee, *op. cit.*, p. 98.
7. C.S. Venkateswaran, "The Ethics of the Puranas', *The Cultural Heritage of India*, Vol. II, p. 293.
8. T.R. Venkatarama Sastri, *op. cit.*, pp. 331-32.
9. V. Raghavan, *op. cit.*, p. 341.
10. Wm T. de Bary, *Sources of Indian Tradition*, pp. 220-22.
11. *Ibid.*
12. *Ibid.*
13. *Ibid.*
14. *Ibid.*

15. T.R. Venkataramana Sastri, *op. cit.*, p. 333.
16. C.S. Venkateswaran, n. 7.
17. H.C. Chakladar, *op. cit.*, p. 571.
18. *Ibid.*
19. C.S. Venkateswaran, *op. cit.*, p. 296.
20. H.C. Chakladar, *op. cit.*, pp. 557-58.
21. C.S. Venkateswaran, *op. cit.*, p. 294.
22. *Ibid.*
23. *Ibid.*
24. *Ibid.*
25. T.R. Venkataramana Sastri, *op. cit.*, pp. 331-32.
26. V. Raghavan, *op. cit.*, p. 348.
27. R.C. Majumdar, *op. cit.*, pp. 81-84.
28. *Ibid.*
29. *Ibid.*
30. *Ibid.*
31. *Ibid.*
32. *Ibid.*
33. *Ibid.*
34. *Ibid.*
35. *Ibid.*
36. *Ibid.*
37. *Ibid.*
38. *Ibid.*
39. *Ibid*
40. *Ibid.*
41. N.N. Bhattacharyya, *The Ancient Indian Rituals and their Social Contents*, pp. 25-45.
42. *Ibid.*, pp. 1-24.
43. R.C. Majumdar, *op. cit.*, pp. 81-84.
44. *Ibid.*
45. Wm. T. de. Bary, *op. cit.*, pp. 231-32 (Yaj., I. 95-105, 115-16).
46. *Manu*, III/79.
47. Sri Aurobindo, *op. cit.*, p. 101.
48. Bary, *op. cit.*,
49. Bary, *op. cit.*
50. *Ibid.*
51. Sri Aurobindo, *op. cit.*, p. 101.
52. Wm. T. de Bary, *op. cit.*, pp. 217-32.
53. *Ibid.*
54. Sri Aurobindo, *op. cit.*, pp. 198-200.
55. Wm. T. de. Bary, *op. cit.*, pp. 231-32.
56. *Ibid.*
57. *Ibid.*
58. R.C. Majumdar (ed.), *The Classical Age*, p. 582.
59. R.B. Pandey, "The Hindu Sacrament (Samskaras)", *The Cultural Heritage of India*, Vol. II, pp. 390-13.
60. *Ibid.*
61. *Ibid.*
62. *Ibid.*

63. *Ibid.*
64. *Ibid.*
65. *Ibid.*
66. *Ibid.*
67. *Ibid.*
68. *Ibid.*
69. *Ibid.*
70. *Ibid.*
71. *Ibid.*
72. *Ibid.*
73. D.C. Bhattacharya, "Penances and Vows", *The Cultural Heritage of India*, Vol. II, pp. 381-389.
74. *Ibid.*
75. *Ibid.*
76. *Ibid.*
77. *Ibid.*
78. *Ibid.*
79. *Ibid.*
80. *Ibid.*
81. *Ibid.*
82. *Ibid.*
83. *Ibid.*
84. *Ibid.*
85. V. Raghavan, *op. cit.*, p. 356.
86. H.C. Chakladar, *op. cit.*, p. 560.
87. *Ibid.*
88. *Ibid.*
89. Swami Prabhavananda (tr.) *Smat Bhagavatam*, p. 254.
90. V. Raghavan, *op. cit.*, p. 359.
91. *Ibid.*
92. *Ibid.*
93. *Ibid.*
94. V. Raghavan, *op. cit.*, pp. 359-60.
95. *Ibid.*
96. *Ibid.*
97. T.R. Venkataramana Sastri, *op. cit.*, p. 332.
98. *Ibid.*
99. *Ibid.*, pp. 333-34.

# 6

# Marriage, Sex-Relations and Status of Woman

Having become a *Snātaka* three courses were open before a man : he could marry and enter upon *Gārhasthy-āśrama*; he could become a *Parivrājaka* or else he could become an ascetic or hermit.[1] If he chose the first, that is the family life, he was to marry a girl of his own *varṇa* but of different *gotra*.[2] For, marriage was considered to be an instrument of *dharma* for the discharge of ordained duties. According to Manu, the wife is the main source of *dharma*, *artha*, *kāma* and so an unmarried man, irrespective of his *varṇa* to which he belongs, is unfit for the discharge of his duties of householder (*Gārhasthy-āśrama*). If the wife of a man died, he was to go for *vānaprastha*, i.e., to retire from life; but if he chose to remain in the house he must marry immediately after the period of impurity, following the cremation of his wife.[3] Life meant sacrifice and "there is no sacrifice for a man without a wife", declares the *Taittirīya Brahmaṇa*.[4] The *Aitareya Brāhmaṇa,* however, states that a widower can continue his sacrifices even if he remained unmarried, his devotion will be his figurative wife. *Vīshṇu* also provides for that.[5]

Marriage was regarded as a *saṁskāras*, *sahadharminī-saṁyoga*. The *Smṛtis* hold it to be bond of union between two persons for their eternal progress through the performance of duties in family life.[6] The marital union was regarded as a divine dispensation, a heaven ordained relation. "The wife stood by the side of the man in life and through death in the gladder life beyond; she was verily the half of man."[7] But the *Arthaśāstra* school held marriage as a contract.[8]

Marriage was usually negotiated and the father of the girl or her guardian decided whether to marry the girl to a particular suitor or not.[9] According to Nearchus, the Indians "marry without taking dowries but the women, as seen as they are marriageable, are brought forward by their fathers and exposed in public to be selected by the victor in wrestling or boxing or running or by one who excels in any other manly exercise."[10]

In the selection of the bride and the bridegroom their family, age, traits of the body, learning, wealth and resourcefulness were considered.[11] The examination of the bride and the bridegroom was a regular item in the negotiation for marriage. The selective principles were of domestic and eugenic importance. A great stress was laid on biological, intellectual and spiritual homogeneity between the bride and the bridegroom. Normally a person was expected to marry within the same *varṇa* but outside the same *gotra* (clan) and *svapiṇda* (consanguinity), and on the whole marriage between agnates and cognates up to a limit was forbidden.[12] A remarkable exception was the custom of marrying the maternal uncle's daughter in South India,[13] which is generally forbidden in the *Smṛtis*, except Bṛhaspati who also sanctions the marriage of the widow to the younger brother of the husband prevalent possibly at that time in Northern India.[14]

Daṇḍins *Daśakumāracharita* gives an idea of a girl usually considered best for marriage in the form of Gomini.[15] None of her limbs was too fat or too thin, too short or too long, rough or unclean. Her fingers were pink on the ineer side, and her palms marked with good signs such as the barley corn, the fish, the lotus and the pitcher. Her ankle-joints were even, the feet were lump and not stingy and the calves were tapering as the cow's tail. The knees slipped into the plumpness of the thigh almost unobserved. Gomini's hips were symmetrical, squarish, beautiful for the demarcating the cavities of the loins and were shaped like chariot-wheels. Her navel was fine and flat but deep. The lower part of the body *(udara)* was adorned with three plicatures, and the breast had emergent nipples with broad bases and covered the entire chest. The creeper-like arms had hands marked with the lines promising wealth, rich harvests and many sons, glossy with soft nails resembling jewels, and straight, tapering and copper-colour fingers. These arms were again exquisite and without the knobbing of joints, and they slipped smoothly into the low region of the shoulder. Gomini's neck was slender with the curve of a conch-shell. Her lotus-like face had roundish lips with the pink colour demarcated in the middle by the whiteness of the teeth, and a broad and a fine chin. The region of the cheeks was full and firm, and the creeper-like brows joining each other were curved, dark, blue and glossy. The nose resembled a half-blown seasamum blossom, and the big gentle eyes had a wet, but fickle, glance flashing with three colours—pure black, white and pink. The forehead was as beautiful as the crescent moon, and the charming curls resembled sapphires. The ears were adorned with the pending double-rings of a lotus-stalk, and the locks were slightly wavy, abundant, not brownish even at the end, long of equal length, glossy blue in colour and fragrant.

The *Dharma-śāstras* which include both the *Dharma-sūtras* and the metrical codes, otherwise known as the *Smṛtis*, provide for eight forms of marriage.[16] They are *Brahma*, *Daiva*, *Ārsha*, *Prājāpatya*, *Āsura*, *Gāndharva*, *Rākshasa* and *Paiśācha*. Father may give away the daughter, bedecked with ornaments and having first offered a libation of water, to a learned man of good conduct, and this is called as the *Brahma* form of marriage. The father may give away his daughter bedecked with ornaments to an officiating priest in *Yatishṭoma* sacrifice and this is known as *Daiva* form of marriage. In *Arsha* form of marriage the girl is married after receiving a cow and bull. Practice *dharma* together—a marriage performed with this commandment on the bride and the bridegroom is said to be *Prājāpatya* form of marriage. *Āsura* form of marriage provides for obtaining of a wife on payment of money to both the parents and the girl. In *Gāndharva* form of marriage the couple consummate their marriage in mutual understanding in secret. Forcible seizure of a bride by killing the relatives of the girl who herself means the death of her near ones is called *Rākshasa* form of marriage and *Paiśācha* form is that in which a girl is kidnapped while she is asleep or is intoxicated or insane.

Of these the first-six forms are considered valid for the *Brāhmaṇas*, *Āsura* to *Paiśācha* valid for the Vaiśya and for the Kshatriya the first-seven forms. For the *Śūdra* *Asura*, *Gāndharva* and *Paiśācha* are noι forbidden.[17] A son born of the first-four was believed to possess *Brahmateja*, noble character and longevity. Children born of the rest were supposed to be of bad character.[18] One of the objects of marriage was to beget a son. The son was to make the man debtless to his ancestors, providing oblation in future after the death of his father. For the purpose son born of *Brahma* form of marriage was supposed to sanctify ten generations on both sides of his parents, besides his own-self; son born of *Daiva* form of marriage was considered to sanctify seven generations, son born of *Prājāpatya* six, *Ārsha* three, in all other cases, besides the self, of the man.[19] *Āśvalāyana*, however, holds that son born of *Brahma* form of marriage sanctifies twelve, *Daiva* ten, *Prājāpatya* eight, *Ārsha* seven generations of the ancestors and the successors of both sides of his parents.[20]

*Gāndharva* form of marriage conceded to the Kshatriyas and other lower orders was not very much respected and not allowed to the Brāhmaṇas.[21] Vātsyāyana provides details of this process of courtship. Where the suitor cannot meet his beloved, he should engage the daughter of his nurse for negotiating with the beloved. When the girl is ready for the marriage, she should come for meeting the man in time fixed before-hand. The marriage is then to be settled by thrice going round the fire brought from the house of a Srotriya and fed with oblations according to the *Smṛti* rules. After the consummation of the marriage the parents and relatives are to be informed for formal bestowal of the girl. Of course, marriage performed before the fire is solemn and cannot be annulled in any way. This sort of courtship of the girl who is styled the *Abhisārikā* provided themes to many romantic Sanskrit works in ancient India.

The marriage ritual was, however, most gorgeous and elaborate. The bridegroom bedecked in great fancy attended by a train of friends and relatives proceeded to the bride's home and was received by her father or male guardian with a *madhuparka*, auspicious ceremonial drink of honey and curd. Usually the ceremony was held in a gaudy temporary pavilion in the court of the house. Bride and groom entered the pavilion separately and sat on either side of a small curtain in the accompaniment of sacred verses muttered by the officiating Brāhmaṇa; then the curtain was removed and the couple saw one another for the first time. The bride's father stepped forward and formally gave her to the groom who promised that he would not behave wrongly to her in respect of the three traditional aims of life—piety, wealth and pleasure. Next, offering of the *ghee* and rice was made in the fire. The groom then grasped the bride's hand while she offered grain in the fire, round which he then led her, usually with their garments knotted together, after which she trod on a mill-stone. The couple then took seven steps together, the bride treading on a small heap of rice at each stage. Then they were sprinkled with holy water and the main part of the ceremony was complete.[22]

The newly married couple then returned to the bridegroom's house where a further sacrifice to the fire was performed. In the evening, it was incumbent upon them to look at the Pole Star, a symbol of faithfulness. For three nights the couple were expected to remain continent, in some cases they were allowed to sleep together with a staff between them. On the fourth night the husband performed a rite to promote conception and the marriage was consummated.[23]

Sexuality was not looked on as a mere vent to the animal passions of the male; it was regarded as a refined mutual relationship for the satisfaction of both the parties.[24] The sophisticated town's man for whom the *Kāmasūtra* was written was advised to consider the satisfaction of his wife as well as of his own, for she was as passionate as he and it was even said by some that her pleasure in sex was greater than his loveplay was manifold and thoroughly classified; thus the *Kāmasūtra* defined no less than sixteen types of kiss. There was much tenderness in love-making, though it often culminated in violent embrace. It was a favourite poetic convention to describe lovers of both sexes, whether married or simile, as displaying the tokens of their passion to their confidential friends in the form of marks of nail and teeth.[25]

Yet a good deal of precaution was provided for to avoid any misunderstanding. It was advised that[26] "for the first-three days after their marriage husband and wife should sleep on the floor and abstain from intercourse; for the next seven days they should bathe to the sound of music, adorn themselves, dine together and pay their respects to their relatives and to other people who attended their wedding. . . On the evening of the tenth day the husband should treat gently to his wife . . . to give her confidence. Vātsyāyana recommends that a man should at first refrain from intercourse until he had over won his bride and gained her confidence, for, women, being gentle by nature, prefer to be won over gently. If a woman is forced to submit to rough handling by a man, whom she scarcely knows, she may come to hate sexual intercourse, and even to hate the whole male sex . . . or she may grow to detest her husband in particular. . . ."

The Ṛgvedic hymns express the feeling of the couple who were united in marriage and gods were invoked to shower their blessings on them as they would jointly offer sacrifices to them. The spirit of the union is beautifully expressed in the marriage ritual when the groom addresses the bride thus :[27]

> "A friend be thou, having paced these seven steps with me; the couple who paced seven steps together became friends. May I gain thy friendship, may I never fall off from thy friendship; let us resolve together that, bound in love and ever radiant in each other's company, meaning well towards each other, sharing together all enjoyments and pleasures, we may unite our thoughts, our duties and our ideals."

In the *Atharva Veda* we find the husband and the wife offering a similar prayers for unity of mind. "The eyes of us two be of honey aspect; our faces be ointment; put thou me within thy heart; may our mind verily be together." Another hymn likewise inspires the unity of the heart and mind. "Like-hearted, like-minded no hostility do I make for you; do show affection, the one towards the other, as the inviolable cow towards her calf when born. Be the son submissive to the father, like-minded with the mother, let the wife speak to the husband words full of honey, beneficent. Let not brother hate brother, nor sister hate sister, becoming accordant, of like-minded, speak ye words auspiciously. Your drinking be the same, in common your share of food; in the same harness do I join you together, worship ye Agni united, like spokes about a nave. United, like-minded, I be you, of one bunch, all of you, by conciliation; be like the gods defending nectar (*amarta*); late and early be well-willing yours."[28]

As a wife woman is highly placed in the Vedic literature. She is identified with the house and the home. "The home has verily its foundation in the wife, the house is not the home, the mistress of the house is called the home."[29] It would appear that a virtuous wife was always desired for all comforts of the home and fulfilling all requirements that a householder needed. Manu ordains[30] that the wife should be entrusted with material and financial resources of the home, with collecting and spending. There is no difference between the house-wife and the goddess of fortune; both illumine the home and are to be adored as such. Everyone in the house, the parents-in-law, brothers-in-law and the husband, shall honour her and keep her happy and bedecked if they want to prosper. "Where women are honoured, there the gods revel; where they are not honoured, all religious acts become futile; that home perishes in which daughter-in-law suffers; homes cursed by them come to grief."

Society was by and large monogamous but the determining factor of the number of wives of a person was perhaps the economic condition. The *Smṛtis* do not prohibit polygamy, rather provide for the rules of determining the status of the wives that one might have married from the different *varṇas*. Of course they discourage on the whole, *pratiloma* marriage. Manu provides[31] that a Brāhmaṇa should marry first a girl from his own *varṇa* and then girls of successive *varṇas*. Similarly a Kshatriya should first marry a girl of his own *varṇa* and then might marry girls of other *varṇas*. The rule for marriage of a Vaiśya was similar. But a Śudra was supposed to marry within his own caste only.[32] The marriage sacraments and rite for such inter-caste marriages are not provided for, in the *Manusmṛti* though the status of such inter-caste marriages and the children born of such unions are specified in detail. Manu also provides that a *Brahmachāri* should pay due homage by touching the feet of the wife of the *Guru* who belonged to the same *varṇa*, apparently Brāhmaṇa wife, but to the rest he might pay homage by touching the ground from a distance.[32] It shows that the *Gurus*, who were supposed to be men of noble birth, had profound knowledge, were engaged in teaching of the Vedas, probing into the Truth and translating Truth in their daily life by the performance of the prescribed rites and ceremonies, could have more than one wife.

That the rich persons had more than one wife as also some of the Brāhmaṇas can be guessed from the *Smṛtis*, *Purāṇas* and secular literature. In the *Mṛchchhakaṭika* of Śūdraka we find Chārudatta, a virtuous Brāhmaṇa, who took to business and had become poor, did not hesitate to marry a Ganikā Vasantasenā though he had his first wife living with him. In Kālidāsa's works such examples are abundant. In his drama *Malavikāgnimitram* we find king Agnimitra married successively two girls (though he had his first wife and son by her), the first of which happened to be his maid servant and second a slave girl who was born in a royal family but sold as a slave and eventually brought to the court of king Agnimitra. In the *Vikramorvasīyam* king Vikrama married Urvasi though he had his wife at home. Again in the *Avijñānaśakuntalam* we find king Dushyanta marrying Śakuntalā in the hermitage of Kaṇva where he had gone casually in hunting excursion. Such examples are seen in plenty in Sanskrit literature of the Classical period. Not only did a man have his wives of different *varṇas*, Vātsyāyana's *Kāmasūtra* provides for marriage of a widow to a *Bhogī*.

But a man's desire was not confined to his wives or the remarried widow called *punarbhū*, he might have prostitutes or *gaṇikās* either in his own house or association with such public women living in the city. The position of prostitutes or public women was by far the better than that of the married wives or the *punarbhūs*. As in Greece the Metaira was usually a qualified lady well trained in sixty-four arts of *Kāmasūtra* and her manifold charms made her not only attractive but her company or association was regarded as a mark of social prestige.[33] Jātaka story tells us the accomplished *gaṇika* of the Lichchhavi tribe was visited by king Bindusāra in disguise and even Lord Buddha accepted her invitation in preference to the city council fathers.[34] Kings and chiefs retained in their palaces prostitutes on salary who attended on them, acted even as guards and accompanied them when they went into battles. In some cases they turned into concubines. In the *Dharma śāstras* the public women have not been favoured; they were not to participate in any religious rites and Gautama even states that murder of a *gaṇika* is no sin and involves no punishment, though in some rituals, soil from their house is till required.[35] In Mauryan time the prostitutes were protected and supervised by the State and two days' earning was collected from them as tax.[36] In lieu teachers and trainers were provided by the State.

A typical *ganikā* was beautiful, accomplished and wealthy, enjoying fame and honour comparable to that of the Aspasias and Phrynes of classical Greece.[37] The distinctive qualities of a *ganikā* is given in the *Daśakumāracharita* of Dandin.[38] This formed a stocklist which included not only music, dancing and singing, but also acting, the composition of poetry, impromptu. . . and otherwise, flower-arrangement and garland-making, the preparation of perfumes and cosmetics, cooking, dress-making and embroidery, sorcery, conjuring and sleight of hand, the composition of riddles, tongue-twisters and other puzzles, fencing with sword and staff, archery, gymnastics, carpentry and architecture, logic, chemistry and mineralogy, gardening, training, fighting cocks, partridges and rams, teaching parrots and mynas to talk, writing in cipher languages, making artificial flowers and clay modelling.[39] No wonder that such a courtesan of pleasant disposition, beautiful and otherwise attractive, who had mastered the arts, should have the right to a seat of honour among men. It was also quite natural that she should have been honoured by the kings and praised by the learned and people sought her favours and treat her with consideration.

In between the virgins and the wedded women there was a class of girls who were attached to temples of various gods as servants or wives of the gods and they were usually styled as *devadāsis*.[40] Many people offered their daughters to the temples who were supposed to serve the gods in the temples as the wives serve their husbands. Usually their duty was to sing and dance before the gods of the temples. They were provided with grants of lands or maintenance allowance by the temple authorities for their services. Often these girls turned into temple prostitutes. The earliest record of *devadāsi* is found in the Rāmgaṛh cave inscription of Vindhya hills, some 160 miles to the south of Vārānasī.[41] In later years the institution did not find much favour in the North but continued to flourish in the South till recent times. Chālukya king Mahendravarman styled Vikramāditya VI founded a temple in memory of his mother with quarters for the *devadāsīs*.[42] Four hundred of them were attached to the great temple of Tanjore during the reign of Rājarāja I of the Chola dynasty.[43]

In spite of provision of having more than one wife or a *punarbhu* or prostitutes for the satisfaction of one's sexual desire we find people taking to sedulous means for the fulfilment of carnal desire or appetites. Not only did men of ordinary walks of life but gods, *ṛshis* and kings took to unusual means to have sexual intercourse with virgins, public women and wives of other people. There is a story that Creator Brahmā attempted to mate with Tilottamā, the divine nymph but also his own daughter Usha; Lord Śiva is said to have mated with thousands of the wives of the *ṛshis*, Lord Kṛṣṇa is stated to have dallied with sixteen thousand *gopis*; sage Parāśara mated with a daughter of a fisherman on the ferryboat; sage Atri even assumed the form of a deer to satisfy his carnal desire by copulating with a deer.[44] The most interesting point is that neither the society nor the caste censured the person who took to such means to have sexual satisfaction nor did the person concerned loose his social position. Sexual urge was regarded as a natural phenomenon and if anybody lose self-control or took to unusual means for its satisfaction people took little note of that.

**Status of Women**

Regarding the position of women, Manu states[45] that a woman should never desire to live separately from her father, husband or son because, for, if she lives independently she would peril both the father's and the husband's family. Even if the husband is displeased with the wife she should live happily and attend to domestic works; she should keep things of the house in good condition and should not spend lavishly. She should attend to her husband to whom her father or brother had given her until death and after death of the husband she should not leave his family; whatever sacrifices are performed these are performed for the religious merit of both husband and wife. Wife does not have any separate sacrifice without her husband, she cannot go to heaven without him. Wife should not do anything which is not approved by her husband whether he is dead or alive. After the death of her husband she should live on roots and fruits like a *brahmachārī* and should never think of another man. If a woman thinks of another man for a son other than her husband she is condemned and goes to hell; no child by another man is recognised. If she goes for another man she is hated and is attacked by many diseases, she becomes a jackal after death; but if she is found devoted to her husband she is praised and goes to heaven or *patiloka*.

Regarding the position of woman, Manu further holds:[46] "Woman, be a young or an adult or an old, should not do anything independently, without permission of her guardian. Before marriage girl should be under the father, in youth under the husband and if the husband dies under the son; she should never be independent." The father protects her (woman) in childhood, the husband in youth and the son in advanced years; a woman is never fit to depend upon herself', says Baudhāyana; exactly the same words are repeated in the *Mahābhārata*. Vaśishṭha also corroborate the same view when he says: "A woman is not independent, she is dependent on man"

The *Vishṇu Purāṇa* holds: "A man is required, of course, to earn unstained money, to do sacrifice and make donations to noble persons—all these are very difficult job; a man can go to *prajāpati-loka* by such onerous discharge of duties. But a woman by serving her husband physically with devotion goes to such a place, she (woman) can earn all merit by service alone."[47] Women usually have been depicted as physically incapable of defending themselves from molestation. Even the *Ṛg Veda* observes that their mind is difficult to be controlled and the epic *Mahābhārata* casts an aspersion on their moral strength.[48] Kālidāsa, a poet of world fame, states that the mind of woman cannot be guessed even by gods, not to speak of men.[49] Again Daṇḍin writes that the mind of woman is the hardest; he gives a story to establish that through the mouth of a man in his *Daśakumāracharita*.[50]

The position of woman, nay any person, depends to a large extent on his or her qualities, utility and serviceability. As such education and personality are matter of considerable importance in determining her position in the family and the society. In an age of large scale illiteracy and supremacy of the males in patriarchal society where a male child was put on premium, the birth of a daughter passed almost unnoticed and very little care was taken for her education. Exception was there in case of rich and noble families of the Kshatriyas and Brāhmaṇas and Vaiśyas where the girls were given education. Rich persons engaged tutors to instruct their daughters as there was no system of public education in ancient India whatsoever. Art of dancing and singing were supposed to be provided to the girls for amusement to their husbands. We learn from Vātsyāyana that the husband usually appointed his wife to keep accounts of the household, to receive and spend money and pay to the servants.[51]

The daughters of the kings or princes or ministers were given instructions at home. We know the instance of Prabhāvatiguptā who acted as the Regent of her minor son Divākarasena, and Gautamī, who acted as Regent during the minority of her son.[52] The daughters of the sages in the hermitages were in a better position to acquire knowledge. The poetess Vijayāṅkā of Karṇāṭaka was a great poet who was second only to Kālidāsā; Avantisundari, wife of well-known poet Rajaśekhara was a literary critic and earned reputation as a great poetess; tradition relates that Maṇḍana Miśra's wife Ubhayabhāratī served as an umpire in the debate between her husband and Śankara Āchārya; a lady Rushā wrote a book on the diseases of woman which was translated into Arabic in the 8th century.[53] But the general picture of education of woman is neither glorious nor considerable.

The ideal of Indian womanhood, as daughter, sister, wife, even as mother, has never been depicted in terms of equality with men or independence. In a society of the prominence of the male-beings, the women were taught to accept a position of subordination, listening to the stories of Sīta and Sāvitrī who personified the virtues of the Indian womanhood, glaring examples of subordination, service and sacrifice; they were taught that their life was meant for the happiness of their husbands and children.

On the question of her marriage she was neither consulted nor given any option. She was given away to a man by her legitimate guardian. Of course, if she was not married in time she could wed herself by *Gāndharva* system of marriage. Here also the consent of the guardian had to be obtained before solemnising the formal marriage.[54]

The *Dharma-śāstras*, especially Manu, discourage widow remarriage. Manu holds that the girl's father gave her away to her husband to whom she belonged for ever. . . . The husband dies, but really he is not dead; he is waiting on the other side where she is sure to go if she does not insult his memory."[55] Bṛhaspati recommends self-immolation on the funeral pyre of her husband by a widow as an alternative, but Śankha, Aṅgiras and Hārīta urge her to burn herself strongly.[56] But Nārada recommends not only remarriage of widow but also the remarriage of a woman whose husband is lost or impotent or has become an ascetic or expelled from the caste. Parāśara also approves of what Nārada says but he prefers the life of *brahmcharya* for such a woman.[57] Vātsyāyana also preferred *brahmcharya* for widow but he recommends to a widow, who could not restrain herself, to get married to a *bhogī*, a seeker after pleasure, of her choice.[58] A widow could not inherit any property of her husband; she could only possess her own property, *stridhana*.[59] If a woman became widow before bearing a child she could have one or two by association with the brother of her husband or a *svapiṇda*.[60] After 300 B.C. the practice began to disuse.

The widow is prescribed a rigorous course of discipline and an austere life to progress towards the spiritual goal.[61] She is supposed to sleep on the floor and not to use a cot. She could not put on bodice and colourful garments. She was not to use collyrium in the eyes or yellow pigment on the face or any kind of scent. She was to take only one meal a day and offer oblation everyday in memory of her husband. Bana's *Harshacharita* refers to the tying of tuft of hair by the widow.[62]

The woman as mother is given heavy responsibilities and painful duties. In return, the mother is paid highest respect in the *Dharma-śāstras*. Manu and Vaśishṭha hold that the teacher is ten times more respectable than an *upādhya* or tutor, the father is hundred-times more than a teacher; but the mother is a thousand times more than the father.[63] Yājñavalkya says that the mother is superior to the teacher and even to the priest participating at the sacrifice.[64] A father who has violated a social injunction and faces loss of caste is to be cast off; but a mother never becomes an outcaste to her son under any circumstances.[65] Even an expectant mother was respected everywhere and she paid no ferry toll like an ascetic and *brahmchāri*.[66] But in spite of all these eulogies and respect shown towards the mother she was always dependent on her son in case she became a widow or husband left home for *vānaprastha*.

The status of woman as wife, married according to the *Smṛti* sacrament or *Sūtra* ritual, was nothing beyond that of complete dependence on her husband; but her position as a remarried widow called *punarbhu* to a *bhogī*, as shown by Vātsyāyana, was comparatively better.[67] The wedded wife, who participated with her husband in the religious rites, lives in comparative seclusion in the inner apartments of the house and she never came out to receive the friends of her husband; nor did she join her husband in parties. But the *punarbhū* in her new home assumed the role of a mistress, patronised the wives of her new husband, commanded his servants and treated his friends with a degree of familiarity unknown to the wedded wives. She cultivated a greater knowledge of arts and crafts, took part in sports and festivals, drinking parties and picnics, etc. She might leave her husband but even if she was driven out she did not give back anything. Her position in the house where there were different quarters for the wedded wives, and the prostitutes, was between the two, that is, in the middle between the wives and the prostitutes. Thus her position is not that of complete dependence on the husband and one of exclusiveness from the gaities of life, though she was not allowed to participate in the religious rites and sacrifices.

That the status of woman was completely subordinated to the man towards the end of the Hindu period is evident from the following quotation: "Though destitute of virtue, or seeking pleasure (elsewhere), or devoid of good qualities, (yet) a husband must be constantly worshipped as a god by a faithful wife. She who shows disrespect to (a husband) who is addicted to (some evil) passion, is drunkard, or diseased, shall be deserted for three months, (and be) deprived of her ornaments and furniture." But the husband is not required to follow a similar line of conduct. For, "she, who drinks spirituous liquor, is of bad conduct, rebellious, diseased, mischievous or wasteful, may at any time be superseded (by another wife)". Nay, more; the husband could supersede his wife on much less serious grounds. "A barren wife may be superseded in the eighth year, she whose children (all) die in the tenth, she who bears only daughters in the eleventh, but she who is quarrelsome without delay." And the poor wife was to bear his degradation with stoic calmness; for, "a wife who, being superseded, in anger departs from her husband's house must either be instantly confined or cast off in the presence of the family." Sometimes she could be beaten with a rope or a split bamboo. The poor wife was expected to follow her husband even in death by burning herself alive, but the husband "having given sacred fire to his wife, who dies before him, could marry again, and again kindle the fire."

Thus the story of Hindu woman is a story of gradual suppression of her position in society and she lost the position of superiority of the earliest times.

**REFERENCES**

1. H.C. Chakladar, *op. cit.*, p. 563.
2. R.B. Pandey, *op. cit.*, p. 409.
3. *Ibid.*
4. H.C. Chakladar, *op. cit.*, pp. 572-73.
5. A.S. Altekar, *The Position of Women in Hindu Civilisation*, pp. 110-11.
6. A.S. Altekar, *op. cit.*, pp. 110-11.
7. *Ibid.*
8. R.C. Majumdar (ed.), *The Age of Imperial Unity*, p. 565.
9. *Ibid.*
10. *Ibid.*, p. 560.
11. R.B. Pandey, *op. cit.*, p. 409.
12. *Ibid.*
13. R.C. Mujumdar (ed.), *op. cit.*, p. 558.
14. *Ibid.*
15. M.M. Sen & others (ed.), *Sanskrita Sahitya Sambhar*, Vol. II, pp. 186-90.
16. R.B. Pandey, *op. cit.*. p. 408.
17. *Manu*, III/21f.
18. *Ibid.*
19. *Ibid.*
20. R.B. Pandey, *op. cit.*, p. 409.
21. R.C. Mujumdar (ed.), *The Classical Age*, p. 566.
22. A.L. Basham, *op. cit.*, pp. 167-73.
23. *Ibid.*
24. *Ibid.*
25. *Ibid.*
26. *Ibid.*
27. H.C. Chakladar, *op. cit.*, p. 572.
28. *Ibid.*
29. *Ibid.*, p. 574.
30. V. Raghavan, *op. cit.*, p. 354.
31. *Manu*, II/219f.
32. *Ibid.*
33. A.L. Basham, *op. cit.*, pp. 184-86.
34. *Ibid.*
35. *Ibid.*, p. 187.
36. *Ibid.*, pp. 184-86.
37. *Ibid.*
38. M.M. Sen & others (ed.), *op. cit.*, pp. 138-40.
39. A.L. Basham, *op. cit.*, pp. 185-87.
40. *Ibid.*
41. *Ibid.*
42. *Ibid.*
43. D.C. Ganguly, "Some Aspects of the Position of Women in Ancient India", *The Cultural Heritage of India*, Vol. II, p. 600.
44. M.M. Sen and others (ed.), *op. cit.*, pp. 138-40.
45. *Manu*, V/147f.
46. *Ibid.*
47. *Vishnu Purāṇa*, V/28f.

48. H.C. Chakladar, *op. cit.*, p. 577.
49. Kalidasa,-*Datrinsatputtalika*, 18/10.
50. M.M. Sen & others (ed.), *op. cit.*, pp. 186-87.
51. R.C. Majumdar (ed.) *The Classical Age*, p. 568.
52. D.C. Sircar, *Studies in the Society and Administration of Ancient and Medieval India*, pp. 234-35.
53. D.C. Ganguly, *op. cit.*, p. 594.
54. R.C. Majumdar (ed.), *The Classical Age*, p. 514.
55. H.C. Chakladar, *op. cit.*, p. 578.
56. R.C. Majumdar (ed.), *The Classical Age*, p. 571.
57. H.C. Chkladar, *op. cit.*, p. 578.
58. *Ibid.*
59. V. Raghavan, *op. cit.*, p. 354.
60. Manu, IX/59f; A.S. Altekar, *op. cit.*, p. 144.
61. H.C. Chakladar, *op. cit.*, pp. 577-78.
62. D.C. Ganguly, *op. cit.*, p. 598.
63. *Manu*, II/142f.
64. H.C. Chakladar, *op. cit.*, pp. 354-80.
65. *Ibid.*
66. *Ibid.*
67. R.C. Majumdar (ed.), *The Classical Age*, pp. 514-15.

# 7

# Spirituality, Religion and Philosophy

## Basic Ideas that governed Ancient Indian Society

Right from the dawn of civilisation people in India attempted to understand the Universe and the Cosmic Principle and developed an attitude of life and the world in accordance with the experience that they acquired. The *Śvetaśvatara Upanishad* pondered:[1]

किं कारणम् ब्रह्म कुतः स्म जाता
जीवाम् केन क्व च स्मप्रतिष्ठाः।
अधिष्ठाताः केन सुखेतरेषु
वर्तामहे ब्रह्मविद्यो व्यवस्थाम्।।

(Those in quest of the *Brāhman* queriéd : Hath the *Brāhman* created the universe? Where are we from? Why should we live? Where do we inhabit? Who hath conditioned enjoyment and suffering to us?)

The *Kena Upanishad* echoes the same query:[2]

केनेषितं पतति प्रेषितं मनः। केन प्राणः प्रथमः प्रैति युक्तः।।
केनेषितां वाचमिमां वदन्ति। चक्षु श्रोत्रं क उ देवो युनक्ति।।

(By whom missionied falls the mind shot to its work? By whom yoked moves the first-life-breath forward on its path? By whom impelled is that word that man speak? What God set eye and ear to their workings?)

The *Ṛshis* arrived at the conclusion, having an insight into the Truth of the Cosmic Principle:[3]

न तत्र चक्षुर्गच्छति न वाग् गच्छति नो मनो:।
न विद्मो न विजानीमो यथैतदनुशिष्यात्।
अन्यदेव तद्विदितादथो अविदितादधि।
इति शुश्रुम पूर्वेषां ये नस्तद्वाचचक्षिरे।।

(There sight travels not, nor speech nor the mind. We know It not nor can distinguish how one should teach of It; for It is other than the known, It is there above the unknown. It is so we have heard from men of old who declared that to our understanding.)

To pursue this Truth the people developed an attitude to life which is commonly called Hinduism. It governed the development of beliefs and practices, aspirations and achievements, speculations and standards of the society in which we live today. Though in the 6th-5th centuries B.C. there emerged some protestant movements against Hinduism, such as Buddhism and Jainism, the governing principle, controlling ideas and the deep-dynamic links, which governed these protestant religions, were the same as those established by Hinduism. In fact, the people of India be the Brāhmaṇical Hindus or the Buddhists or the followers of Mahavira-Jina had accepted certain basic truths of existence and adhered to some fundamentals which govern their thought and action in life.[4]

Of this, the first is the belief in the existence of a Basic Reality, or a Being or God, beyond the mental and physical appearances.[5] There is a spirit, beyond the mind, life and body, containing all that is relative, a Supreme Absolute, originating and supporting all that is transcendent and eternal:[6] ईशा वास्यमिदं सर्व यत् किञ्च जगत्यां जगत्।[7] (All this is for the habitation of by the Lord, whatever is individual universe of movement in the universal motion.) In other words One transcendent, Universal, Original, Sempiternal, Divinity or Divine Essence or Consciousness or Force is the fount and continent of an inhabitant of things. Soul, Nature, Life are only a manifestation of or partial phenomenon of this self-aware Eternity and Conscious Eternal: ऊर्ध्वमूलोऽवाक्शाख एषोऽश्वत्थ सनातनः। तदेव शुक्रं तदब्रह्म तदेवामृतमुच्यते। तस्मिँल्लोकाः श्रिताः सर्वे तदु नात्येति कश्चन। एतद्वै तत्।।[8] (This is an eternal Ashvattha tree whose root is above but its branches are downward. It is He that is called the Bright one and Brahman and Immortality, and in Him are all the worlds established, nothing goes beyond Him). In the words of Radhakrishnan:

"There is a community and continuity of life between man in his deepest self and God."[9]

But this cannot be seen as a physical phenomenon by eyes or felt by any of the other senses including the mind:[10] न तत्र चक्षुर्गच्छति न वाग् गच्छति नो मनो। (There sight travels not, nor speech nor the mind). The Supreme Truth of all is a Being or an Existence beyond the mental and physical appearances:[11] न चक्षुषा पश्यति कश्चनैनम्। (Neither by vision doth anybody behold him). The unseen Reality is arrived at either by intuitive faith or by intellectual ratiocination or by both reason and faith:[12] अस्तीत्येवोपलब्धाव्यस्तत्त्वभावेन चोभयो:। अस्तीत्येवोपलब्धस्य तत्त्वभाव: प्रसीदति।। (One must comprehend God in concept. He is and in his essentials but when one has grasped Him as the Is, then the essentials of God downs upon him). But this realisation cannot be pinned down to a particular description:[13] न संदृशे तिष्ठति रूपमस्य।। (It is that He hath no likeness nor image). This force or Principle or Order of Consciousness can be attained by mam when he rises above his material personality:[14] एषोऽणुरात्मा चेतसा वेदितव्यो यस्मिन् प्राण: पञ्चधा संविवेश।

Followers of one religion or of a sect or denomination might consider the self of man to be indivisibly one with the Universal-Self or the Supreme-Spirit. Another might consider man as one with the Divine in essence but different from Him in nature. A third might hold God, Nature and Soul of man to be eternally three different powers of the Being. But, for all, the truth of the soul and self is held with equal force.[15] Even for the dualist God is the Supreme-Self and Reality by whom Nature and man live.[16] The Spirit, its Universal Nature and the Soul in the living Jiva are the three Truths which are universally admitted by all the many religious sects and denominations of India.[17] Universal is also the admission of the fact that some kind of living unity or uniting contact or absolute unity of the soul in man with God or Supreme-Self or Eternal *Brahman* is the condition of spiritual perfection.[18]

This truth was to be lived upon and even to be made the governing idea of thought, life and action. In other words the *summum bonum* in the life of a man was to pursue the truth under whatever conception or form, to attain it by inner experience, to live in it by consciousness.[19] "Man lives in the physical cosmos subject to death and much falsehood or mortal existence. To rise beyond this death, to become one of the immortals, he has to turn from the falsehood to the truth; he has to turn to the light and to battle with and to conquer the powers of the Darkness."[20] One has to realise that he is a potential divine Being and his soul is veiled by *māyā* or *avidyā* suggested in the *Gītā*.[21]

Indian religions then placed four necessities before human life: First, it imposed upon the mind a belief in a highest consciousness or a state of existence, universal and transcendent of universe, from which all come, in which all live, and to which all must return. Secondly, it laid upon individual life the need of self-preparation by development and experience till man is ready to grow into the truth of the greater existence. Thirdly, it provided it with a well-founded, well-explored, many branching and always enlarging way of knowledge and of spiritual or religious discipline. Lastly, it placed before man a framework of personal and social discipline and conduct of mental and moral development, according to his own nature, to become eventually ready for the greater existence.[22]

To give fuller play to the above ideas people of India evolved a basic system of Individual life in the social framework. This was the double system of the four *Varnas* and four successive *āśramas* in the life of a man.[23] All men cannot follow in all things—one common and invarible rule. Differing with the type of man and the type of function *Dharma* would differ. चातुर्वर्ण्यं मया सृष्टं गुणकर्मविभागशः।[24] (I have created the four orders according to the division of the *Guṇa* and *Karma* or quality and works). *Dharma* special for special person according to his stage of development and pursuit of life, but universal too in broad-lines, would lead towards his aim of spiritual liberation and perfection, *mukti, moksha*:[25] स्वे स्वे कर्मण्यभिरतः संसिद्धिं लभते नरः।।[26] (Doing one's own work (according to own *Guṇa* and *Karma* one attains salvation). Not only people were divided in four classes or groups but the life of an individual was also ideally divided into four stages—*Brahmachārya*, *Gārhasthya*, *Vānaprastha* and *Sannyāsa*.[27] A man in order to be a full man was to be trained properly for discharging his duties and responsibilities. This he does as a celibate student. Then he must be a householder and perform his duties and pay his debt to all concerned by marrying and raising a family. In the next stage he should gradually withdraw from *Saṁsāra* passing on the torch to his next generation. Finally he severs connection with the *saṁsāra* by asceticism.

But life as an intermediate reality was never denied. "Man was allowed to fathom on his way all experience, to give to his character and action a large reign and heroic proportions and to fill in life opulently with colour and beauty and enjoyment." For the purpose *āśrama-dharmas* were provided.[28] The scheme of *Grāhasthy-āśrama* is based on the ethical principle that man should discharge his debt to the Gods, to the *Ṛshis*, to *Pitṛis*, to the world around, before aspiring liberation from the bonds of the flesh and blood, and his hedonistic desires—*artha* and *kārma*.[29] The *Brahmachary-āśrama* prepared and trained the would-be *Gārhasthya*;[30] the *Gārhasthy-āśrama* provided for *pañcha-ṁahāyajña* to achieve *Purushārtha*;[31] the *āśramas* of *Vānaprastha* and *Sannyāsa* for the transition to the spiritual existence.[32] Thus *āśrama-dharma* provided for the discipline of an inward growth of man from the physical through the psychic to the spiritual.

The theory of *Karma* and rebirth or transmigration of soul also plays a fundamental role in Hindu philosophy. The soul does not begin with the body; nor does it end with it. The Lord tells Arjuna:[33] बहूनि मे व्यतीतानि जन्मानि तव चार्जुन। (Oh Arjuna you and myself had so many births before this); its long pilgrimage through dying bodies and decaying worlds. The great purpose of redemption is carried over without break from one life to another. All systems of Indian thought accept the idea of the continuous existence of the individual as axiomatic. "Our mental and emotional make-up is reborn with us in the next birth forming what is called character. Our strivings and endeavours give us the start."[34] This continuity will go on until the soul attains destiny of freedom which is the goal of human evolution.[35] बहूनां जन्मनामन्ते ज्ञानवान्मां प्रपद्यते। (After several lives the wise comes unto me). The idea of *Karma* has been found to be an incentive to further noble action, and it has impelled people to try to rise above what they felt has been ordained by their previous *Karma*. By *Purushākāra* or personal enterprise fatalism or abject surrender to Fate or adversities in life has been sought to be fought. This sentiment accepted by the people of India has been put in the mouth of Karṇa in the *Veṇīsaṁhāra* by Bhaṭṭa Nārāyaṇā in the following words:[36]

> "Whatever I may be by caste—a Sūta or the son of Sūta—birth in a particular family is in the hands of God. But success as a man is in my control."

Life is an education in the moral sphere, no less than the physical;

whatsoever a man soweth that shall he also reap. Every act produces its natural result in future character. It does not accept the theory of predetermination or the idea of an overruling providence.[37] The *Garuḍa Purāṇa* says : "No one gives joy or sorrow. That others give us these is an erroneous conception : Our own deeds bring to us their fruits. Body of mine repays by suffering." The law of morality is fundamental to the whole cosmic drama. *The Law of Karma* holds that man can control his future by creating in the present what will produce the desired effect. "Man is the sole and absolute master of his fate."[38]

People in India also believed that realisation of this ultimate truth would come through a righteous living, by following *Ṛta-Dharma*. *Ṛta* or Eternal Law or Moral order is also called *dharma* which means the Principle which holds together all existence. "One might say that *Ṛta* is the Divine Order in itself and Dharma is its outward manifestation in life."[39] The Ultimate Reality is a Principle of Order (*Ṛta*) as much as it is the Supreme Force or Spirit and it operates in the Universe—in worlds of both the animate and inanimate as *dharma*.[40] *Dharma* is, thus, the Divine Principle which acts as the moral principle in the mind and soul of man as the still small voice of God or conscience. *Dharma* is at once religious law of Action and deepest law of Nature.[41]

## Religion

"The task of religion and spirituality is to mediate between God and man, between the Eternal and Indefinite and this transient, and yet persistent finite, between luminous Truth-consciousness not expressed or not yet expressed here and the mind's ignorance," says Sri Aurobindo.[42] Radhakrishnan holds: "Religion for the Hindu is experience or attitude of mind. It is not an idea but a power, not an intellectual proposition but a life conviction. . . . The aim of all religions is the practical realisation of this highest truth. It is intuition of reality (*brahmasānubhava*); insight into the truth (*brahmasadarśana*); contact with the supreme (*brahmasaṁsparśa*), direct apprehension of the reality (*brahmasākshātkāra*).[43] Religious practices and institutions were founded for the practical realisation of these ideas.

### *Vedic Religion*

Man's first and primitive idea of God, however, came only through his vision of the world around him. The simple hymns of the *Ṛg Veda* reveal to us an age when man was still alive and when the trees in the forest could speak, and the waters in the rivers could sing and man could listen and understand.[44] The spells and the charms to be found in the tenth book of the *Ṛg Veda* and in most of the *Atharva Veda* suggest a type of religious practice based on fears and association with the spirits of the dark.[45]

The Vedic deities were conceived of as names, powers, personalities of the Universal Godhead and representation of the essential puissance of the Divine Being. The gods who were thirty-three in number manifested the cosmos and were manifest in it.[46] Indra, Varuṇa, Agni, Marut, *Ūshā* and host of other deities in the Vedas represent only manifestation of the forces of Nature.[47] It was believed that the gods recognised in the soul of man his brother and desired to help and increase him by themselves increasing in him so as to possess his world with their light, strength and beauty. The gods call man to a divine companionship and alliance; they attract and uplift him to their luminous fraternity, invite him his aid and offer their against the sons of the Darkness and Division.[48] Gods live in the sky and Agni or Fire was their messengers.[49] "Man calls the gods to his sacrifice; offers to them the shining cow, distilled juices of the plant of joy, the horse of the sacrifice, the cake of the wine, the grain for the God-Mind's radiant courses. He receives them into his Being and their gifts into his life, increases them by the hymns and the wine and forms perfectly . . . as a smith forges iron, says the *Veda*—their great and luminous godheads."[50] The idea is very simple and primitive, "I give, so that you may give in return". The Sumerians and the Semitics following them had a similar practice of burning of offerings in sacrificial fire.[51]

In the period the Brāhmaṇas Vedic sacrifice began to be regarded as an end in itself. It was only through sacrifice that the gods were said to have attained to godhead and overpowered the demons. Therefore, the people to attain earthly prosperity imitated the gods in sacrifice and through these sacrifices they envisaged Divinity.[52] The Brāhmaṇas raised sacrifice to the position of the omnipotent world-principle and employed several mythical legends with sacrifice as the central theme to illustrate their cosmogonical, ethical exhortological and other teachings.[53] The freedom afforded by the early Vedic practices to religious matters was curtailed and a very elaborate and complicated system of rituals which required rich patrons and professional priests became necessary.[54] As a result there developed a stronger tendency of intellectual culture in opulent, political and social set-up of later times.

In the Upanishads the main teaching generally presented is the background of narratives which tell about the doings of the gods, their relation of human worshippers or incidents in the life of different sages, lessons, to illustrate transcendental concepts.[55] The six systems of philosophical speculations were developed from them for the liberation or enlightenment of man. But its high intellectual aim and vigorous spiritual discipline coupled with their individualistic attitude, mysticism, preaching of utility of worldly existence, lack of consistent uniform doctrine failed to appeal to the common man. Taking advantage of this favourable condition created by the Upanishads, through their non-acceptance of the authority of the Vedas, the Buddhism and the Jainism grew up.[56] They regarded spontaneous renunciation and practice of *yoga* as the best means of attaining the supreme bliss.

### *Buddhism*

Hindu religion is said to be *Sanātana* or eternal which was not propagated but revealed. It was revealed to its followers by god himself. But both Jainism and Buddhism are historical religions which were propagated by human beings in Magadha or adjoining territories during the reigns of king Bimbisara and his son Ajātaśatru.[57] Buddhism was propagated by Gautama who was the son of a Kshatriya chief Śuddhodana of the Śākya clan. Unhappy with priestly rituals he shared the pessimism of the day and after practising rigorous asceticism obtained Buddha-hood taking rice from a girl; he concluded that the ills of the world could neither be cured by asceticism nor by luxurious living but by means of the 'golden mean' between the two *majjhimapanthā*.[58]

Starting with the prevailing Hindu ideas of rebirth and *karma*, the Buddha held that to be born is an evil, that the highest good is deliverance from rebirth, that good *karma* will effect such deliverance and that acquisition of good *karma* requires a strictly moral life based on meditation and wisdom or knowledge.[59] His disciples were required to aim at purity, in deed, word and thought, observing ten vows, namely, not to kill or injure living beings, not to steal, to remain celibate, not to lie or slander, to abstain from intoxicants, not to eat after noon, to abstain from dancing, singing and entertainments, to abstain from the use of garlands, scents and ornaments, not to sleep on a raised bed and not to receive any money or valuables.[60] The first-five were binding on laymen for when the third law was modified to have a lawful marriage, special stress was laid on virtues of truthfulness, reverence to superiors and respect to ancient life.[61] He held that men should follow Noble Eight-fold Path practising right belief, right thought, right speech, right action, right means of livelihood, right exertions, right remembrance and right meditation. Men and women of laity could attain much success in travelling the way of holiness but full satisfactions could only be attained only by joining the *Saṁgha* or the order of monks.[62]

The person of the Buddha inspired his disciples to such an extent with affections and devotion that soon he was regarded as being something more than a man to whom prayer might be offered by deliverance.[63] After his death, primitive Buddhism which ignored the Divine and efficacy of prayer and held fast to the ideal of *Arhat*, the worthy who achieved *Nirvāṇa* and would be reborn no more, began to be regarded as *Hīnayāna* or the Lesser Vehicle, while those who recognised the value of prayer and acknowledged the Buddha as Divine incarnate were regarded as *Mahāyāna* or the Greater Vehicle.[64] A schism which had developed over minor points of monastic discipline soon after the death of Buddha now divided the Buddhists over doctrinal issues. The *Mahāyānists* soon introduced a belief in Bodhisattvas. "If there had been the Buddhas before Gautama there would be the Buddhas after him."[65] The Jataka stories show that the Bodhisattvas can be incarnated as men or even as animals; but the advanced Bodhisattvas who help the suffering world are Divine Beings in the heavens.[66] The future Baddha called Maiterya is worshipped as Bodhisattva. Of the other numerous Bodhisattvas important ones are Avalokiteśwara also called Padmapāni; Mañjuśrī and Vajrapāṇi.[67] Special attribute of the first is compassion; his helping hand reaches to Avīchi, the deepest of Buddhist purgatories. Mañjuśrī stimulates understanding destroying falsehood and error and helps development of Pāramitās. Vajrapāṇi with the thunderbolt in his hand like the Hindu god Indra strikes at sin and evils.[68] From the beginning of the Christian era the image of the Buddha had begun to replace his symbols and all sects of Buddhism took to worship with flower, incense, waving of lamps, though the old practice of prostrations and circumambulation in clockwise direction of the old days continued.

Pilgrimage to places connected with the life of the Buddha from the time of Aśoka had also been added for earning religious merit.[69]

The *Vajrayāna* or the Adamantine Vehicle or the Diamond Vehicle, associated with Tantra as predominantly yogic and magical in character, began to develop in Eastern India from the 8th century and was firmly established in Tibet in the 11th century.[70] The *Hinayānists* believe that *Nirvāṇa* can be achieved by gradual loss of self-identity through self-discipline and meditation; the *Mahāyānists* believe that the grace and help of the Buddha and heavenly Bodhisattvas help the process; the followers of the Diamond Vehicle hold that by pronouncing the right formula (*mantra*) in the correct manner and by drawing the correct symbol (*Yantra*) under the guidance of *Guru*, who is regarded as the Buddha, one could attain Buddhahood in a short time.[71] The last phase of this Vehicle is known as *Sahajayāna* or the Vehicle of the Innate. They stress the view that all pleasures including copulation are positive helps in attaining *Nirvāṇa*.[72]

Both as a philosophy and a religion Buddhism adapted itself to the needs of the foreigners and spread over the world, though it nearly died out in India. From the time of the Imperial Guptas devotional form of Hinduism made very vigorous appeal to the ordinary man. The Buddhist laity who supported the local monasteries began to employ the Brāhmaṇa priests at births, marriages and deaths like the Jains. For the ordinary man Buddhism was one of the many cults and faiths of Hinduism and the Buddha was nothing but an incarnation of the great Hindu God Vishṇu.[73]

The Buddha did not nominate anybody to succeed him. He said to his disciples: the truth and the rules, of the order which I have set forth and laid down for you, let them, after I am gone, be the teacher to you.[74] "Shortly after the death of the Buddha his disciples met together at Rajagriha and made a collection of his teaching. These collections which took final shape centuries later is known as *Tri-piṭaka* or three baskets.[75] The first is the *Vinaya-piṭaka* which laid down rules and regulation for the guidance of the monks and their order of the Church. The second is *Sutta-piṭaka* which contain the religious discourses of the Buddha; the third *Abhidharma-piṭaka* contained an exposition of the philosophical principles underlying the religion.

Buddhist *Saṁgha* or the Church consisted of all followers of the Buddha above fifteen years of age, male or female, except the afflicted, criminals, debtors and slaves,[76] though strictly speaking monks are the only Buddhist in proper sense of the term. But in each area local communities or *Saṁgha* had an executive which met fortnightly to transact organisation and religious business. The organisation and meeting of the Buddhist order was democratic and office-bearers of the orders were elected to secret ballot and deviation from *Dharma* or negligence of duty were punished in open meetings.[77] But though the Buddhists allowed women to have their separate Church, the order of the nuns was practically subordinate to the community of the males.[78] In the rainy season the monks were supposed to live in a particular residence, fixed area-wise, for three months. This *Varshāvāsa* or Retreat brought together the monks for three months which they utilised for increasing their knowledge of *Dharma* by discourses. From this institution developed the universities of ancient India.[79]

*Jainism*

Vardhamāna, a junior contemporary of Gautama Buddha, was the son of a sister of Lichhavi chief of Vaiśālī. He was born about 540 B.C. and was the son of Siddhārtha, a chief of Jñātṛka. He was educated, married and had a daughter. At the age of thirty when his parents died Vardhamāna left his home and joined an ascetic sect called *Nirgrantha* founded by Pārśva; after twelve years he attained supreme knowledge. Henceforth he was styled as Mahavira or Jina or *Nirgrantha*, one who was free from fetters.[80]

Jainism as it is today seems to have been reformed by Mahāvīra who added or altered some practices established during the time of Pārśva. Jains regard Mahāvira as the founder of Jainism though they hold Mahāvīra to be the last of the Twenty-four *Tirthankaras* (or Ford-makers across the stream of existence). Pārśva was a historical figure who was born some two hundred years before the birth of Vardhamāna. Pārśva had enjoined four commandments, viz., thou shalt tell the truth; thou shalt possess no property; thou shalt not injure any living being; thou shalt not receive thing which is not freely given. To these Vardhamāna added, thou shalt observe chastity.[81]

In Jainism there is no place for God as creator and distributor of prizes and punishments. Jain view of life is essentially materialistic. The Universe functions through interaction of living souls (*jīva*) and five categories of non-living (*ajīva*) entities. The number of lives or souls is infinite and the process of transmigration continues eternally and the Universe passes through an infinite number of phases of progress and decline. It also rejects the Vedantic doctrine of the Universal Soul. *Nirvāṇa* is defined as being "only the highest, the noblest, and the fullest manifestation of all the powers which lie latent in the soul of man".[82] From that point of view Jainism is said to anticipate Comte's religion of humanity.[83] Jainism is thus a moral code, rather than a religion in modern sense of the term.[84]

According to Jain tradition a serious famine at the end of Chandragupta Maurya's reign led to an exodus of Jain monks from Pāṭaliputra to the South in which Chandragupta himself had joined. At the time of this migration Bhadrabāhu who led the migrants insisted on the retention of the practice of nudity established by Mahāvīra but Sthūlabhadra who remained in the North allowed his followers to wear white robes. This divided the Jains into two sects, viz., the *Śvetāmbaras* or the white robbed and the *Digambaras* or the naked.[85] Each sect has its separate scriptures. A further division of the *Śvetāmbaras* called the *Sthānakavāsīs* rejects the use of idol in worship.[86]

The close parallelism of the career of the two prophets, Gautam Buddha and Mahāvīra Jina, combined with certain superficial resemblances between the doctrines of their philosophies or religions which they propagated misled many to regard Jainism as a mere branch of Buddhism.[87] Both started with a frank recognition of the fact that the world is full of sorrows and salvation of a man means his deliverance from the eternal chain of birth and death; both derived their basic principles from the Upanishads, although they denied the authenticity of the Vedas as an infallible authority and the efficacy of the rites prescribed in them for the purpose of salvation; both ignored the idea of god; both led great stress upon a pure and moral life, especially non-injury to animals and living beings, rather than worship of and devotion to god as means of salvation; both emphasised the effect of good or bad deeds upon man's future births and ultimate salvations, both decried caste; both preached their religion in the language of the people and, lastly, both encouraged the idea of giving up the world, and organised church for the monks and nuns.[88]

But in spite of so much of resemblances there are fundamental differences in conceptions and philosophies of the two. Jain conception of soul is radically different from the Buddhist; Jainism laid great stress upon asceticism and practised it in a rigorous whereas Buddhist followed the middle path between luxury and asceticism.

Jainism differs from Buddhism in that its lay folk are expected to subject themselves to a more rigid discipline under the care of Jain clergy. In theory at least the layman is expected to spend in fasting and penance on new and full-moon days in Jain monastery. At the end of Jain ecclesiastical year, Jains observe *paryūsana* which lasts eight days for the *Śvetāmbaras* and fifteen days for the *Digambaras*.[89] The year ends with a general penance in which all Jains both layman and monk alike are expected to confirm their sins, pay their debts and ask for forgiveness of their neighbours for any offences whether intentional or unintentional.

Buddhism and Jainism seemed to reject all spiritual continuity with the Vedic religion. But they were no revolution or iconoclastic reformation. They adopted from Vedic mythology, Brāhmaṇic ritualism and Upanishadic spiritualism all that was necessary for them. The Buddhist ideal of *Nirvāṇa* was, for example, no more than a negative and exclusive statement of the highest Vedantic spiritual experience. The ethical system of the eight-fold path taken as the way to release was an austere sublimation of the Vedic notion of the Right. Truth and Law followed as the way to immortality, *ṛtasya panthā*. The strongest note of *Mahāyāna* Buddhism, its stress on universal compassion and fellow-feeling was as ethical application of the spiritual unity which is the essential idea of the Vedanta; with belief of *Karma* and *Saṁsāra* both Buddhism and Jainism can be termed sects of Hinduism.[90]

V.A. Smith holds that instead of religions, Jainism and Buddhism may be termed as sects of Hinduism since both Gautama Buddha and Mahāvīra Jina started like Hindu reformers and accommodated much Hindu practices.[91] Neither Mahāvīra nor the Buddha asked their followers to give up their belief in Hindu gods. Jains of the present day employ Hindu priests "for performance of birth and death ceremonies, and even sometimes they go for temple worship (to get temporal benefits). Jainism has never cut itself away from its roots in Hinduism". "Indra, Brahmā and other gods play a prominent part in Buddhist legend and belief."[92] Thomas holds that Buddhism and Jainism retained the spirit of Hinduism.[93]

### *The Ājīvikas*

A third heterodox denomination of the Ajīvikas flourished contemporaneously with the Buddhists and Jains. The founder of the sect Gośāla Maṅkhaliputra, a contemporary of Mahāvira and Gautama, is believed to be of humble origin and died near Śrāvastī. It was a flourishing religion in the Mauryan times. Aśoka and his successor Daśaratha made endowments for them.[94] The Ājīvikas seemed to be rivals of Buddhism and Jainism even after two centuries of Gautama and Mahāvīra. Though it is referred to as late as the 14th century the sect declined quickly after the Mauryan times.[95]

The Ājīvikas have not left behind any literature of their own. The informations called for from the Buddhists and Jain sources establish that they were strict determinists. According to them the Universe was conditioned and determined to the smallest detail by an impersonal cosmic principle *Niyati* or destiny.[96] It was not possible to change the course of transmigration in any way as preached by the Brāhmanas, Buddhists and the Jains. Though nothing could be done to influence the course of future events the Ājīvikas practised severe asceticism holding the view that they were ordained by the destiny to do so. The followers of other sects, however, accused them of licentiousness and immorality.[97]

The Dravidian Ājīvikas developed their doctrine in way resembling the *Mahāyāna* Buddhists and Gośāla, the founder of the sect, was raised to the status of divinity by them. They held that all changes and movements were illusory and the world was, in fact, eternally and immovably at rest. This view resembles the doctrine of "void" or *Śūnyatā* of Nāgārjuna.[98]

### *Purāṇo-Tāntric Religion or Neo-Hinduism*

Between the heterodox religious of Buddhism and Jainism and Vedic religion there grew up another current of theistic movement which established Purāṇo-Tāntric denominations of Hinduism. The Purāṇic religion worshipped the psychological forms of the God-head within men and expressed them in symbolic figures and housed them in temples. It centred round the idea of a supreme God conceived either as Śiva or Vishṇu or Kṛṣṇa, as the ultimate reality, the creator, destroyer. Salvation could be achieved through His Grace (*Prasāda*) having Bhakti or intense love and devotion, by complete surrender to Him. The devotion to the god might be purely spiritual but it was usually manifested by *Pūjā*, the ritual of worship and service of an idol of the god by bathing, offering food, water, flower, light, music and dance. A life of activism and social solidarity were the ends of spirituality. Just as sacrifice (*yajña*) was characteristic of Vedic religion or sacrificial Brāhmaṇism, renunciation (*sannyāsa*) of the Upanishad and asceticism of Jainism-Theravāda Buddhism, *pūjā* was the characteristic of neo-Hinduism. The trends of thought are embodied in the *Purāṇas* composed in veneration of these gods. The chief representatives of this system were Bhāgavatism, Śaivism, Śāktism, Gaṇapatism, Saurapatism and Smārthaism.[99]

*Bhakti-cult or Devotionalism*

Bhāgavatism "owed its origin to the stream of thought which began with the Upanishads and culminated in the east in Buddhism and Jainism". It conceived the idea of a supreme god, god of gods, called Hari or Vishṇu, and emphasised the necessity of worshipping Him with devotion, in preference to older methods of sacrifices and austerities.[100] This religion received a strong impetus from Vāsudeva Kṛshṇa, son of Devakī, of the Vṛshṇi race which was probably another name of Satvatas, a branch of the Yādavas of the Mathurā region. A passage in the *Chhāndogya Upanishad* refers to sage Kṛshṇa, son of Devakī, who was a disciple of Ṛshi Ghora. He preached moral virtues as *etona* (charity), *arjava* (piety), *ahiṁsā* (non-injury), and *satya vachana* (truthfulness) and laid stress upon *tapas* (meditation and asceticism) deprecating *yajñā* (or sacrifice). All these are emphasised in the *Gītā* incorporation in the *Mahābhārata* by Kṛshṇa.[101] It also absorbed the cult of Nārāyaṇa and Saṇkarshaṇa prevalent and popular in the region, in course of time. This combination of religious tradition with the epic resulted in an exuberant growth of this new Kṛshṇa cult or Bhāgavatism.[102]

Bhāgavatism spread far and wide as a result of reconciliation between the two Vedic gods, viz., Vishṇu, originally a satellite of the Sun but recognised as a great god in later Vedic period, and Nārāyaṇa, probably a deified sage who was regarded as Hari, the deity, eternal supreme and lord. That this identification was complete before the second century B.C. is evidenced by the Garuḍadhvaja of Heliodorus dedicated in honour of Vāsudeva.[103] The progress of this religion continued unabated henceforth and penetrating beyond the Vindhya, it gained a firm footing in deep South. Vaishṇava faith was popularised in the South by a clan of devotees called the 'Alvars' whose devotion songs known as *Nālāriya Prabandham* enriched Tamil literature and the depth of their feeling and piety made it the Vaishṇava Veda.[104] This reconciliation of Bhāgvatism with orthodox Brāhmaṇism gave a new turn to Hindu religion. Image worship, unknown in the Vedic period, now became a regular feature of Hindu religion. Henceforth, Bhāgavatism more popularly known as Vaishṇavism, with Śaivism, formed the main planks of Brāhmaṇism in its contest with Buddhism and Jainism.[105] A further change occurred in Bhāgavatism by the addition of two more chapters in the life of Vāsudeva Kṛshṇa. The first related to the story of child Kṛshṇa brought up among the cowherds of Gokul and the second is his amorous dalliance with the *Gopīs* or cowherd girls.[106]

The doctrine of Vaishṇavism underwent further change by the adoption of the theory of *Avatāra* or incarnation, i.e., the birth of the Divine Being in human form. Originating in early historic period it gradually gained ground in later Hindu period. The number and nature of these *Avatāras* are variously given in different treatises. But the number generally accepted rose to ten incorporating the Buddha within its fold.[107]

### *Śaivism*

The existence of Śaivism is traced by some scholars from the Indus Valley civilisation, where a three-faced male deity meditating, wearing a horned head-dress, seated cross-legged and flanked by animals has been taken by some as the prototype of Śiva. If this view is accepted, then Śaivism would have to be accepted as India's earliest religion. However, it is equally probable that a definite Śaiva system was founded like the Vaishṇava cult by a person called variously as Lakulin, Lakutin, Lakulīśa and Nakulīśa after the rise of Buddhism. This Saiva movement was originally named after its founder Lakula and then termed Pāśupata or Māheśwara.[108] Temples were dedicated to the image of Śiva.

The reconciliation of Śaivism with Brāhmaṇical Hinduism was effected by the identification of Vedic God Rudra with Śiva. The *Rg Vedic* God Rudra was a malevolent spirit who destroyed the cattle and caused disease to the people. But he was given a benign character in the *Yajur Veda*.[109] It is said in the latter Veda that when his worthful nature is thoroughly appeased he becomes Śambhu or benign Śaṅkara or beneficent and Śiva or auspicious."[110] In the *Atharva Veda*, this Rudra is looked upon as a supreme god and in the *Śvetāśvātara Upanishad* this active God assumes the characteristic of impersonal *Brahmā*.[111] "Śiva, the God, the creator and destroyer, is said to be known as Bhāva (faith, love and the pure heart). Those who see him, dwelling in the heart by heart and internal consciousness, become immortal."[112]

The Śaiva cult became universally popular in the South through the exertions of the Śaiva saints called the Nayanmārs whose devotional songs, called the *Thevarams*, appealed to the hearts of the common people like the *Nālāriya Prabandham* of the Vaishṇava saints.[113] The image of Śiva was replaced in many places by Liṅga or phallus and that gained wide currency throughout the country.[114]

The votaries of theism developed not only the cult of Vishṇu or Nārāyana-Kṛshṇa and Śiva but they established a host of other deities either as spouses of dominant gods or as satellite offsprings of the popular gods.[115] These were *Śakti* or Durgā, wife of Śiva; Gaṇapati and Kārtikeya or Skanda, sons of Śiva. Brahmā who formed with Vishṇu and Siva the famous trinity was regarded as Paśupati, the Creator, and occupied the position of the impersonal *Brahmā*. Besides, primitive beliefs in the earth and the mountains, the Yakshas and Gandharvas and Nāgas, beasts and trees continued to hold the popular imagination.[116]

But the concept of female devinities led to the development of Tāntricism. The idea of the productive activity of the Divine thought in terms of sexual union, however, is as old as the *Ṛg Veda*.[117] As developed in Tantra it held that the supreme knowledge and bliss could be obtained by the ten great paths or *Daśa Mahāvidyā*.[118] The deity worshipped by the initiate should be compelled rather than persuaded to confer on the initiate magical power and bliss.[119] By pronouncing the right formula (*mantra*) in the correct manner and by drawing correct manner and by drawing correct symbol (*yantra*) under the guidance of *Guru* it was possible to attain supreme bliss in a short time. The *mantra* was regarded as the sound body of the deity while the *yantra* as its form-pattern.[120] Even incest was permitted and taking of meat and alcohol was regarded as positive helps on the way to realisation.[121] Beginning with the imagination that the initiate was born from the womb of the deity worshipped he would gradually assume the role of his father, the male counterpart of the deity and thus become a *siddha*.[122] The Tantra deems it essential to inculcate the doctrine that no worship of the deity is complete without the worship of the deity's body in a material image—an idol or a picture or a symbol in the physical world.[123] The supreme deity of the Tantra is the Primordial Mother, not only of the created world but of the universe but also of all gods and goddesses.[124]

In the long and diversified history of man's quest for reality represented by Hinduism the Infinite has been evisaged in different ways. God manifests himself and fulfils himself in the world in many ways, but each is the way of the Eternal. The Infinite creates and it is *Brahmā*; it preserves and is Vishnu; it destroys and is Rudra or Śiva. The supreme energy beneficent in upholding and protection formulates itself as the Mother of the World, Lakshmi or Durgā; or beneficent even in the work of destruction is Chaṇḍī or Kālī, the Dark Mother.[125] The one god has different powers and personalities and manifests himself in various names and forms. Though it is quite impossible to describe the Ultimate Reality it is quite possible to describe that by means by symbol though the symbolic description is not a substitute for the experience of God. Though God is formless yet He informs and sustains countless forms.[126]

The Purāṇo-Tāntric religion was a catholic attempt to draw towards the spiritual truth of mind of all qualities and people of all classes.[127] It combined elements of *Āgama* and *Nigama* traditions. *Āgama* tradition embodies Tāntric doctrine, *Pūjā* ritual and *yoga* ideas whereas *Nigama* tradition of the Aryans was a cultural imposition of the Fire ritual or *Homa* practice. The *Pūjā* ritual is meant for a personal communion with the divine installed within an image or a pot or a tree or a picture or a design or even a symbol. Called through a rite the spirit comes into the symbol and then it becomes a living presence for the worshipper and it is treated as guest.[128] Water is poured over the symbol; flowers; leaves and fruits, grams are offered to it; cooked food, delicacies of all sorts are offered to it to become consecrated food with special sanctity. Arms, ornaments and jewellery are used to bedeck the symbol and it is regaled with incense and with music and dance. Lights are waved before it in homage. When the Divinity is worshipped under a terrible aspect, animals are sacrificed before it by decapitating and the blood of the victim is offered to the symbol. The worshipper is then allowed to come to a personal relationship with the god by prayer and appeal and meditation. The *pūja* may be followed by *Homa* ritual of the *Nigama* tradition when the worship is thus over. By another ritual the spirit of the god may be released from the symbol which then becomes useless material object with no further spiritual or religious potency.[129]

A conspicuous feature of the Neo-Hinduism is its temple worship. To the Hindu, the temple is not only a place of worship but a centre of social life.[130] The outward physical sense was satisfied through its asthetic turn by a picturesque temple worship, by numerous ceremonies, by the use of physical images; but these were given a psycho-emotional sense and direction that was open to the heart and imagination of the ordinary man and not reserved for the deeper sight of the elect or the strenuous *tapasyā* of the initiates. The secret initiation remained but now a condition for the passage from the surface psycho-emotional and *religions* to a prefounder psycho-spiritual truth and experience.[131]

The Hindu thinkers from the beginning of history attempted to bring god closer to the needs of man. A religion in order that it may become popular needs a simple and uniform spiritual doctrine a good deal of mythology, certain easy practices of worship and a sort of generally elastic attitude. The Purano-Tantric revival absorbed all that it would of Buddhism but rejected its exclusive positions.[132] Again it transformed the symbol and ritual and ceremony of the Vedanta by the substitution of new kindred figures. The Vedic gods rapidly lost their deep original significance. At first they kept their hold by their outer cosmic sense but were over-shadowed by the great Trinity—Brahmā-Vishṇu-Śiva—and afterwards faded altogether.[133] A new pantheon appeared which in its outward symbolic aspect expressed a deeper truth and larger range of religious experience, an intense feeling, a vaster idea. The Vedic sacrifice persisted only in broken and lessening fragments. The house of Fire was replaced by the temple; the Karmic ritual of sacrifice was transformed into the devotional temple ritual; the vague and shifting mental images of the Vedic gods figures in the *mantras* yielded to more precise conceptual forms of the two great deities Vishṇu and Śhiva and their Satis and their off-shoots. It may be stated that Hinduism as it stands today is a growth of ideas, rituals and beliefs so comprehensive as to include anything between atheism and pantheism. It is said generally that the Hindus have no theology, they only have mythology and philosophy; mythology is the religion of the masses and philosophy of the intellectuals. The two, however, are so blended that it is difficult to say where the one begins and the other ends.[134]

## Philosophy

We have already referred to the fact that the people of India acknowledged the existence of some basic reality behind Life and the Universe. This unseen reality we arrived at by intuitive faith or by intellectual ratiocination or by reason and faith, both.[135] With these assumptions they developed six principal systems of philosophy (*shaḍdarśana*) linked together in pairs of three. They are *Sāṅkhya* and *Yoga*, *Nyāya* and *Vaiśhika*, *Mīmāṁsā* and *Vedānta* or *Uttara Mīmāṁsā*.

The *Śaṅkhya* is probably the earliest Indian attempt at systematic philosophy.[136] Though some elements are found in the Upanishads, Kapila by his contribution to systematisation became virtually its founder. This school is divided into two: theistic and non-theistic or atheistic. The theistic *Sāṅkhya* is now based on the *Mahābhāshya* of Patanjali (2nd century B.C.) and is now called *Yoga* system. The basis of the school, however, is the compendium of *Īśwara-kṛshṇa* (3rd century A.D.)[137]

*Sāṅkhya* and *Yoga* systems supplement each other. The *Sāṅkhya* supplies the metaphysics and *Yoga* delineates the psychological discipline, by which the result contemplated in philosophy may be actually achieved. They hold that the world is evolved out of an eternal feminine principle *Prakṛti* which consists of three qualities *sattva*, *raja* and *tama*; when *Prakṛti* comes in contact with *Purusha* world begins to unfold through a series of stages. *Purusha* is conscious but inactive but *Prakṛti* is unconscious but active.[138]

According to both *Sāṅkhya* and *Yoga*, individual mind has a beginningless history of emotional volitional tendencies integrated or interwoven, as it were, in its very structure as passes from one cycle of life to another. The determination of the mind in pursuance of its end as desire, will or action is called *Karma*. Any one inclined towards cessation of the life-cycle must seek the extinction of the conditions that determine the mind structure.[139] The followers of *yoga* practise a system of moral and religious restraints, such as non-injury, truthfulness, purity, sincerity, sex-control, self-containment and virtues called *yamas* and *niyamas* for the external purification of the mind. As an accessory process the *yogi* learns to steady himself in a particular posture (*āsana*) and gradually arrests the process of breath (*prāṇāyama*). He purifies the mind resorting to *dharma* and *dhyāna* and acquires *prajñā*. Ultimately *avidyā* and misuse of the mind is thus destroyed and the fabric of the mind is disintegrated leaving the pure *purusha* in his transcendent loneliness (*kaivalya*) which is regarded as the ultimate aspiration of the human mind.[140]

The *Yoga* believes in the existence of god and thinks that, had it not been for the will of god, the potentialities of the *guṇas* might not have manifested themselves in the present order; the *Sāṅkhya*, however, thinks that the necessity inherent in the potentialities is sufficient to explain the present order and the existence of god is both unwarrantable and unnecessary.[141]

Next come the *Nyāya* and *Vaiśeshika*. They believe in soul, god and reality of the outside world as also the Vedas. The *Nyāya* school is essentially a school of logic which maintains that clear thinking is essential for salvation. The famous parable of the salt in the *Chhāndogya Upanishad* is typical of its analogical argumentation. As salt dissolves in water so the individual dissolves in the Absolute *Brahma*. On the basis of this *Nyāya* logicians developed very subtle and different doctrines which influenced the West considerably in the twentieth-century.[142]

The basic tenets of *Vaiśeshika* held in common with Jainism and some schools of Buddhism are based on a system of atomism. The things of the world made of atoms are individual and is distinguishable from one another by a quality of its own which is *viśesha* but they also form classes and have some common qualities which is called *Sāmānya*.[143] In the world of things changes take place in regular principles on following another. The things, their qualities and their relationship in thing of space are real. They hold that there is a soul that, like the *Sāṅkhyas*, is wholly different from the cosmos, and salvation lies in realising this difference.[144]

The two *Mīmāṁsās* appear to have constituted one system. It is primarily concerned with Vedic exegesis and attempt to prove the complete truth and accuracy of the sacred texts.[145] The world view of this school is not distinctive but its adherents produced interesting theories of semantics and made some contribution in the field of law. They believe that there is a soul and it is uncreated. It enjoys the fruits of its action. The soul has to be saved and when liberated it lives a life of blessedness. The *Mīmāṁsā* held that duties belonging to the *varṇa* and *āśrama* were imperative and must be performed till death.[146]

Out of the *Mīmāṁsās* emerged *uttara-mīmāṁsā* commonly known as Vedānta. Unlike the *Mīmāṁsākāras* who put much emphasis on literature, the Vedāntis stress the significance of the Upanishads and harmonise the teaching of these texts into a consistent body of doctrine. The basic text of the school, however, is the *Brahmasūtra* of Bādarāyaṇa and most prominent exponent of the school is Śaṅkara.[147]

Śaṅkara is famous for his doctrine of *Advaita*, maintaining that the universal phenomenon including the hierarchy of gods, is *māyā* or emanations of the Ultimate Absolute Being which consists of *sat-chit-ānanda. Brahma* unchanging and eternally stable while everything else being unreal is subject to change and the individual beings manifested in *Saṁsāra* are subject to transmigration. Śaṅkara did not reject gods but held that one was to go beyond to realise the Absolute to be found in one's own self (*Ātma*).[148]

*Materialists*

The Upanishadic philosophical speculations gave rise to these Indian philosophical schools; some of which drifted away from the Vedic sacrifices. Those who accepted the authority of the Vedas were known as *āstikas* and who denied their authority were known as *nāstikas*.[149] The Buddhists and Jains were thus *nāstikas* as were the followers of Chārvāk. We do not know definitely whether there was any person called Chārvāk; nor do we know his probable date, if he did exist at all.[150] But the teachings associated with his name have been partially preserved. This school held that the Vedas were the work of three kinds of men, viz., cheats, hypocrites and flesh-eaters, and were the vapouring of the fools and rascals. They held that perception was the only source of knowledge and that which could not be perceived by the senses did not exist.[151] The *āstika* contended that when Chārvāka went out of his home his wife could not see him for a time. Did she become a widow and began to mourn his death? So even that which is not seen or known may exist, as Chārvāka did exist even when his wife could not see him.[152]

*Buddhist Philosophy*

It has often been debated whether Buddhism is a religion or Buddhist Philosophy. The answer is that so long as religion is thought of in exclusive theistic terms and philosophy remains divorced from any kind of ethical and spiritual discipline Buddhism is neither. Assuming four *ārya-satyas*—Noble truth of suffering, origins of suffering, cessation of suffering and cessation way of suffering Buddhism is based on the concept of conditioned co-production, representing two different trends of things.[153] In one of them reaction takes place in a cyclic order between two opposites, such as pleasure and pain, virtue and vice, good and evil. This system is the wheel of life. In the other reaction takes place in progressive order between two counterparts.[154]

The first process is set forth in the first and second of the four *Ārya-satyas* or Noble Truths, viz., the truth of suffering and the truth of the origin of suffering and the twelve *nidānas* or links. Conditioned by spiritual ignorance (*avidyā*) arises the *karma* formations (*saṁskara*); conditioned by the *karma*-formation arises consciousness (*vijñāna*); conditioned by name and form arise the six sense-fields (*shaḍāyatana*);conditioned by six sense-fields arises contact (*sparśa*); conditioned by contact arises feeling (*vedana*); conditioned by feeling arises thirst (*trishṇā*); conditioned by thirst arises grasping (*upādāna*); conditioned by grasping arises becoming (*bhāva*); conditioned by becoming arises birth (*jāti*); and conditioned by birth arises decay and death (*jarāmaraṇa*) with sorrow, lamentation, pain, grief and despair. These twelve Nidānas are distributed over three life-times, the first two belonging to be past life, the middle eight to the present and the last two to the future.[155]

The path of deliverance and *Nirvāṇa* represent the second. This process is set forth in the third and fourth *Ārya-satyas*, the growth of suffering and the way to the cessation of the suffering in another set of twelve links. Conditioned by suffering (*duḥkha*) arises faith (*śraddhā*); conditioned by faith arises delight (*premodayya*); conditioned by delight arises joy (*prīti*); conditioned by joy arises serenity (*praśānti*); conditioned by serenity arises bliss (*sukha*); conditioned by bliss arises concentration (*samādhi*); conditioned by concentration arises knowledge and vision of things (*yathā bhūta jñānadarśana*); conditioned by knowledge and vision arises disgust (*nirvid, nirveda*); conditioned by disgust arises dispassion (*virāga*); conditioned by dispassion arises liberation (*vimukti*); and conditioned by liberation arises knowledge of destruction of the intoxicants (*āśravakshya-jñāna*).[156]

But it should be remembered that the doctrine of conditioned co-production is not a theory of causation in the philosophical sense. It signifies that one who is reborn, the one who died and the one who followed the path are, in reality, neither the same nor different persons. "Rebirth takes place but nobody is reborn; *Nirvāṇa* is attained but nobody attains it."[157]

Psychologically, *Nirvāṇa* is a state of absolute illumination, supreme bliss, infinite love and compassion, unshakable serenity and unrestricted spiritual freedom.[158] Ontologically, it is for the *Hīnayāna*, an eternal, unchanging, extramental spiritual entity wholly unconnected with the cosmic process, and for the *Mahāyāna* the Absolute Reality transcending all oppositions including that between itself and *Saṁsāra*.[159]

*Jain Philosophy*

Jainism starts with two principles, the living (*jīva*) and the non-living (*ajīva*) or soul and non-soul, which comprise all that exists in the Universe.[160] The living is in contact with the non-living being, an account of thoughts, words and acts, to the influence of (*āśrava*) fresh energies known as *karmas* which are conceived as subtle matter.[161] This influx can be counteracted (*samvara*) by religious discipline; and the existing stock (*bandha*) of *karmas* can be exhausted (*nirjara*) through severe austerities. Then salvation or perfection can be attained.[162]

A person begins with five vows, viz., *Ahimsa*, *Satya*, *Asteya*, *Brahmachārya* and *Aparigraha* and conquers anger, pride, deception and greed; virtues to be cultivated in step are divided into eleven *pratimas* and fourteen stages called *guṇasthānas*.[163] The soul marches from bondage and gross ignorance to final liberation and omniscience, gradually overpowering at different stages wrong belief, unrighteousness, negligence, passions and of activities. Both change and permanence are facts of experience. Soul with its consciousness is permanent even when it is changing through various bodies in different births.[164]

The aspiring soul has to practise austerities, external and internal-penances are extremely rigorous. But it is pure meditation that leads the soul to liberation. There is a complete cessation of physical, verbal and mental activities, and the self—or *ātmā*—is absorbed in it. With the entire stock of *karmas* exhausted, the soul rises to the top of the Universe where it remains for ever retaining its individual identity.[165] The doctrine of *karma* and theory of transmigration of soul are accepted. The soul is characterised by sentiency or consciousness, in its embodied state it has sense organised; the non-living substance is devoid of sentience and is of five rids. The *jīva* and *ajīva* are uncreated and eternal.[166]

REFERENCES


1. *Svetasvatara Upanishad*, I : I : 1.
2. *Kena Upanishad*, I: I: 1.
3. *Ibid.*, I: I: 3.
4-6. S.K. Chatterjee, *op. cit.*
7. *Isa Upanishad*, 1.
8. *Katha*, II/III/1.
9. A.L. Basham, *A Cultural History of India.*
10. *Keno.*, I/I/3.
11. *Ibid.*, I/I/2.
12. *Katha*, II/III/13.
13. *Ibid.*, II/III/9.
14. *Mundaka*, III/I/9.
15-19. S.K. Chaterjee, *op. cit.*
20. Sri Aurobindo, *op. cit.*, p. 98.
21. *Ibid.*
22. Sri Aurobindo, *op. cit.*, p. 98.
23. *Infra*, p. 124.
24. *Gita*, IV: 13.
25. Sri Aurobindo, *op. cit.*, p. 130.
26. *Gita*, XVIII: 45.
27. *Infra.*
28. Sri Aurobindo, *op. cit.*, p. 102.
29-32. *Infra.*
33. *Gita*, IV: 5.
34. S. Radhakrishnan, 'Hinduism', *A Cultural History of India*, p. 77.
35. *Gita*, VII: 19.
36. S.K. Chatterjee, *op. cit.*
37-38. S. Radhakrishnan, *op. cit.*
39-40. S.K. Chatterjee, *op. cit.*, pp. 59-60.
41-42. Sri Aurobindo, *op. cit.*, p. 139.
43. S. Radhakrishnan, *op. cit.*, p. 63.
44-51. Sri Aurobindo, *op. cit.*, pp. 141-46.
52-56. Sri Aurobindo, *op. cit.*
57-64. V. Smith, *op. cit.*, pp. 76-81.
65-68. A.L. Basham, *op. cit.*, p. 275.
69-70. *Ibid.*, pp. 275-82.
71. A.L. Basham (ed.), *A Cultural History of India*, p. 95.
72. G. Sen Majumdar, *Buddhism in Ancient Bengal*, pp. 105-10.
73. A.L. Basham, *op. cit.*, p. 275.
74-76. R.C. Majumdar, *op. cit.*, pp. 162-63.
77. *Ibid*
78. *Ibid.*
79. *Infra*, Chap. III.
80. R.C. Majumdar, *op. cit.*, p. 168.
81. *Ibid.*
82. A.L. Basham (ed.), *A Cultural History of India*, pp. 103-08.
83. V. Smith, *op. cit.*, p. 79.
84. *Ibid.*

85-88. V. Smith, *op. cit.*, pp. 78-79.
89. R.C. Majumdar, *op. cit.*
90. Sri Aurobindo, *op. cit.*, p. 150.
91-92. V. Smith, *op. cit.*, p. 78.
93. P. Thomas, *op. cit.*, p. 51.
94-98. A.L. Basham, *op. cit.*, pp. 291-98.
99. P. Thomas, *Hindu Religion, Customs and Manners*, p. 27.
100. D.C. Sircar, 'Vaishnavism', *The Classical Age*, pp. 419-26.
101. B. Majumdar, *Krshna in History and Legend*, p. 102.
102. R.N. Dandekar, *op. cit.*, p. 234.
103. D.C. Sircar, *op. cit.*, pp. 425-26.
104. K.R. Srinivas Iyengar, 'Tamil'; *The Classical Age*, pp. 327-28.
105. *Ibid.*
106-107. D.C. Sircar, *op. cit.*, p. 419.
108. R.C. Majumdar, *op. cit.*, pp. 175-76.
109-12. R.K. Siddhantashastree, *Saiviam through the Ages*, p. 85.
113. *Ibid.*
114. R.K. Siddhantashastree, *op. cit.*
115-16. H.D. Bhattacharyya, "Minor Religious Sects", *The Classical Age*, pp.440-453.
117. A.L. Basham, *op. cit.*, p. 282.
118. *Ibid.*
119-22. *Ibid.*
123. S. Shankaranarayanan, *Sri Chakra*, p. 45.
124. S. Shankaranarayanan, *Quintessence* of Sri Vidya, p. 5.
125. Sri Aurobindo, *op. cit.*, p. 137.
126. S. Radhakrishnan, *op. cit.*, pp. 67-69.
127. Sri Aurobindo, *op. cit.*, p. 152.
128-129. S.K. Chatterjee, *op. cit.*, pp. 197-99.
130. P. Thomas, *op. cit.*, p. 66.
131. Sri Aurobindo, *op. cit.*, p. 152.
132. Sri Aurobindo, *op. cit.*, pp. 151-53.
133. *Ibid.*
134. P. Thomas, *op. cit.*, p. 24.
135. *Infra.*
136. A.L. Basham, *op. cit.*, p. 325.
137-39. R.C. Mujumdar (ed.), *The Age of Imperial Unity*, pp. 467-69.
140-42. *Ibid.*
143. A.L. Basham, *op. cit.*, p. 326.
144. R.C. Majumdar (ed.), *op. cit.*, p. 465.
145-146. *Ibid.*, pp. 469-70.
147-52. *Ibid.*
153-55. A.L. Basham (ed.), *op. cit.*, pp. 83-98.
156-59. *Ibid.*
160-66. *Ibid.* pp. 100-10.

# 8

# Language and Literature

Indian literary tradition goes back to third millennium B.C.[1] In ancient times it was largely dominated by Sanskrit which is one of the most magnificent, perfect and wonderfully sufficient literary instruments ever developed by human mind.[2] The Tāmils, of course, claim a more antiquarian origin of their language and literature.[3] Pending the consideration of their claim, let us first see the development of North Indian languages and literature, particularly Sanskrit.

The beginning of Sanskrit may be sought somewhere around 1300 B.C. with the formulation of *Ṛg Vedic* hymns which were probably completed by 1000 B.C.[4] After these, hymns were no longer composed in old poetic tradition; instead there developed an intensive prose literature of the Brāhmaṇa, entirely oral and remarkably uniform. The period of the old Brāhmaṇas may be put roughly around 1000-800 B.C., though it continued for two or three centuries more.[5]

The next milestone in Sanskrit literature is the grammar of Pāṇini's, *Ashṭādhyāyī*. Fourth century B.C. is usually accepted to be the probable time when Pāṇini composed his grammar, possibly on the basis of the language of the scholars of his days.[6] There is, however, no dearth of theories placing Pāṇini earlier. His book is a marvel of human intellect, consisting of over 4,000 grammatical rules classified in some 2,000 mono-syllabic roots which by addition of prefixes, suffixes and inflaxions provide all the words of the language.[7] It gained universal popularity among the scholars of the day. The book was later on annotated and commented upon by Kātyāyana (3rd century B.C.) and Patañjali (2nd century B.C.) and set up norms of Sanskrit grammar once for all.[8] As a result Sanskrit assumed a stylised form after the beginning of the Christian era.

### Literature

Earliest Sanskrit literature consists of the four Vedas—*Ṛg Veda*, *Yajur*

*Veda*, *Sāma Veda* and *Atharva Veda*—metrical hymnal parts of which are called *Saṁhitās*, several expository ritual texts to each of these Vedas are called *Brāhmaṇas* and speculative treatises on them are known as *Upanishads*.[9] In their literary aspect much of this literature is of high merit, especially some hymns of *Ṛg Veda* and some parts of the early *Upanishads*.[10] The *Ṛg Vedic* Sanskrit bears the same relation to the classical Sanskrit as does Homeric to Classical Greeks.[11] The 1,028 hymns of *Ṛg Veda*, divided into ten *maṇḍalas* or books, are the works of many authors and show a great variation of style and merit. Composed over centuries the hymns follow a strict metrical scheme and an accepted literary convention.[12] The *Vedic* singers believed that they were in possession of a high mystic and hidden truth, claimed to be the bearer of speech acceptable to a divine knowledge and expressly so speak of their utterances as secret words which declare their whole significance only to the seer '*Kavaye nivachanāni ninya vachāṁsi*'.[13]

The *Ṛg Vedic* hymns centred on many deities which were names, powers and personalities of the Divine. Indra stands out as a pre-eminent god and core myth of *Ṛg Veda*.[14] In terms of this creation proceeded when Indra slew the serpent Vṛtra who had enclosed the waters and the sun, requisite for human life. When Indra split open the belly of the Vṛtra, moisture, heat and lıght were released and cosmic order (*Rta*) was established under the administration of god Varuṇa. Gods and men then had specified functions (*vṛata*) to perform in accordance with this cosmic order. Those who performed their specified functions went to a heavenly abode presided over by Yama, the first mortal after death. Two dogs guarded the righteous on the path to heaven but the sinful were fettered and fell prey to various demons.[15] The story bears a close relation to the myth of creation prevalent in Mesopotamia where the god Mārduk slew the demon Tiāmat and created the Universe.[16] Number of other hymns express deep feeling for nature. The most beautiful of these is the hymns to Ushā, the goddess of dawn; others were addressed to Rātri, the personification of night, and Araṇyāni, the spirit of the forest.[17] Some of the *Vedic* hymns were secular.[18]

The contents of the *Atharva Veda* relate mainly to religion.[19] Yet it contains a few poems of great merit. The Brahmana or liturgical prose literature, i.e. *Śrauta Sūtras*, manuals of *Vedic* sacrifice and the recensions of *Yajur Veda*, were written in simple straight forward language, very different in style from Classical Sanskrit. The story of

Urvaśi, referred to in *Ṛg Vedic* hymn, told in prose in *Śatapatha Brāhmaṇa*, is typical of the *Vedic* prose literature. The story is as follows:[20]

"The nymph Urvaśi loved Purūravas, the son of Ila; when she married him she said: `You must embrace me three times a day, but never lie with me against my will. Moreover, I must never see you naked, for this is the proper way to behave to us women'.

"She lived with him long, and she was with child by him, so long did she live with him. Then the Gandharvas said to one another: "This Urvaśī has been living too long among men! We must find a way to get her back!'

"She kept an ewe with two lambs tied to her bed, and the Gandharvas carried off one of the lambs. "They are taking away my baby', she cried, `as though there were no warrior and no man in the palace'. Then they took away the second, and she cried out in the same way.

"Then he thought to himself: `How can the palace, where I am, be without a warrior and a man?' And naked as he was, he leapt up after them, for he thought it would take too long to put on a garment. Then the Gandharvas produced a flash of lightning, and she saw him as clearly as it were a day and she vanished. . ..

"Bitterly weeping he wandered all over Kurukshetra. There was a lake of lotuses called Anyatahplaksha. He walked on its bank and there were nymphs swimming in it in the form of swans.

"And she noticed him, and said: "That is the man with whom I lived'. Let us show ourselves to him', they said, 'Very well', she replied, and they appeared to him (in their true forms).

"Then he recognised her and entreated her :

*'O my wife, with mind so cruel,*
*stay, let us talk together*
*for if your secrets are untold*
*we shall have no joy in days to come'.*

"Then she replied:

*'What use is there in my talking to you'*
*I have passed like the first of dawns,*
*Purūravas, go home again!*

"Mournfully Purūravas said:

*Today your lover will perish*
*he will go to the furthest distance and never come back.*
*He will lie in the lap of disaster*
*and fierce wolves will devour him.*

"She replied:

*'Purūravas do not die! do not go away!*
*do not let the fierce wolves devour you!*
*Friendship is not to be found in women,*
*For they have hearts like halftamed jackals!'*

"And then she said to him:

*'When I dwelt in disguise in the land of the mortal,*
*and passed the night of four autumns,*
*I ate a little ghee once a day,*
*and now I have had quite enough!'*

"But her heart pitied him, and she said: `come on the last evening of the year, then, when your son is born you shall lie one night with me'.
"He came on the last night of the year and there stood a golden palace. They told him to enter, and brought her to him."

This story provided the theme of Kālidāsas celebrated drama *Vikramorvaśīyam*, which is a romance par excellence.[21]

*Upanishads*

The Upanishads represent the final stage in the development of the *Vedic* literature. They are *Vedānta*, a book of knowledge in a higher degree, even than the *Vedas*, but knowledge in the founder Indian sense of the word '*Jnāna*'. They are epic hymns of self-knowledge and world-knowledge and god knowledge and are at once profound religious scriptures.[22] Whatever is written in verse or condensed prose they are the record of the deepest spiritual experiences—documents of revelatory and intuitive philosophy of an inexhaustible light, power, and largeness. Here the intuitive mind and intimate psychological experience of the *Vedic* seers pass into a supreme culmination in which the spirit, as it is said in a phrase of the *Kaṭha Upanishad*, discloses its own very body, reveals the very word of its self-expression and discovers to the mind the vibration of rhythms which repeating themselves within it, the spiritual hearing seems to build up the soul and set it satisfied and complete on the height of self-knowledge.[23] The *Upanishads* are the creation of a revelatory and intuitive mind and its illumined experience, and all their substance structure, phrase, imagery, movement are determined by and stamped with original character.[24] There is no revolutionary departure from the *Vedic* mind and its temperament and fundamental ideas, but a continuation and development and to a certain extent enlarging transformation of all that was held in the symbolic speech as a mystery and secret. The *Upanishads* have been the acknowledged source of numerous profound philosophies and religions that flowed from it.[25] The ideas of the *Upanishads* can be rediscovered in much of the thought of Pythagoras and Plato and form the profoundest part of Neo-Platonism and Gnosticism which profoundly influenced the philosophical thinking in the West, and *Sufism* only repeats them in another religious language.[26]

### *The Dharma Śāstras*

The *Veda* is the spiritual and psychological seed of Indian culture and the *Upanishads* express the truth of highest spiritual knowledge and experience. The *Vedic Gṛhya Sūtra* and *Dharma Śāstras* written in aphoristic method were meant to govern life and desire by the social and ethical law, the *Dharma*, so that it might be made all vital; economic, aesthetic, hedonistic, intellectual and other needs being satisfied duly and according to the right law of nature—a preparation for spiritual existence.[27]

*Dharma-sūtras*, written over a period between *c.* 600 B.C. to 300 B.C., were manuals written by the teachers of the *Vedic* schools for the guidance of their pupils. The *Dharma-śāstras*, also called *Smṛtis*, expanded the *Dharma-sūtras* by incorporating the current local customs and usages of the *śishṭas* (learned and cultured) after this period and extending over eight hundred years. It may be assumed that the *Smṛtis* were based on *Dharma-sūtras* but the *Smṛtis* were later declared to be of divine origin and claimed to be the sole authority for Aryan or

Hindu law, which cover the whole life of the individual, the class and the people.[28] Although the *Vedas* are regarded as the ultimate source of *dharma*, in practice the *Smṛtis*, by the Hindus all over India, are regarded as the real exposition of religious duties and social customs.[29]

However, the *Smṛtis* contain passages of literary merit and were considerably influenced by the epics, particularly the *Mahābhārata*; for unlike the prose form of the *Sūtras*, the *Smṛtis* were written in poetry, the style and metre being the same.[30] *Manusmṛti* was possibly composed between 200 B.C. and A.D. 200. The *Smṛtis* of Yājñavalkya, Nārada, Bṛhaspati and Kātyāyana were re-edited during the Classical Age to adjust the changed social practices.[31]

The stream of religious poetry flows separately in *Purāṇa* and *Tantra*. The *Purāṇas* were originally bardic stories eighteen in number narrated by *Sūtras* which were condensed to writing in different periods bringing the history of the ancient Indian dynasties up to *c*. A.D. 350.[32] They are essentially true religious poetry. There is much waste substance, dull and dreary, but on the whole they are rich and end in a style which is unique. *Padma Purāṇa* classified the *Purāṇas* into three categories of *Sattva*, *Raja* and *Tama*.[33] In the first category may be placed Vishṇu, Nārada, Bhāgavata, Garuḍa, Padma, Varāha. Brahmāṇḍa, Brahmavaivarta, Mārkaṇḍeya Bhavishya, Varāha and Vāmana are of *Raja* category; and Matsha, Kūrma, Liṅga, Śiva, Skanda and Agni are of Śaivite category of Tāmasa nature. Possibly in the first phase of growth of *Purāṇic* literature they dealt with Hindu rites and customs which formed the subject matter of the *Smṛtis*; in the second phase new topics relating to gifts, glorification of holy places, *vrata* (vow), *pūjā* (worship), sacrifice to planets, etc., were included.[34] Thus they tried to bring the theistic religions like Vaishṇavism and Śaivism within the pale of orthodoxy by combining *Vedic* rituals with non-*Vedic* beliefs.

However, *Vishṇu Purāṇa* is a remarkable literary creation and stands at the height of old epic style.[35] *Bhāgavata* coming at the end is strongly affected by learned and more ornate literary form of speech, full of subtlety, rich and deep thought and beauty.[36] An immense and complex body of psycho-spiritual experience is embodied in the Tantras, supported by visual images and systematised in forms of *yogic* practice.[37] But their literary style was not new or important. *Purāṇa* and *Tantra* aiming by their simplicity at a wider appeal prolonged the traditions of the epics.

*The Epics*

One of the elements of old *Vedic* tradition was a knowledge of significant tradition, *itihāsa*, and it is this word that was used to dīstinguish the *Mahābhārata* and *Rāmāyaṇa* from the *Purāṇas*. *Itihāsa* was an ancient historical or legendary tradition turned to creative use as significant myths or tales expressive of some spiritual or religious or ethical or ideal meaning and thus formative of the mind of the people.[38] The *Mahābhārata* and *Rāmāyaṇa* are *itihāsas* of this kind on a large scale and with a massive purpose.[39] The epics, however, did not originate among the priestly class. The Sūtas who witnessed the battle first hand as charioteers, described them in their ballads. It may be mentioned that Sanjoy who described before Dhṛtarashtra the *Mahābhārata* battle was such a Sūta. Kuśilavas who popularised *Rāmāyaṇa* were travelling singers and not Brāhmaṇas.[40] To the original bardic poetry many myths and legends of Brāhmaṇical origin in the fashion of the *Purāṇas* were fitted in later on. The two poems are epical in their motive and spirit, but they are not like any other two epic of the world, and are entirely of their own kind and subtly different from others in their principle.

*The Mahābhārata*

The *Mahābhārata* has been spoken of as a fifth *Veda*. It has been said of both these poems that they are not only great poems but *Dharmaśāstras*, the body of a large religious and ethical and social and political teachings. Their effect and hold on the mind and life of the people have been so great that they have been described as the *Bible* of the Indian people.[41] It is said of it that whatever is in India is in the *Mahābhārata*.[42]

The kernel of the *Mahābhārata* is the family-feud of the Bhārata tribe now divided into Kauravas and Pāṇḍavas.[43] Paṇḍu had been consecrated emperor of the Bhārata dynasty because his elder brother Dhṛtarāshṭra was blind. As Pāṇḍu died first, Dhṛtarāshṭra assumed imperial prerogative as Pāṇḍu's sons were minor. Yudhishṭhira, Pāṇḍu's eldest son, was made a crown prince and later on given a fiat to rule. He formed a marriage alliance with Kṛshṇa and assumed imperial prerogative. Duryodhana, eldest son of Dhṛtarashṭra, envious and ambitious, challenged Yudhishṭhira to a gambling match. Yudhishṭhira lost everything in gambling, even his wife Draupadī, who was publicly stripped by Duryodhana's brother. Draupadī was restored by elders who arranged terms that Yudhishṭhira and his brother would go to exile for twelve years and one year *incognito*. After the expiry of the terms of exile and *incognito* Yudhishṭhira sent Kṛshṇa to negotiate terms of restoration but Duryodhana refused to give even one village without war. Yudhishthira marshalled his allies against Duryodhana which resulted into a war of eighteen days fought at Kurukshetra in which almost all kingdoms in the then India participated.[44] To this original bardic poetry many pieces of legends connected or unconnected with life of the epic heroes, numerous myths and Brāhmaṇical origin, large sections devoted to philosophy and ethics, cosmologies and genealogies in the fashion of the *Purāṇas*, legends of the Śiva and Vishṇu cult, fables and parables were added over hundreds of years till these were redacted in the present form in the Classical period.[45] In point of form it is not a single book but a whole literature and in point of time it stretches over a vast period. "The *Mahābhārata* is the creation and expression not of a single individual mind, but of the mind of the nation, it is a poem written by a whole people."[46]

It is told in the epic itself that Vyāsa imparted this epic first to his pupil Vaiśampāyana, who in his turn recited it in 24,000 verses before king Janmjaya while the latter was performing snake-sacrifice. It was then heard by Sūta Ugraśravā and recited it in 100,000 verses at the assembly of the *Ṛshis* at the time of the sacrifice arranged by Śaunaka in the Naimisha forest.[47] In its present form it has come down in two recensions, one in the North and the other in the South. It is now believed that the battle to Kurukshetra was fought between 1400 and 1000 B.C. But Dr Winternitz holds: "The *Mahābhārata* cannot have received its present form earlier than 4th century B.C. and later than the 4th century A.D."[48] This conclusion is based on the facts that on the one hand we have numerous references to Buddhism and the Jāvṭanas in the present form of the epic and on the other hand the works of such classical authors as Bāṇa and Kumārila and the epigraphic records of the 5th century A.D. onwards testify to the epic having at that time assumed a form of *Smṛti*.[49]

### *The Rāmāyaṇa*

The second epic, the *Rāmāyaṇa*, is ascribed to Vālmīki whom Bhavabhuti and other call the first *Kāvi*, the author of first *Kāvya*.[50]

In this epic we find the palace intrigue at Ayodhyā by queen Kaikeyi resulting in her step-son (1) Rāma's exclusion to succession to his father's throne and a sentence of fourteen years' exile, and (2) Rāma exiled in the South, finds its inhabitants oppressed by the raids of the demons (*Rākshasas*) from Lankā (e.g., Śrī Laṅkā), the kingdom of the demon king Rāvaṇa who abducts Rāma's wife Sītā. he raises an army of the monkeys and invades Laṅkā, kills Rāvaṇa, frees Sītā and returns home in triumph; the period of exile having elapsed his noble step-brother Bhārata surrenders the throne to him. This poem, too, like the *Mahābhārata*, contains interpolations, but they are brief and mostly deductive.[51] Valmiki's finest notes are surely those of the palace intrigue, with the psychological study of the characters of Kaikeyī and her confidant. The apocryphal last book of the *Rāmāyaṇa* adds a tragic ending: Sītā's new exile on suspicion of unchastity, when a captive, and final disappearance. This changes the main *rasa* which is 'heroic' to 'compassionate' resulting from Rāma's sufferings.[52]

The *Rāmāyaṇa* is different from the *Mahābhārata* in style and contents. The diction of the *Rāmāyaṇa* is shaped in a more attractive mould, a marvel of sweetness and strength, lucidity and warmth and grace; its phase has not only poetic truth and epic form and diction but a constant intimate vibration of the feeling of the idea, emotion or object. There is an element of fine ideal delicacy in its sustained strength and breadth of power. It is little more than a quarter of the size of the *Mahābhārata*. Metrically it is certainly later than the *Mahābhārata* — it is also more homogeneous and nearer to Classical Sanskrit lyric.[53] The main body of the poem gives the impression of being the work of a single hand, sometimes in the first century B.C.[54]

**The Classical Sanskrit**

Sanskrit literature reached its zenith in the Classical period. Most of this literature was written by men integrated with society, with few of the complex psychological difficulties of the modern English writer; hence the spiritual anguish of a Cowper, the heart-searching of a Donne and the social pessimism of an early T.S. Elliot are almost entirely absent[55] and no counterpart of Shelly and Swinburne are found. Hindu thought and literature are fundamentally optimistic and the tragic drama of the story with unhappy ending did not find favour of ancient India.[56]

The chief themes of the writers were love, nature, panegyric, moralising, and story telling love was passionately physical. Nature was usually treated in its relation to man—phenomena of the seasons, day and night, birds and beasts and flowers were used to evoke human emotions.[57] Yet throughout the literature a deep love of nature is implicit. Panegyrics in praise of kings and their ancestors provide historical materials. Elements of moralising is also prominent in some of the writings.[58]

The technic of poetry was thoroughly studied and rules were laid down in numerous text-books.[59] The unit of poetry was *śloka*, the sufficient verse of four quart or *pada* and each *śloka* a perfect art of itself.[60] *Śloka* must be a content development by addition of completeness to completeness—a progression of definite movements building a complete harmony. The purpose of poetry was considered to be prerogative, the emotion aroused not of the pity or terror of Aristotle but a calmer experience, an aesthetic sensation.[61] The basic *rasa* or flavour from which this experience could arise were—love, courage, loathing, anger, mirth, terror, pity, surprise and poise. Poetry was supposed to arouse some of these flavours.[62]

*Dhvani* and *alaṁkāra* were two other characteristics of Classical poetry.[63] The great and subtle and musical rhythms were roused by carefully choosing the words; the poets could say something more than the usual meaning of the world by suggestion and incantation. And free use of ornamentation resulted in poetry of great floridity. This was encouraged by the use of synonyms and by the universally accepted stock epithets.[64]

The earliest Classical Sanskrit poetry is *Buddhacharita* of Aśvaghosha who is believed to have lived in the first century A.D.[65] Aśvaghosha was an ardent Buddhist so the ultimate significance, he wishes to convey, through the delights of poetry, was the shallowness of the world and the true happiness of renunciation and peace of mind. But he describes most realistically the pleasures of the world.[66]

Classical poetry reached its acme of perfection in the poetry of Kālidāsa who is believed to have flourished during the reign of Chandragupta II and Kumāragupta I (A.D. 376-454).[67] He was the author of three dramas—*Mālavikāgnimitram*, *Vikramorvaśīyam* and *Abhijñānaśakuntalam*, two long poems (*kāvya*) *Raghuvaṁśam* and *Kumārasambhavam*, two shorter poems (*kāvya*) *Meghadūtam* and *Ṛtusaṁhāram*, as well as several others which have not survived. His authorship of *Naladamyantī* and *Betāladvātriṁśat* are, of course, disputed. The subjects which found favour with Kālidāsa were high actions of gods and kings, the nobler or the more delicate human sentiments, the charm and beauty of women, the sensuous passion of lovers, the procession of the seasons and the scenes of nature. *Mālavikāgnimitram* is a musical play which gives the story of a love intrigue at the Śuṅga court. Dramatically, it is the best and least lyrical. Vikramorvaśīyam is also a musical play based on the *Ṛg Vedic* story. It is romantic lyrical drama, half human and half mythical—the hero being an earthly king and heroine being a nymph depicted in human colour. The third *Abhijñānaśakuntalam* is based on a story of the *Mahābhārata*. It is admired for its lyricism, and realism, though both the hero and heroine appear to be mere tools in the hands of the supernatural forces. There is no real action but a sense of helplessness, plaything of supernatural powers.[68]

Kālidāsa's most popular poem is *Meghadūtam* or Cloud-Messenger. A distracted lover Yaksha exiled for year in Rāmagiri from his beloved in the Himalayan abode of Yaksha attempts to send a message to his beloved by a passing cloud at the beginning of the rain. Kālidāsa gives to the cloud guidance for his journey and describes along with their denizens and erotic charms which sublimate in the spiritual atmosphere of the temple of Mahākāla on the Śipra in Ujjain and Alakā in the Himalaya where his beautiful wife, weak from sorrow and longing, awaits him.[69] *Ṛtusaṁhāra* unrolls the series of the six seasons of the Hindu year.[70]

His great literary epic, the *Raghuvaṁśa* or the "House of Raghu", treats the story of line of ancient kings of Ayodhyā as representative of the highest religious and ethical culture and ideals of the race containing many passages of great beauty.[71] The short unfinished epic *Kumārasambhavam* or Origin of Kumāra gives a humorous plot of Indra, the god of the gods, to make a father of lord Śiva, the gods having been defeated by a demon whom only a son of Śiva can kill. Here Kālidāsa gives a remarkable description of Himalaya which reminds one of John Donne and Gastave Dore.[72]

The literary epics of Bhāravi and Māgha reveal the beginning of the decline marked by the progressive encroachment of a rhetorical and laborious standard of form, method and manner that heavily burdens and is bound eventually to stifle the poetic spirit, an artificiality of tradition and convention. Nevertheless Bhāravi has high qualities of grave poetic thinking.[73] His *Kirātārjunīyam* is based on a short episode of *Mahābhārata*. He tells the story of Śiva in the guise of a Kirāta fighting with Arjuna over a hunting incident which reaches its sudden climax when the former grants the decisive weapon which will enable the Pandavas to win the Bhārata battle. The narrative style is heroic and epical, customary description of the beauty of Himalaya is brought to a climax when the nymphs attacks Arjuna, the ascetic.[74] *Śiśupalabadha* of Māgha is also based on a story of the epic *Mahābhārata* where Kṛshṇa kills Śiśupāla at Yudhisṭhira's *rājasuya* consecration. It is essentially a lyrical poem which is like an anthology of verses.[75]

Kumāradāsa's *Jānaki-haraṇa* and Bhaṭṭi's poem *Rāvaṇabadha* known as *Bhaṭṭikāvya*, an exercise to illustrate rules of grammar, continued the classical tradition but poems were now display of verbal ingenuity. A well-known example of this genre is the *Rāmacharita* of Sandhyākara of 12th century A.D.[76]

The best poems of the later period of Classical literature is represented by single stanza poems called 'Champū' either by one or many hands.[77] Each *śloka* is independent and complete and expresses a thought or significant incident of life. The first poet of this genre is Bhartṛhari who is believed to have lived in the 7th century.[78] In the midst of *amours* he feels the call for religious life though he convinces himself that love is not a futile waste of time. Triple motive of his poems are interest in life, enjoyment of senses and spiritualisation.[79] Another poet of Bhartṛhari's time is *Amaru* who described poignant moments of human love in a single verse. His stanzas are voluptuous, humorously tender and show all understanding of feminine psychology.[80]

Lyrical poems of Classical period found once again a distinction in the *Gīta Govinda* of Jayadeva in the 12th century. It is a dramatic, lyrical poem, beautifully rhymed; commencing with an introductory stanza in one of the more used Sanskrit metres, the final stanza introduces the poet's name. It describes the love of Kṛshṇa for Rādhā and the milk-maids or Gopīs.[81]

### *Narrative Poetry*

Besides the epical, lyrical and *Subhāshita* poems in Classical Sanskrit, there are some narrative poems. They either describe stories in poetry or biography of some chiefs in panegyrical manners.[82] In the first category may be placed *Bṛhatkathā* of Guṇāḍhya now available in Somadeva's *Kaṭha-Saritsāgara* written in the eleventh century. The stories are told with comparative simplicity and directness, punctuated with humour and pathos. In the next category may be placed *Harshacharita* of Bāṇabhaṭṭa (7th century) *Vikramāṅkadevacharita* of Bilhāṇa (6th century), *Hammīramahākāvya* of Nāyachandra Sūri, *Rāmacharita* of Sandhyākara Nandī (12th century A.D.).[83] But besides these two types, there are some historical poems, like Kalhāṇa's *Rājataraṅgini*, giving the history of Kāshmir.[84]

*Sanskrit Drama*

Right from the Vedic period dramatic performances were held at festivals in dance and mime.[85] But regular drama (*nāṭaka*) began possible with Aśvaghosha who lived in the Classical period.[86] His only work in manuscript was discovered in the desert of Central Asia in fragments. But Indian drama attained both maturity in form and theme with Bhāsha whose thirteen plays were found in Trivandrum.[87] His plays *Swapnavāsavadattā* or the Dream of Vāsavadattā and *Pratijñā-yaugandharāyaṇa* or vows of *Yaugandharāyaṇa* are the best of the lot. Most of his dramas, however, were short, based on epic stories in simple and vigorous style.

Next dramatist in whose all characteristics of maturity and realism are found is Śūdraka.[88] His play *Mṛchchhakaṭika* or Claycart unravels a complicated plot, is rich in humour and pathos and crowded with actions. The love-story of Chārudatta with Vasantasenā is interwoven with one of political intrigues leading to the overthrow of a wicked king Pālaka. It is notable for its realistic depiction of the city life and a host of minor characters who are drawn form different walks of life and portrayed in their proper skill and individuality. But the greatest dramatists of Sanskrit literature was Kālidāsa whose three plays *Mālavikāgnimitram*, *Vikramorvaśīyam* and *Abhijñānaśakuntalam* have already been referred to. As in English literature so also in Sanskrit the greatest poet was also the greatest dramatist. Shakespeare and Kālidāsa were both poets and dramatists.[89]

Kālidāsa is followed by Viśākhadatta who possibly flourished in the 6th century and was a dramatist of politics.[90] His *Mudrārākshasa* or the Minister's Signet Ring shows how Chāṇakya, the minister of Chandragupta Maurya, foiled the plot of Rākshasa, the leading businessman of the capital and minister of the Nanda, to place his royal master on the throne of Paṭaliputra. His other play found in fragments *Devīchandraguptam* tells the story of the rise of Chandragupta II in power after slaying the Śaka king in the guise of his sister-in-law.[91]

King Harshavardhana of Pushyabhūti dynasty and Mahendra Vikramavarma, the contemporary Pallava king, were good litterateur. The former has three plays : *Nāgānanda*, *Priyadarśikā* and *Ratnāvalī*. The last two are dramatic comedies named after the heroines and the first one is a play of religious support.[92]

Mahendra Vikramavaman's *Mattavilāsa* is one-act play. It shows a drunken Śaivite ascetic who loses his begging bowl, a human skull, accuses a Buddhist monk for stealing it. After much satirical and humorous dialogues, in which many dissolute ascetics of other persuasions of both sexes are involved, it was found that the lost skull was taken away by a dog.[93]

In the eighth century Bhavabhuti who is considered second only to Kālidāsa composed three great dramas—*Mālatī Mādhava*, *Mahāviracharita* and *Uttara Rāmacharita*.[94] The themes of the first is love story, full of incidents of an exciting type in which more than once the heroine is rescued from death, while the latter two tell the story of Rāma, the epic hero. His greatest merit is his deep understanding of sorrow and treatment of the pathetic and terrible in which he possibly excels Kālidāsa.

Subsequent dramatists like Bhaṭṭa Nārāyana (8th century), Murāri (9th century), Rājaśekhara (9th-10th centuries) and Kṛshṇamiśra of 11th century continued the dramatic tradition yet the quality of Sanskrit drama as a whole declined.[95]

Sanskrit dramas were numerous and varied ranging from one-act plays to very long plays in ten acts. The main dialogue of the play was in prose but this was interspersed with verses which were intended to be intoned but not sung. Normally dramas were performed either in the palaces or in temple courts on special occasions. Tragic and pathetic scenes were common but endings were invariably happy — Indian players delighted in melodrama and pathos. Legends of gods and epics or ancient hero formed the mine of dramatic materials.[96]

The earliest classical Sanskrit prose literature is the description of Rudradāman in the Girnar Hills of Gujarat.[97] The prose story style, however, is foreseen in the *Vedic* literature and Pāli *Jātakas*. But the classical Sanskrit prose flourished in the Gupta and post-Gupta periods, only. In this category may be placed Subandhu, Bāṇa, Daṇḍin, Vishṇuśarmā and Nārāyaṇa. *Pañchatantra* or Five Treatise of Vishṇuśarma is a work on '*nīti*' or conduct intended mainly for statesmen and chiefs, written in the fourth century A.D. *Hitopadesa* of Nārāyaṇa written in the twelfth century was intended for students of Sanskrit.[98]

Subandhu's *Vāsavadattā* is a romantic novel while the *Daśakumāracharita* or Tales of Ten Princes of Daṇḍin is an adventure.[99] Subandhu tells the vicissitudes of love of his heroine Vāsavadattā in her love with prince Kandarpa Ketu. His work abounds in ornate description punctuated with alliterations assonances, puns etc. He shows mastery over language but lacks in brevity and directness. The *Daśakumāracharita* of Daṇḍin, however, is a romance parexcellence of the seventh century. The stories are secular, humorous and sometimes a moral and the characters are well developed in the stories. They are realistic and the entire cross-section of the contemporant society—chiefs and princes, merchants and prostitutes, thieves and crafts, peasants and wildmen with their behaviour and practices are well-delineated. Bāṇabhaṭṭa's style is similar to that of Subandhu. His works *Harshacharita* and *Kādambarī* represent his personality.[100] The first work is of autobiographical nature—something unique in Sanskrit literature—and *Kādambari* is a romantic novel presented in a series which shows an advance upon Subandhu's work *Vāsavadattā* but the work was incomplete.

Besides the poems, plays, novels, fables and romances there were numerous works on every aspect of life.[101] There were works on grammar and lexicons, medicine and mathematics, astronomy and astrology. Pāṇini, Kātyāyana, Vārttikas and Patañjali's *Mahābhāshya* laid the foundation of grammar which were supplemented by *Chāndra-Vyākaraṇa* of Chandragomin. Amara Singha's *Amarakośha* is the important lexicon of Sanskrit language; on politics and economics there are *Arthaśāstra* of Chāṇakya and *Śukra Kāmandaka*. *Bṛhatsaṁhita* of Varāḥamihira (6th century) is an encyclopaedic work on chemistry and metallurgy; there were works on astronomy and astrology and even on metre. Charaka's and Śuśruta's *Saṁhitās* works on medicine; while Āryabhaṭṭa made significant contribution to the knowledge of mathematics and astronomy.[102]

The classical age of Sanskrit literature covers a period of about ten centuries,[103] and the classical Sanskrit is the most remarkably finished and capable instrument of thought yet fashioned, . . . lucid with the utmost possible clarity, precise to the farthest limit of precision, always compact and at its best sparing in its formation of phrase, but yet with all these never poor or bare: there is no sacrifice of depth to lucidity, but matter of pregnant opulence of meaning, a capacity of high richness and beauty, a natural grandeur of sound and diction inherited from the ancient days. It is marked off from the earlier literature in the moulding and colour of its thought, temperament and language. The difference in spirit and mould between the epics and the speech of Bhartṛhari and Kālidāsa is enormous yet it is still spiritual, philosophical, religious and ethical. The inner austerer things, of course, seem to draw back a little and to stand in the background and the curious intellect, the vital urge, the aesthetic, urbanely active and hedonistic sense of life stand out in the front.[104]

The Sanskrit literature with its drama, poetry, prose, romances, monographs like Bāṇas *Harshacharita* collection of religious or reomantic tales, the *Pañchatantra* and *Hitopadeśa*, the *Jātakas* and *Kathā Saritasāgara* and Pāli and Prākrit literature are remnants of what must have been a continuous immense literary activity of many sided rich and opulent and vigorous life-movement of ancient India.[105] Gupta period is compared to Elzabethan period of English history and regarded as the classical period of Indian history. This period produced the best authors is all branches of literature including sciences. It is in fact a period of florescence, not of revival or renaissance of Sanskrit literature as is evinced by a continued and sustained growth proved by the works of Aśvaghosha, Bhāsa, Harisena and Vatsabhaṭṭi preceding Gupta period.[106]

### *Pāli and Prākrit Literature*

While Sanskrit was the language of the educated and medium of literary activities, Pāli and Prākrit were, probably, the languages of the common people. The Buddhists and Jains, to start with, carried on their proselytising activities in Māgadhi dialect but soon took to Pāli and Prākrit for more direct approach to the common people. The development of these two literatures range over a period from 500 B.C. to A.D. 1000 in three stages.[107] Pāli a western type of dialect current in Mālwa and Saurāshṭra, mainly continued to develop as the official language of the Theravāda school of Buddhism. It is represented by the Aśokan inscriptions and some other local rulers till the beginning of Christian era.[108] Prākrit was adopted as the language by the Jains. Its Māhārashṭrī dialect was adopted by the Svetāmbaras and Śauraseni or the dialect of Mathurā region was adopted by the Digambaras. Prākrit literature continued to flourish till A.D. 600.[109] There was yet another dialect of Prākrit known as

Paiśāchī in which *Bṛhatkathā* of Guṇāḍhya was originally written.[110] In the last phase of the Prākrit language Apabhraṁśa developed and mothered the vernacular languages of northern India after A.D. 1000.[111] When Pāli and Prākrit languages began to be progressively used for literary purposes some grammars were written. The Prākrit grammar of Vararuchi called *Prākraprakāśa* and Chaṇḍa's *Prākṛtalakshaṇa* were written in Sanskrit. But Pāli grammar *Kātyāyanaprakaraṇa* was written in Pali language.[112]

Pāli literature consists mainly of the canonical texts of the Buddhist. The elaborate and exhaustive *Tripitakas* and commentaries on them are the kernel. The next important work in Pāli literature is *Milinda-Pañho* which is a dialogue between the king Menander and monk Nāgasena. Mostly repetitive and prosaic they are pressed into service for religious purposes.[113] The narrative portions are of much merit. The style of the Pali poems is simpler and show a love of nature. Śrī Laṅkā chronicles *Dipavaṁśa* and *Mahāvaṁśa* written in the 5th century are important works in Pāli language.[114]

The Prākrit literature is both enormous and interesting but dull and dry like the Pāli canonical literature. It abounds in lengthy stock phrases and descriptions and have very little literary value though occasionally there are grace and beauty. But like the Buddhist Jātaka stories we get from them pictures of prosperous cities and populous villages, kings and merchants, tīrthaṅkaras and monks.[115]

The poetry of the Jains is a little better than their prose literature. While the prose is terse, poetry is sometimes punctuated with humours.[116] But by far most important literary works in Prakrit is *Saptaśatakas* of Hāla, the Śātavāhana king.[117] This work based on south Indian folk-song is a collection of self-contained stanzas of great charm and beauty. They are notable for their brevity and like *Amaru* suggest a whole story in four short lines.[118] The story of *Samarāditya* written by Haribhadra in the seventh century is a lengthy story in mixed prose and verse of parable nature.[119] Hemachandra Sūri (A.D. 1089-1172) is the most distinguished of the Jain authors.[120]

Jain monks were encouraged to write secular works provided those had ethical value.[121] Such works like *Setubandha* or Building the Causeway of Pravarasena II, *Gauḍabadha* (or Slaying of the king of Bengal) of Vākpati of the 8th century are important.[122] Besides, the Jain scholars have works on politics, mathematics and even on poetics with a little Jain slant. *Kālakāchārya-Kathānaka* provides an account of the conquest of Ujjain and *Kathākośa* is a collection of works which provides information of countries outside India.[123]

Sawnyahtisekaumudi describes how a merchant with his eight wives attained *samyukta* (perfection) in religion.[124]

*South Indian Languages and Literature*

Tāmil is the oldest language of South India; it may be even older than Sanskrit.[125] And Tāmil is the mother of all South Indian languages, e.g., Kaṇṇada, Telugu and Mālayālam, which began to assume distinctive forms in the 8th, 11th and 14th centuries, respectively.[126] The history of the Tāmil literature goes back to hoary past and its development in the Tamilians show in three stages or periods, old (500 B.C. to A.D. 500), middle (A.D. 500) and modern (from A.D. 800).[127] The oldest period is known as the Saṅgam age which, according to Tāmilians, ranges between 4290 B.C. to B.C. 2706 in three stages. But modern scholars hold that all the three academics of the first period of Tāmil literature ended before the rise of the Pallavas of Kañchī between 500 B.C. to A.D. 500.[128]

However, the Tāmils say, the first Saṅgam period covered 4,400 years; the seat of the Sangam was at old Madurā and 89 Pallava kings were its patron. Its membership consisted of 549 legendary sages and gods to whom 4,499 authors submitted their works for approval. None of these works is available.[129] The second Saṅgam covered a period of 3,900 years and had its headquarters at Kapātpuram. It had a library which housed 8,149 works and in its membership there were some 3,700 poets, and 59 Pāṇḍyan kings patronised this Saṅgam. Of this period one work known as *Tolkāppiyam* has come down to us. It is a grammatical work in three parts each with nine sections written in the form of Sūtras, though it contains a lot of informations on manners, customs, thoughts and beliefs of the people.[130] The third Saṅgam had its headquarters at present Mādurā and covers a period of 1,850 years. Its president was Nākkirār and its membership rose to 49 but some 449 poets were associated with it. The output of this last Saṅgam may be divided into two categories—anthologies and the epics. The first is divided into three—

(i) Ten Idylls or *Patthuppātu*,
(ii) *Ettuthokāi* or eight collections, and
(iii) *Padinenkitkanakku* or Eighteen Minor Didactic poems.[131]

Of the ten, Idylls Nedunalvādai of Nākkirār is known for its story of the Pāṇḍyan king Nedun-jeliyan. It draws a contrast between the king's life in battle-field and his queen pinning for him at home.[132] Another Idyll by Rudran Kannanār, Perumpanattrupadai beautifully depicts the internal struggle of the hero suffering from two opposite emotions calling him to the battle-field and the other to his beloved at home.[133]

*Ettuthokai* or eight collections consists of 400 short lyrics in a haval metre; *Karunthokai* consists of 400 stanzas on love written by 200 poets; *Ainkurunuru* is a collection of 500 love poems composed by five poets; *Panditrupāttu* or Ten Tens of 10 poems of 10 stanzas show the powers and virtue of the Chera kings and customs and manners of the people; *Paripadal* of 70 poems is famous for peacock dance; *Kalithokāi* comprises of 150 love songs in Kāli metre; *Ahananuru* consists of 400 love lyrics and *Parunanuru* of 400 poems by 150 poets. The last one is best known for its literary merit and data on social history of Tamil Nadu.[134]

*Tirukkural* or *Kural* of Tiruvalluvar is most popular of the Minor Dialectic poems and it is considered to provide eternal inspiration and guide to the Tamilians. The text is divided in three parts dealing with *dharma*, *artha* and *kama*, the three objects of life, and devoting ten stanzas to each of the 113 topics bearing upon different aspects of human life.[135]

Of the ten epics of the last Saṅgam only seven are extant and two of these *Silappadikāram* and *Maṇimekhalāi* occupy a high place in Tamil literature and are compared to the *Rāmāyana* and the *Mahābhārata* of Sanskrit literature.[136] The story of the former centres round an anklet. The hero Kovalan by name squanders his fortune after a courtesan Mādhavī and being disappointed returns to his chaste wife Kaṇṇakī. The couple then comes to Madura to live there and pursue a trade. He goes to a goldsmith to sell the anklet of his wife to raise necessary fund. But the goldsmith, who had stolen a similar anklet of the queen, accuses Kovālan for the theft and the king executes him. His distracted wife thereupon breaks open the other anklet to prove the innocence of her husband and curse the city of Mādurā for the injustice done to her husband. The city is consumed by flame according to the curse of the faithful and honest woman. Kaṇṇakī rejoins her husband in heaven where she is proclaimed as the goddess of chastity.[137] The other epic *Maṇimekhalāi* is a sequel to the former epic written in later times. Its heroine Maṇimekhalāi, the daughter of Kovālan by Mādhavī, through the vicissitudes of fortune drew inspiration from her step-mother Kaṇṇakī and becomes a Buddhist nun.[138]

The poets of the Saṅgam Age divided their poems into two broad categories — those dealing with love were called *Agam* and those composed on the praise of the kings were called *Puram.*[139] A further division was based on regional basis.[140] Tamils divided their love poems into five divisions—*kurinchi* or hills, *pālai* or dry land, *mullai* or jungle land, *maaruntham* or cultivated lands and *neithal* or coastal land. Each of these is connected to a particular theme of poetry. Thus on the background of hills are composed poems on pre-nuptial love and cattle-raising; lamentations of lovers are shown on dry lands; the jungles provide the background of brief parting of lovers and raiding expeditions; on the background of the valleys are shown post-nuptial love or the wiles of courtesans; and parting of fishermen's wives and pitched battles are shown on coastal regions. To each region was given its appropriate flowers, animals and people.[141]

The Tāmil literature of the Saṅgam age holds a unique place in the whole range of Indian literature including Sanskrit for its universal link between nature and human relations.[142] Many scenes of daily life in the town and the country, shops and fields, temples and palaces, households and fishermen's huts—all are represented in it with rare economy of words.[143]

The Tāmil literature of the second period beginning from *c.* A.D. 500 and continuing till eighteenth century consists of a large number of secular works resembling those of the Saṅgam Age and the devotional poems or songs of the Śaivite and Vaishṇavite saints.[144] The devotional songs are collected and preserved by Nāmbi-Andar-Nāmbi and Sri Nāthamuni. The former arranged the Śaiva hymns into eleven Tirumurāi, the first seven of which are collectively called *Teveram*. Likewise Sri Nāthamuni arranged the extant Vaishṇava hymns into a colossal collection called *Nālāriya Prabandham* which consists of 4,000 hymns. Put together these embody the teachings of the Upanishads and are regarded as the Tamil Veda.[145] These songs are still sung in the temples of South India in different melodic tunes.

The Śaiva saints were called Nāyanārs. Their songs represent the spiritual excellence of Śaivism at its best. Among the saints Tirumular, Sambander, Appar, Sundarar and Mānikkavāchakar lived between 7th and 8th centuries and are held in great veneration by the South Indian saints.[146] It is said that one who is not touched by the Tiruvāchakam of Mānikkavāchakar is verily a stone. The biographies of the Śaiva saints were collected together in a work called *Periyapurānam.* It includes men and women of all classes and castes, even untouchables; all of them are venerated irrespective of caste and this shows the catholicity and universality of devotional Śaivism.[147]

The Vaishṇava saints were known as Ālvār—one in deep wisdom—who also belonged to different sexes and castes ranging from a king to Vellala and Kalla. Contemporaries of the Śaiva saints traditionally are regarded as twelve.[148] Their songs as collected in *Nālāriya-Prabandham* consist of 4,000 stanzas. Four poems of Nammālvār, the most popular of the Vaishṇavites, is regarded as the Tāmil redaction of the four Vedas. Six poems of Tirumangai, the last Ālvār, are regarded as the six Vedāntas. Perumāl-Tirumoli and Mukundamālā of Ālvār Kulasehhara, a king of Mālābār, excels in its lyric beauty and his later work is compared to Sanskrit work *Gīta Govinda* of Jayadeva.[149]

The secular literature of this period was enriched by *Tiruttakhadevar*, *Yayangordav*, *Ottakhuttan* and *Kamban*.[150] *Tiruttakkadevar*, *Jivahachintamani* of tenth century, is a romantic poem which describes the love of hero Junaka ending in marriage; *Lalingottupparani* of Jayangoutar is a war poem which describes the Kalinga War of Kulottuṅga I; Ottakkatan wrote laudatory poems on the three successors of Kulottuṅga I. But by far the greatest author was Kamban who composed Tāmil *Rāmāyaṇa* during the reign of Kulottuṅga III. It is regarded as the greatest epic in Tamil literature.[151]

The literatures in Kaṇṇada, Telugu and Mālayālam began to be written towards the end of ancient Indian history as already observed. Kaṇṇada literature begins with Kavirājamārga, a work on poetics of Amoghavarsha (A.D. 814-88), but it attained celebrity in the next century with the poems of Pampa Ponna and Ranna.[152] The Telugu literature began in the eleventh century with translation of the *Mahābhārata* by Nannaya.[153]

## REFERENCES


1. A.L. Basham (ed.), *A Cultural History of India*, p. 162.
2. Sri Aurobindo, *op. cit.*, p. 225.
3. R.C. Majumdar (ed.)., *The Age of Imperial Unity*, p. 290.

4-9. A.L. Basham (ed.), *A Cultural History of India*, p. 162.

10. Sri Aurobindo, *op. cit.*, p. 225.

11-12. A.L. Basham, *op. cit.*, pp. 388-401.

13. Sri Aurobindo, *op. cit.*, p. 261.

14-17. A.L. Basham, *op. cit.*, pp. 202-04.

18. Sri Aurobindo, *op. cit.*

19-21. A.L. Basham, *op. cit.*, pp. 407-08.

22-27. Sri Aurobindo, *op. cit.*, pp. 259-284.

28-29. R.C. Majumdar, *op. cit.*, p. 437.
30. Sri Aurobindo, *op. cit.*
31. R.C. Majumdar, *op. cit.*
32-34. R.C. Majumdar (ed.)., *The Classical Age*, pp. 291-98.
35-37. Sri Aurobindo, *op. cit.*, pp. 313-314.
38-39. *Ibid.*, p. 285.
40-42. *Ibid.*, pp. 284-85.
43-44. A.L. Basham (ed.), *A Cultural History of India*, pp. 170-71.
45-46. Sri Aurobindo, *op. cit.*, p. 287.
47-49. A.L. Basham (ed.), *A Cultural History of India*, pp. 170-71.
50-52. *Ibid.*
53-54. Sri Aurobindo, *op. cit.*
55-65. A.L. Basham, *op. cit.*, pp. 417-18.
66. A.L. Basham (ed.), *A Cultural History of India*, p. 177.
67. A.L. Basham, *op. cit.*, p. 420.
68-70. *Ibid.*, pp. 420-25.
71-72. *Ibid.*
73. Sri Aurobindo, *op. cit.*, p. 301.
74. A.L. Basham (ed.), *op. cit.*, p. 183.
75. A.L. Basham, *op. cit.*, p. 425.
76. *Ibid.*
77-81. *Ibid.*, pp. 427-30.
82-84. S.P. Sen (ed.), *Historical Biography in Sanskrit Literature* (1979), pp. 1-24.
85-87. *Ibid.*, p. 437.
88. A.L. Basham (ed.), *op. cit.*, p. 179.
89. A.L. Basham, *op. cit.*, p. 437.
90-93. *Ibid.*, p. 443.
94. A.L. Basham (ed.), *op. cit.*, p. 186.
95-96. A.L. Basham, *op. cit.*, pp. 435-444.
97-98. *Ibid.*, p. 417.
99-100. *Ibid.*, pp. 435-449.
101-02. R.C. Majumdar, *op. cit.*, pp. 441-42.
103-05. Sri Aurobindo, *op. cit.*, pp. 295-97.
106. R.C. Majumdar (ed.), *The Classical Age*, p. 291.
107-11. A.L. Basham (ed.), *A cultural History of India*, pp. 164-65.
112. R.C. Majumdar (ed.) *The Classical Age*, p 325.
113-16. A.L. Basham, *op. cit.*, pp. 455-461.
117-18. *Ibid.*, pp. 462-63.
119-20. R.C. Majumdar, *op. cit.*, pp. 445-48.
121-22. R.C. Majumdar (ed.), *The Classical Age*, p. 326.
123. R.C. Majumdar, *op. cit.*, pp. 445-48.
124. *Ibid.*
125-27. A.L. Basham (ed.), *A Cultural History of India*, pp. 167-68.
128. R.C. Majumdar, *op. cit.*, p. 193.
129-31. R.C. Majumdar (ed.), *The Age of Imperial Unity*, pp. 292-93.
132-34. *Ibid.*, pp. 293-302.
135. R.C. Majumdar, *op. cit.*, p. 194.
136-39. A.L. Basham, *op. cit.*, pp. 477-85.
140-41. R.C. Majumdar (ed.), *The Age of Imperial Unity*, p. 296.
142-43. *Ibid.*
144-45. R.C. Majumdar, *op. cit.*, pp. 448-49.
146-51. R.C. Majumdar (ed.), *The Classical Age*, pp. 327-39.
152-53. A.L. Basham (ed.), *A Cultural History of India*, pp. 168-69.

# 9

# Art

P.S. Rawson observes :

> "Very few people yet realise how great a debt the art of the world — especially that of the Eastern world — already owes to India. It is true to say that without the examples of Indian forms and ideas the art of the whole of South-East Asia, or China, Korea, Mongolia, Tibet and Japan would have been radically different, and would have lost by that difference. So, too, modern Western art, especially architecture and painting."[1]

Very little, however, of the visual art of early period of ancient India has survived. After the end of the Indus Valley there is a wide gap and nobody knows for certain when the Indus Valley art began. Historically, Indian art begins with the ceramic wares and figurative terracottas made in the cities of the broad Gaṅgā basin during the last centuries of pre-Christian era.[2] From about 299 B.C. onward large number of miniature reliefs, either hand-modelled or pressed in mould, set the key for what comes after. Its flowery and opulence, combined with erotic charms, appear full-fledged in the ivories representing gorgeous girls and fantastic animals.[3] But these are scattered fragments of what must have been a wide spread and flourishing activity.

Literary sources and the friezes on Buddhist stupas provide some idea of ancient Indian architecture. The Milinda-pañho describes a city, fine and regular, measured out into quarters with excavated moats and ramparts about it, with stout gatehouses and towers, with market places, cross-roads, street comers and public squares, with cleanly and even main roads, with regular lines of open shops, well provided with parks, gardens, lakes, lotus-ponds and wells, adorned with many kinds of temples of the gods, free from every fault and standing in all its glory.[4] Excavation at Ahichchhatrā, the capital of the Pañchāla country, appears to be a city of this type. Its walls built of burnt bricks still rise to a height of 40 to 50 feet. At the centre of the city stood a temple where main thoroughfares crossed.[5] The city of Rājgir was enclosed by a Cyclopean wall (of 6th century B.C.) and at Kauśāmbī (3rd century B.C.) there was a palace with substantial tunnel vault.[6]

Further idea of the ancient cities can be gleaned from the representations in the reliefs of Bhārhut, Sāñchi, Amarāvatī, Mathurā, and other places.[7] In these, the cities of Rājagṛha, Śrāvastī, Vārāṇasī, Kapilāvastu, Kuśīnagara, etc., have been shown. Outer view shows the city wall with its gatehouse and defensive towers and glimpses of the buildings inside. Moat surrounds the city which is enclosed by wall made of bricks or wooden wall of palisade which are finished at the top either by a coping or battlements. The gatehouse is flanked by two high towers, projecting from the gatehouse joined to each other by a porch. Quite distinct from the gatehouse stand occasionally 'toraṇas' situated at the end of the bridge communicating with the gateway.[8]

The buildings represented usually consisted of several storeys having a wagon-vaulted roof on the top with gables at either end and pointed finials at the top. They usually face a court, occasionally enclosed on either side by subsidiary structures, but left open in front (as in Sāñchi east gate).[9] Sometimes a *toraṇa*, consisting of two upright pillars surmounted by two or three architraves, leads to the court in front of the buildings (as in Amarāvatī). The above picture of the cities was corroborated by the writings of the classical writers and Fa-hsien. Descriptions by Megasthenes of the city of Pātliputra and Chandragupta's palace leave no trace of doubt about the representations.[10] The excavation of the Mauryan palace shows that how it resembled the Achaemenid Hall of hundred cloumns at Persepolis.

The rise of new religious sects like Buddhism and Jainism provides new impetus to Indian art and architecture. The stūpas, the Chaitya Halls and Vihāras are important monuments of the Buddhists and Jain denominations. The rise of Bhakti cult provided impetus to the Hindus to construct images and *Deva-gṛha* as well.[11]

Before the introduction of images, the stūpa was the centre and focus of adoration of the Buddhists. The stūpa originally was a domed mound near the crest of which relics of Buddha and his saints were enshrined. The stūpa was, to start with, a plain simple structure consisting of a hemispherical dome (*aṇḍa*) placed on a low circular base and surmounted by a square-box (*hārmika*) which is further crowned by a parasol or umbrella (*chhatra*), the symbol of universal paramountcy. The dome was surrounded by a passage for circumambulation (*pradakshiṇapatha*) fenced off by a railing or wall.[12] This original form is seen at Sāñchi. A study of the evolution shows that there was a general tendency towards elevation of each component part conceived over life-size couples on the facade. The original brick stūpa at Sāñchi was later on refurbished with stone masonry and richly decorated with carved railings and beautiful gateways. The stūpa at Bhārhut is similar in design but the rails of the stūpa and gate in this place is richly carved. This art lies at the root of all Buddhist styles of South-East Asia and the Far East.[13] The stupa which obtained greatest celebrity was the relic-tower which Kanishka erected at Peshawar.

From the third century B.C. all stūpa rites have one constant feature, a large hall aligned with the stūpa with an internal colonnade which separates a nave from two aisles, linking them across the closed end by an ambulatory.[14] With very few exceptions the Chaitya halls were hewn out of rock. The early halls were certainly built of wood. The earlier Chaitya of Bhāgā near Poonā was completed with actual wooden feature roof-ribs, window, latices and portico. But about 50 B.C. they were being cut entirely in stone, faithfully retaining wooden architectural pattern. In addition these were sculptured with ornamental figures in reliefs including attractive women sitting on balconies. At Kārle and Kānheri (A.D. 100) they were opulently connaived over life-size couples on the facade.[15]

The monks who preached the doctrine at these cave-halls were gradually settling down to live on the sites. It is probable that in the last century B.C. the Buddhist texts were written down and the monks, depending on the support of the laity, were unable to read anyway. So adjacent to the Chaitya halls Vihāras were constructed to provide accommodation to these monks who were provided with regular instruction. Even at Bhāgā there are a few living caves cut in rock adjacent to Chaitya hall, decorated with legendry reliefs.[16] Ajanta illustrates this process clearly. For here, over about eight centuries from the third century B.C., twenty-six caves were cut, four being preaching halls, the others living caves, which provided accommodation for 600 to 700 monks.[17]

The monastery in India was designed on the same line as a private house—in a square block formed by four rooms of cells along the four sides of an inner quadrangle.[18] The caves of western India show the continuous development of monasteries. Earlier, rock cut

**Plate 1** : Bhārhut (Satna-MP) Stūpa Great railing, western gate, corner pillar, top Panel, worship of Gautam's hair-lock Insc : Celebration of Lord's hair-lock in Sudharma, Assembly hall of Gods 2nd cent BC Sandstone Calcutta, Indian Museum No. 182, *Courtesy* : American Institute of Indian Studies, Vārānasī.

**Plate 2 :** Sānchi (Raisen-MP) Stupa 1 Southern gateway, north side, superstructure, view from north *c* 1st BC Buff sandstone. *Courtesy* : American Institute of Indian Studies, Vāraṇasī.

**Plate 5** : Bhubaneswar (Puri-Orissa) Parasuramesvara temple śikhārā from west Mid 7th cent Kalinga style Sandstone. *Courtesy* : American Institute of Indian Studies, Varanasi.

**Plate 6** : Kumbhakonam (Thanjavur-Tamilnadu) Nāgesvarasvami temple Eastern outer gopurā, view from east *c* 13th cent Late Colanadu style Granita. *Courtesy* : American Institute of Indian Studies, Vārāṇasī.

**Plate 7** : Cave No. 21 (Rāmeswar) General views from south-west *c* 2nd half of 6th A.D.
*Courtesy* : American Institute of Indian Studies, Vārāṇasī.

**Plate 8** : Ellòra (Aurangabad-Maharashtra) Cave 10, Viśvakarmā View of facade *c* first-half of 7th cent Deccan trap. *Courtesy* : American Institute of Indian Studies, Vārānasī.

monasteries are seen at Barābar hills and Nāgārjuna and the Udayagiri and Khandagiri caves of Orissa of the time of Khāravela. The caves of western India also show a continuous process of development. The typical form shows a central hall, proceeded in front by a pillared *verandah* or vestibule, and opening out on the other side into a number of small square cells, carried further into the rock.[19]

Hindu art developed later than Buddhist in India as a whole.[20] Natural tendency of the Indian population has been to adore and make offerings at a place in the country side where the Divine seems to show its presence. Every village has a hallow tree, a sacred hill or a holy spot marked by boulders—where sacrificial rituals are conducted in open. Brāhmanical Hinduism demanded, to start with, no installation. From second century of the Christian era Hinduism seems to have a successful alliance with theory of kingship, whereby the metaphysical principle to which kings might appeal for supernatural patronage was awarded a name and form as a deity. Attempts were made now to Brāhmanise the iconography of religious art and permanent installations for the gods began to be constructed. It is thus natural that the evolution of Hindu stone architecture and temple-curving took place at scattered sites which were each nearer to the capital cities of royal dynasties.[21]

Original pattern of Hindu temple, however, was very simple. "The sacred luminous object stands within an enclosure and a cell; the object is often a Śiva Lingam; it can be also a sculptural image either replacing an older more primitive hallow or ceremonially curved or cast, and dedicated as a new dwelling for sacred."[22] The cell is raised on a plinth and to it may be appended extra features, the commonest being a porch or portico and a decorated door-frame. Then came an ambulatory, a crowning tower, one or more aligned approach-halls, one of which was meant for dancing, and sometimes an encircling layout of lesser cells, or even miniature temples.[23] This last feature, in South India, became a fantastically elaborate sequence of concentric enclosures with towering gateways called *gopurā*.

Each temple was conceived, as the Buddhist stūpa was, as the axis of the world, symbolically transforming into the mythical Mount Meru around which are stung like garlands the heavens and the earth. The heavens are represented on the exterior of the developed temples by bands of sculpture containing icons of gods and other lesser superhuman-figures, which popular legend ascribes to heaven. Among these are the famous erotic carvings which are images of the post-mortem delights awarded by celestial girls called *apsarās* to the spirits of the heroes and sages. These heaven-bands are at the level of raised interior floor, thus converting it into analogous 'courts of heaven', which are naturally adorned with ornamental designs reflecting all that the heart can desire.[24] The principal image in its cell—called 'womb-house'—occupies at this level the place of the enthroned king in his court, to whom the only officiating Brāhmaṇa has direct access. It is dressed, fed and entertained, just as a king might be. From it the originating energy of the cosmos is felt to flow out through the fabric of the temple into the every-day world around its foot.[25]

There are many regional styles in temple architecture. But from about A.D. 650 it is possible to distinguish two main types, the northern and the southern, both of which involved as distinctive patterns out of a previous mixed experience.[26] The fully characteristic northern temple stands on a plinth adorned with elaborately profiled rhythmical horizontal mouldings. It is distinguished by its tall square-planned tower over the main cubical cell; this has a *maṇḍapa* in the front and may have around it complex re-entrant angles, imitative plasters, small duplicate of its own profiles or ogival hood-mouldings. This tower is divided into horizontal bands. Temples of Bhubaneswar, Konārak, Khājurāho and Mount Ābu are best specimens of this style. These temples were plastered and painted and sometimes decorated with painted and dyed cotton hangings and precious metals and gems.[27]

The South Indian style that evolved at Bādāmi under the Chālukyas was standardised by the Pallava dynasty.[28] The temples at Palladakal, Kānchipuram and Mamallāpuram represent this type. Its essential characteristics are a pyramidal tower surmounting the cell, composed of a restricted number of storeys, decorated with miniature pavalions and crowned by a kind of small faceted dome; and exterior wall uniting cell and main portico, which is vertically banded with plasters between foot and lintel, in the panels of which there may be few relief sculptures; a rounding wall often lined with cells, so close to the structure that it creates the feeling of a roofless corridor, pillars supported by lion caryatids, with broadspread capitals; and curvilinear brackets under lintel and caves. Later the porticos gradually developed into corridorous gateway known as *Gopurā* which overwhelmed the main cells.[29]

The external architectural style of the colossal monolithic temple called Kailāsanatha at Ellorā is a marvel of the Indian architectural design. It was cut in two chief stages from a volcanic hill side, curved both inside and out, so that it stands free within an enormous quarry, the walls of which are pierced with flanking cave temples.[30] The fundamental plan of cells with broad colonnaded hall is derived from a late type of Buddhist living cave-monastery of Ajantā. The sculpture, however, is unique. Enormous figures of deep-relief, bound, leap and twist, their energy bursting their architectural frames. They were once plastered and painted; here and there on the fabric few fragments of pure wall paintings are found surviving. This temples is related to Pallava school of art.[31]

Under the Cholas about A.D. 1000 another flowing of art is found at Thānjavur. A stupendous pyramidal shrine dedicated to Śiva was built here. Its tower is nearly 200 feet high and crowned by an eighty-tonne ornate dome-capstone. The temples is 180 feet long; the base of the sanctum is 82 feet square and two storeyed in height; above this rises in 13 storeys the main pyramidal tower of 190 feet high. The exterior wall is richly decorated with sculptures but inner walls of the ambulatory which surrounds the cells under the main tower show original series of wall-paintings illustrating Śiva mythology and celestial female-dancers.[32]

## Sculpture

The first school of Indian sculpture began with the Mauryas in the fourth century B.C.[33] The products of the period are tall footless pillars of polished sandstone, whose capital are carved with symbolic animal figures with three dimensional forepart of animals, like an elephant in Dhaulī. At Sārnāth, polished sandstone railing and dedicatory figures were erected. Buddhist stūpas, which might have been constructed a century earlier, were now enlarged and refurbished — a process which was successfully repeated in later periods. A dynastic guild of sculptors seems to have grown up, able to curve colossal polished stone, dedicatory figures, called *yakshas* and *yakshīs*.[34] The two best known are the male from Parkham and female from Dildārganj, the latter dating from A.D. 500. A number of caves in the Barābar hills were also cut to accommodate members of religious orders which were sometimes decorated with simple sculpture of guardian figures and inscriptions.[35]

But in the decoration of major religious monuments we find the best specimen of Indian art.[36] At a number of places decorative and figural reliefs carving was evolved to ornament Buddhist stūpas and their railing. At first the style was in low and flat relief, the figures being carefully outlined and isolated against their backgrounds; often they were angular and primitive, this owe nothing to the Maurya dynastic style. "All figures are carved boldly against plain surface of the ground. A certain heaviness of form, earth bound and of primitive significance is found emerging at Mathurā; those in action betray a note of sensuality as well."[37] But this low relief style was capable of its own kind of sophistication, as at Bhārhut where the pillars of the railing carried half-life size figures of country godlings, pressed into service at the Buddhist shrines; "its coping carries a continuous-creeper design, framing small reliefs, which suggest that the whole structure was interpreted as an image of the mythical wish-granting tree."[38]

The early years of the Christian era saw the evolution of sculptural style with softly rounded relief to represent virtually three-dimensional figures, as on the brackets and capitals at Sāñchī.[39] These works succeeded in converting in stone what must have been a strongly developing style of two dimensional narrative expression. The scrolled ends to the Sāñchī lintels suggest that the Buddhists succeeded in transcripting into a more permanent medium the stories related to the Buddha from the pictorial story scrolls so popular in India throughout the ages.[40]

The skill of the sculptors to represent figures with a powerful plastic presence and in composing complex narrative scenes, full of overlaps, advanced rapidly, especially in southeast India around Amrāvati. The stūpas with their railings and gateways came to be almost totally clad in panels of white limestone carved with rich ornamental designs or sensuous figural relief.[41] There is no doubt that Vengi carried on the tradition of early Indian art and served as a link between the earlier art of Bhārhut, Bodh Gayā and Sāñchī on the one hand and the later Gupta and Pallava art on the other.[42] The style of these works is closely related to contemporary fragments of paintings in the caves of Ajantā on the other side of the peninsula as well.[43]

The style of Gāndhāra assimilated into the Buddhist schist and stucco sculpture is Romano-Hellenistic and as such seems Classical. The Buddha wears something resembling a draped *toga*; deities develop classical muscular torsos; there are *swags* and *putti*, and even illustrations of Greek legends.[44] But under the Kushaṇas Mathurā gained special importance. At Mathurā, skill of the Maurya dynastic school of sculpture seems to have continued and have been applied to the development of three-dimensional sculpture, first for Buddhist subjects and in second century A.D. to present Hindu gods—Śiva and Vishṇu.[45] The pivot of the Gupta art was the human figure; the rich animal and vegetable world was pushed on to borders or to panels to decorate human figure. The body seems to be disciplined but the inner world had not yet been conquered; for the muscular body seems to pulsate with glow of vital energy. The heavy physicality is soon partly relieved by a relaxation of the flesh and an open-eyed smiling countenance.[46] "The full round breasts and full heavy hips of female figures are no longer just conveyors of idea of fertility but suggest warm and living flesh relaxed or light."[47]

At Sārnāth, body sheds off its toughness, attains full soft roundness and exhales an air of complete ease of serenity, seems to float with an almost uncanny sensitivity. The experiences of Mathurā-Sārnāth were shared all over northern India in varying degrees according to ethnical, social and religious tradition in different parts.[48] "The dignity and beauty of the human figure in the best Indian statue cannot be excelled but what was sought and achieved was not an outward naturalistic, but a spiritual and psycho-beauty, and to achieve it the sculptor suppressed, and was entirely right in suppressing, the obtrusive material detail and aimed instead at purity of outline and fineness of feature", says Sri Aurobindo.[49]

**Painting**

Painting as an art was very popular in India right from the prehistoric times, can be surmised from the references in the Epic *Mahābhārata* and *Jātaka* stories.[50] It is told in the *Vinaya Piṭaka* that Āmrapālī invited painters from various countries to paint on her walls the figures of kings, merchants and traders; and king Prasenajit had picture-halls. But extant specimen of ancient art is only available in a few rows of human figures in yellow and ochre earth colours, arranged in sections in accordance with the shape of the irregularly vaulted ceilings of the Sitābhenga or Jogimārā cave in Rāmgarh hills.[51] Besides the irregular compositional bands, there is also another band with representation of large acquatic animals like *makara*, etc., in same colours. Subsequently these were covered by a layer of painting. Yet this can be assumed that these murals were executed in what is known as *tempera*, that these figures mostly in three-quarters profile are lively and freely rythmical and are well balanced in alignment and third dimension was intelligently understood.[52] These figures establish strong similarities with early Sāñchī (Stūpa II) and Jaggayyapetā reliefs, in form and motiff. This Rāmgarh hill painting bespeaks considerable past knowledge and practice but similarities with Sāñchī and Jaggayyapetā push back the date of these to the first century B.C. and compares favourably with contemporary sculptures.[53]

The next phase of Indian painting is traced in the Ajantā Caves IX and X.[54] Two scenes, one on frieze representing human figures in Cave IX and another representing a group of elephants in Cave X, show the main principles of this phase. Paintings are laid over a fine coat of plaster, finished by another coat of finely polished white priming. The outlines were drawn first in broad sweeps and details were added afterwards. Ajantā paintings are mural and not fresco since the artists of Ajantā painted their scenes when the plaster had set.[55] Natural earth, found locally, formed most, not all, of the pigments, in which real, in different tones, green grey, brown, yellow and white predominate. Both men and animals are modelled in a variety of positions in line and colour. Full masses of figures reach the outermost level where they spread up their limits. Study in shape, of distinct ethnic class and sartorial types, the human figures are detached and reticent, and are very nearer in appearance to figures as carved in Bodh Gaya and Sāñchī.[55]

In the Classical period paintings had become popular and importance of this art is proved by the works on painting. The *Vishṇu-dharma Purāṇa* and Vatsyāyana's *Kāmasūtra* provide both theoretical and practical principles of painting.[56] Buddhist and Jain conceptions of painting hold that painting is the product of the seeing faculty of the mind, or direct institution or '*pratyaksha*' *darśana* activity of the soul. Yasodhara commenting on Vatsyayana's work speaks of '*Śaḍaṅga*' or Six Limbs of painting, viz., rūpabheda, pramāṇas, bhāva, lābaṇya yojanā, sardrisya and varṇikabhaṅga.[57] *Vishnu-dharma Purāṇa* gives directions for 'vajralepa' or method of preparation of the ground for murals, preparation and application of colours, methods of shading the lime, adding highlights, fore-shortening of limbs and features, different methods of treating the volume and expression of mood and movement and classification of painting, according to themes, as 'satya', 'vainika', 'nagara' and 'miśra'.[58] Besides mural paintings, we have *Yamapats*, *Charanachitras* and *Paṭachitras* in this period.[59]

The remains of the paintings of this period are found in the caves at Bedsā (A.D. 300), Kānheri Cave XIX (A.D. 6*c*), Aurangābad Cave II and VI (A.D. 6*c*), Pitalkhora (Chaitya Cave, 1, 206 A.D. 6*c*) —all in the Deccan; in rock cut temples of Tirumalāipuram (Digambara Jain A.D. 7*c*), Malayadipatti (Vaishṇava A.D. 788-840), both in the South; caves at Bāgh (Cave IV, A.D. 500 *c*), Ajantā (Caves I, II, XVI, XVII, XIX), Bādāmi (Caves III, A.D. 6*c*), Sittanavasal

(A.D. 7*c*) and Kuṭamaṭha temples of Kāñchipuram (A.D. 7*c*).[60] All paintings of this period belong to common denominator, the norm being supplied by Ajantā. Only at Ellorā a new tradition seems to emerge in the eighth century.[61]

The materials adopted were powdered rock, clay, cowdung mixed with chaff or vegetable fibres, sometimes with mudga concoction or chaff were made into a paste and plastered on the rock. The plaster was then polished with a trowel and, when still wet, coated with lime wash. After the plaster dried paints were laid and afterwards the surface was burnished. The outlines were drawn first; then colours were laid; then colours were applied in broad shading to give it an effect of rounded three dimensional volume fully modelled. Colour too was invariably fully modelled which showed the figures as it bodied forth in fully rounded and plastic volumes.[62] Principal colours used were lose red active (*draturāga*), vivid red (*kumkuma or sindūra*), yellow ochre (*haritala*), indigo-blue lapis-luzuli blue, lamp black (*kajjala*), chalk white (*khadi-māti*), tena varte (*gera-māti*) and green (*orpiment or powdered verdigris, jangal*).[63]

In both colour and modelling, the Ajantā Cave paintings (Cave II) exhaust the possibility of what colour can achieve in solidity and third dimension. Paintings seemed to parallel sculpture and reached the elevated Classical or Sanskrit being and dignity.[64]

## Terracotta

Terracotta plaques and figurines display another sphere of activity of the Indian artists in ancient India, particularly in the North on the Gaṅga basin. Exterior walls of the residential houses were decorated with plaques representing gods and goddesses, narrative scenes from the Epics and the *Purāṇas*, animals and semi-divine beings, amorous couples, portrait heads, toys and human and animal figures.[65] Bāṇa's *Harshacharita* mentions that a host of clay modellers were employed to make terracotta figures holding auspicious fruits for decoration on the occasion of Rājyaśri's marriage.[66] Of special technical and aesthetic significance were the terracottas from Ahichchhatra, Rājghāt, Pāhārpur and Moinamatī. A cross-section of the society and animal and vegetable world are represented in terracotta figures of these areas. Aware of the iconographic injunctions and religious dictates the artists in clay modelling worked with an intensely playful and joyous freedom of imagination and vision. But the essential plastic treatment is the same as that of contemporary sculpture.[67]

## Other Minor Arts

Ivory carving, coinage, jewellery, clay-seals, pottery, carpentry and metal-casting were other fields of activity of the Indian artists through the ancient period.[68] Gupta coins attained refinement and elegance after the Kushāṇa apprenticeship and the excellence of the jewellery have an aesthetic sense and skilfulness in the art. The clay seals and pottery bespeaks of 36th Greeko-Roman and China excellence of the workers in these spheres. Ivory works and bronze figurines compare equally with the sculpture and painting of ancient India.[69]

## Music and Dance

Music plays a vital role in the religious, social and artistic life of the people. It was considered to be a śilpa, the knowledge of which was essential for a cultured man. There goes an ancient Indian adage that the man, who knows nothing of literature, music and art, is "nothing but a beast without the beast's tail and horns."[70] The origin of music in India is sought from the *Sama Veda* which was chanted in a regular fashion and is still practised by the Brāhmaṇas.[71] But it took bold step further from the time of Bharata's *Nātya Sāstra* which was composed by an anonymous author before the Christian era.[72] This work has set for ever the systems of Indian dance, drama and music. Indian music is based mainly on melody and rhythm. The basic scale of Indian music is heptatonic and its seven notes called *Shaḍaja*, *ṛshabha*, *gāndhāra*, *madhyama*, *pañchama*, *dhaivata* and *nishāda*, abbreviated to *Sā, re, gā, mā, pā, dhā,* and *ni* correspond approximately to European major scale.[73] These may be elaborated with half tones of varying intervals according to the number of *Smṛtis* they contain. The Sruti is a theoretical interval of which the scale contains 22.[74]

Besides the drāma, *rāga*, and *tāla* are the two main tunetypes of Indian music, particularly Classical music.[75] *Rāga* is a melody of five or more notes upon which a melody is based. There are six basic *rāgas* and 36 *rāgiṇīs* personified as wives of the masculine *rāgas*. *Rāgas* are classified according to time which is suitable for each.[76] Thus *Bhairava* is the *rāga* of dawn, *Megha* of morning, *Dīpaka* and *Saraṅga* of afternoon, *Kauśika* and *Hindola* of night.[77] The tune is sustained by one or more drone notes and by drumming.

The *tala* or system of musical time, after *Rāga*, is the next important element of Indian music.[78] The melodic line and the subtle and cross rhythms of Indian music take the place of harmony and counterpoint. The musician could choose his *rāga* and *tāla* and starting from a melody would elaborate his theme in the rapid ornamentation.

Indian music is a reflection of her racial, linguistic and cultured variety and a good deal of it is functional, being associated with the events of everyday life ranging from birth to death. Classical music which is most reflated and suspected has an elaborate musical theory and literature and the musicians are trained in those. Indian people preferred the throaty type of singing, which is more natural, as they do in the present day. The singing voice was often treated as a musical instrument.[79]

Yet a great variety of musical instruments were freely used. The chief musical instrument was vīṇā, a bow-harp with ten strings, a type similar to small harp used in ancient Egypt and Mesopotamia. In the Classical period the vīṇā went out of fashion and its place was taken by lute with a pear-shaped body, played either with fingers or with a plactrum. This instrument can be tuned to a pitch convenient to the singer or instrumentalist. It is played still in South-East Asia where Indian music has disappeared practically. Flutes and reedpipes were widely used as were smaller drums. Larger drums were used for State occasions and there was a wide range of cymbals, gongs and bells.[80]

In ancient India, Dance, like music, was a favourite recreation and pastime, not only of the royal courtiers and princes but of the common people as well. Like music, dance was also functional as well as Classical.[81] Literary sources amplify the fact that on the fine occasions folk dances were arranged as are even now.

It is generally believed that Indian dance had its origin in ritual miming, song and dance. Dance is in fact a form of *abhinaya*, portrayal of eight emotions by gesture and posture in the accompaniment of music. In *adhinaya* proper which is equated with drama (*nātya*) emotion is expressed through gesture and words.[82]

The poses and gestures are classified in detail in Bharata's *Nāṭya Śāstra*.[83] It provides for thirteen postures of the hand, thirty-seven of the head, thirty-six of the eyes, nine of the neck and ten of the body. Later texts on the subject provide for more such postures and gestures. By gestures and postures it was possible to tell stories and it is done even now. This, of course, requires years of training.[84]

The most striking feature of Indian dance is *mudrā* or hand-gesture. Hundred of *mudrās* have been classified and by a combination of this hand-gesture alone it is possible to portray not only emotions

**but gods, animals, men, natural scenery and so on and so forth.[85]**

**Inference**

The fundamental point in Indian Art is that it incorporates a set of ideal canons of form.[85] The different categories of architecture were made according to strict principles of proportion whose patterns were considered sacred; sculptures were made according to clearly laid down principles as was the case with paintings; music and dance were based on religio-spiritual principles.[86] The artist worked with a certain purpose and ideal, a general norm and standard which permitted a good many variations and forms.[87] The multiple and emphatic, but also sophisticated, rhythms of the mouldings, profiles, columns and ornament on architecture were meant to be as vividly executing as the subtle rhythms of Indian music. The brilliant colours of paintings, *rāgas* of music and *mudrās* of dance were intended to strike directly at human feelings. They might evoke sensuous desire even. The sensuous havens of Indian art, however, are the 'heavens'; they do not direct the imagination towards the everyday world insted they arouse desires and focus them into a state beyond this world where their fulfilment is promised. They are incentives to appetite, but indicators of supernatural . . . the vital sense awareness which the art stimulates provides the fuel which is consumed in the transcendental fire.[88]

REFERENCES

1. A.L. Basham (ed.), *A Cultural History of India*, p. 194.
2. *Ibid.*
3. *Ibid.*
4. R.C. Majumdar (ed.), *The Age of Imperial Unity*, pp. 482-502.
5. *Ibid.*
6. *Ibid.*
7. *Ibid.*
8. *Ibid.*
9. *Ibid.*
10. *Ibid*
11. A.L. Basham (ed.), *A Cultural History of India*, pp. 202-03.
12. *Ibid.*, pp. 199-202.
13. *Ibid.*
14. *Ibid.*
15. *Ibid.*

16. *Ibid.*
17. *Ibid.*
18. A.L. Basham, *op. cit*, pp. 354-357.
19. *Ibid.*
20. A.L. Basham (ed.), *op. cit.*, 203-04.
21. *Ibid.*
22. *Ibid.* pp. 204-07.
23. *Ibid.*
24. *Ibid.*
25. *Ibid.*
26. *Ibid.*
27. *Ibid.*
28. *Ibid.*
29. *Ibid.*
30. *Ibid.*
31. *Ibid.*
32. R.C. Mujumdar, *op. cit.*, p. 464.
33. *Ibid.*, p. 521,
34. *Ibid.*, pp. 521-42.
35. R.C. Majumdar, *op. cit.*, pp. 521-42.
36. A.L. Basham (ed.), *op. cit.*, p. 197.
37. *Ibid.*
38. *Ibid.*
39. *Ibid.*
40. *Ibid.*
41. *Ibid.*
42. A.L. Basham. *op. cit.*, pp. 366-71.
43. *Ibid.*
44. A.L. Basham (ed.), *op. cit.*, p. 201.
45. *Ibid.*

46-48. R.C. Majumdar (ed.), *op. cit.*, pp. 521-24.

49. Sri Aurobindo, *op. cit.*

50-53. R.C. Majumdar (ed.)., *The Age of Imperial Unity*, pp. 528-29.

54. *Ibid.*, pp. 529-30.
55. A.L. Basham, *op. cit.*, p. 379.
56. R.C. Majumdar (ed.), *The Age of Imperial Unity*, pp. 529-30.
57. R.C. Majumdar (ed.), *The Classical Age*, pp. 542-44.

58-64. *Ibid.*, pp. 546-49.

65-67. *Ibid.*, pp. 553-56.

68-69. *Ibid.*, pp. 558-59.

70-80. A.L. Basham, *op. cit.*, pp. 384-87.

81-85. *Ibid.*, pp. 387-88.

86. A.L. Basham (ed.), *A Cultural History of India*, p. 209.
87. Sri Aurobindo, *op. cit.*, p. 230.
88. A.L. Basham (ed)., *op. cit.*, pp. 210-11.

# 10

# Living Conditions of the People

Ancient Indian life was rich, varied and full of gaity and splendour is evident from the literature, sculpture, art and architecture and also the accounts of foreign travellers who visited India in that period. An idea can also be gleaned from the architecture and sculptural panels on the buildings, monasteries, stūpas as also from the furnitures, utensils dress and ornaments, foods and drinks, games and sports of the period. The best of these are found in the classical period which is compared to the Elizabethan Age of the English history.

## Buildings and Houses

The reliefs of Bhārhut, Sāñchī, Amarāvati, Mathurā and other places show how buildings in the cities were built.[1] These consisted of several stories, the topmost story having a wagon-vaulted roof with gubles at either end with pointed finiah at the top. They usually face a court, occasionally enclosed on either side by subsidiary structures, but left open in front as shown in Sāñchi east gate.[2] Sometimes a *torana* consisting of two upright pillars surmounted by two or three architraves, leads to the court in front of the building as shown in Amarāvati. The upper storeys were provided with balustraded *veranda* (alindas) in front.

By c. 600 B.C. there were small towns all over North India, the important ones being Srāvasti, Campā, Rājagṛha, Sāketa (present Ayodhyā), Kausāmbi, and Kāsī. In time of the Mauryas Pātāliputra had grown up as a long narrow city, stretching nine miles along the bank of the Gaṇgā, and reaching one and a half miles inland[3] Māduräikkhāñj provides a description of the ancient Indian city of Mādurai[4] But *Milinda-Pānha* speaks of a city fine and regular measured out into quarters, with excavated moats and ramparts about it, with stout gate-houses and towers with market places, cross-roads with regular lines of open shops, provided with parks, gardens, lakes, lotus-ponds and wells adorned with many kinds of temples of the gods, free from every fault and standing in all its glory.[5] The reliefs on Bhārhut, Sāñchī, Amarāvati and other places corroborate this description. Usually cities were surrounded by moats and further protected by walls running all around.[6] These walls were built in cyclopacan fashion of massive block of stones or burnt bricks pierced by gateways approached by bridge across the moat, each flanked by a semi-circular bastion on either side over which rose the watch tower.[7] The cities, however, had two foci, the palace and the temple. [8]

Of the ancient Indian palace architecture we know very little, for the buildings shown in the reliefs were made of impermanent materials like wood. The Greek writers like Arrian write that the cities on the bank of river and other low lying areas were built of wood, mud and brick and in commanding position and less exposed to flood. The Vinaya texts state that common dwelling houses were made of stone, brick or wood and roofing of five kinds—bricks, stone, cement, straw and leaves. The walls and roofs were plastered within and without.[9]

The houses were white-washed, the floors were adorned black, and the walls red. The rooms were decorated with paintings and engraving of human figures, wreath-work and creeper work.[10] There were windows with shutters and curtains, elaborate doors with keyholes, verandahs, covered terraces, inner-verandahs and over hanging eaves, dwelling-rooms, retiring-rooms, store-rooms, closets and wells with lids and covered by sheds with skin roofs. Every house had an attached garden with flowers, cages of pet birds such as parrots and a dola or swing-board.[11]

The buildings with verandahs were supported on pillars with capitals in the forms of heads of animals. Hygienic arrangements were kept in view while constructing privies.[12] R.C. Majundar writes "It should be mentioned that the Indo-Aryans displayed remarkable capacity for assimilation and absorption". But although they borrowed largely, both from the Greeks and Persians, not only technical processes but decorative patterns, animal types and such like notives, the spirit of their productions were always their own.[13]

**Furniture and Furnishing of Household**

From the Vinaya Texts we get a long list of furnitures. There was a large variety of chairs such as rectangular, cushioned, cane-bottomed, straw-bottomed, the one raised on a pedestal or with many legs, armchair and state chair and sofas with or without arms.[14] There were also different types of bed-steads with legs curved to represent animals' feet, and chairs with same design.[15] Some bed-steads had lofty supports with arrangements for rocking backwards and forwards and the bed, comprising mattresses stuffed with cotton and pillows half the size of a man's body, was strewn over with flowers.[16] Bolsters stuffed with wool, cotton cloth, bark, grass or *talipot* leaves and chains and bed-steads covered with upholstered cushions to fit them, were in use.[17] Every bedroom was supposed to contain books, musical instruments, requisites for painting and board for different kinds of sports such as card playing and one for gambling. For poorer people there were mats made of grass and bedsteads made of laths of split bamboo.[18]

For reclining people used lofty and large things such as large cushions, divans, coverlets. White or marked with thick flowers, mattresses, cotton coverlets dyed with figures of animals; rugs with long hair on one or both sides, carpets inwrought with gold or with silk, large woollen carpets with designs such as a nautch-girl's dance, couches covered with canopies or with crimson cushions at both ends.[19] There were also rich elephant housings, and horse-rugs or carriage-rugs, sheep-skin, goat skins and deer-skins were used as coverlets, especially in Avanti and the Southern country, and fine-skins, such as those of lion, tiger, panther or antelope, were either used for reclining[20] or cut into pieces and spread inside or outside the couches and chairs.[21]

The rooms were provided with ceiling cloth, movable screens, curtains that could be drawn inside, cupboards, and bone-hooks for hanging clothes.[22] We also here of sun-shades, mosquito-certains, filters for straining water, mosquito-fans, flower-stands, and fly-whisks (*chāmara*) made of tails of oxen and peacocks or of bark and grass.[23]

Costly uetensils were used such as bowls of various kinds made of beryl, crystals, gold and silver, copper, glass, tin, lead or bronze, and some of them were painted or set with jewels. Even circular supports of bowls were made of gold and silver.[24] For the common people earthen ware was in use and terracotta figurines decorated their bedrooms. The children played with toys made of clay.

## Dress and Ornaments

Regarding dress, Nearchus writes, the Indians used gaments of cotton, and undergarment which reaches below the knee half-way down to the ankles, and an upper garment which they throw partly over their shoulders and partly twist in folds round their head.[25] Possibly this was the *dhoti* (or *Sari*) and *chadar* used by the people of Bengal, Orissa, and Madras and other parts of India now a days. The upper garment was generally not used inside the house, a part of the lower one being wrapped round the upper part or thrown over the shoulders.[26] The *Mahābharata* refers to *Draupadi* in her private aspartment wearing *ekavastra*; she also served in the palace of king Virāta in *akavasha*. Ladies of upper strata generally wore colour garments but the widows are described as clad in white.[27] Higher class usually wore a turban or head-gear consisting of long piece of cloth wrapped round the head in a number of ways according to local custom,[28] Kings, of course, wore crowns.[29]

There was not much difference between the male and female dresses. Both used head-dress and ornaments; gradually the women gave up the former and men the latter.[30] Cotton cloth was commonly used though cloths made of silk, linen and wool were in great demand among the rich.[31] Kautilya refers to extensive textile industry all over India and the Vinaya Texts refer to complete veaving outfit.[32] The sculpture of Bhārhut and Sāñchi provide interesting specimen of dress and ornament as also the paintings of Ajantā.

The Vinaya Texts mention that cloth was fastened at waist by a girdle.[33] Variety of girdles such as those made of many strings, plaited together, those made like the head of a water-snake, those with tambaurines, or beads on them, or those with ornaments hanging from them.[34] On rare occasions we found women putting on the lower garments in Sakachchna fashion like the women of Mahārāstra today.[35] This practice was confined to the North-West India in Ancient times.

The sculptured female figures suggest that women did not wear a veil and the upper part of the body was kept bare, revealing in full the bosom and the navel.[36] The Ajantā paintings also exhibit the same picture. Further the classical Sanskrit literature describe the female bosom and navel in the same vein.[37] This proves that the *purdah* system was not in vogue in ancient India, though some literary description indicate that aristocrat ladies used a veil when appearing in public. The other point that the upper part of the body was nude is refuted by many scholars on the argument that it is against the sense of decencey.[38] The Vinaya Texts mention that Buddhist nuns, together with courtesans, took their bath in a river without any clothing.[39] Further we are told that Buddhist monks when naked saluted one another, and received slalutes, they did service to one another, and received services; gave to one another and accepted, ate both hard food and soft, tasted and drank.[40] Dasakumāra-charita of Daṇḍin tells of a girl whose uppar part of the body was nude as it was the practice in south India even in modern times.[41] The Hindu girls of Bāli island ate still found to wear no upper garment. These conclusively prove that upper part of the body was usually nude.[42]

The rulers like the Greeks, Scythians, Sākas and Hūnas introduced new fashions of dress. The kings are represented as wearing trousers and big overcoats,[43] and this was imitated by the Indians. Women, too, began to wear blouses, jackets and frocks in imitation of the Greeks and Scythians.[44] But this did not become a general practice. The Vinaya Texts, however, show that stitched clothes were coming into fashion, also there is no concrete reference to it in the epics.[45]

Megasthenes has observed that "inspite of the general simplicity of style the Indians love finery and ornament. Their robes are worked in gold and ornamented with precious stones, and they wear also flowered garments made of finest muslin"[46]. The ornaments which decorated the bodies of both men and women were also costly and of various types and designs. Every part of the body from head to foot had its appropriate ornaments made of gold, silver, pearls, gems, and precious stones, [47] One can form and idea of them from numerous sculptures, paintings and actual specimens found out from different excavated sites.[48] Vinaya Texts mention that at first even the monks used to wear ear-rings, ear-drops, stings of beads for the throat, girdles of beads, bangles, necklaces, bracelets and rings"[49] Nearchus says that ear-ring made of ivory were worn by the wealthy people. Waist lands and anklets were, however, worn by women alone.[50]

The Vinaya Texts states that shoes with one, two, three or even more linnet, squirrel and owl; boots pointed with horn of rams and goats, ornamented with scorpion's tails sewn round with peacock feathers; boots, shoes and slipper of all hues such as blue, red, yellow, brown, black and orange.[51] Sometimes the shoes were ornamented with gold, silver, pearls, beryls, crystals, copper, glass, tin, lead or bronze.[52] Poor people used wooden-shoes, shoes made of leaves of palmyra and date-palm, or of various kinds of grass.[53] Shoes were also made of wool.[53] Nearchus tells us that "Indians wear shoes made of white leather, and these are elaborately trimmed, while the sole are variegated and made of great thickness to make the wearer seem so much the tallers".[54]

Cosmetics were used by both sexes. Chief among this was a paste made of finely grained dust of sandlwood, often coloured with lac or other dyes which was smeered over the whole body or applied in patterns.[55] It was supposed to cool the body in hot season.

The Vinaya Pitaka provides a long list of toilette.[56] Hair was besmeared with pomade or hair-oil or bee-wax and then smoothed with a comb or special instrument shaped like a snake's hood. Scents, perfumes, garland and unguents were used and faces were rubbed with ointment and painted. The body was also painted, and feet were rubbed with sandstone gravel and foam. To keep long hair seems to have been the fashion.[57] A Brāhmaṇa generally shaved his head keeping a crest-lock two while an anchorite kept matted hair.[58] Women who had their husband living parted their hair in the middle, the parting being coloured red with vermillion or other powder.[59] Beards were either removed by razor (as in case of a Brāhmaṇa) or allowed to grow long as in the case of hermits). Sometimes they were kept on the chin like a goat's beard, or so cut that they had four corners.[60] The beards were also dyed blue, red, purple or green according to individual's taste. The beard on the ladle was sometimes cut into figures and some had whisker. Nails were polished, or cut with nail-cutters, and tooth-sticks were used.[61]

## Food and Drinks

There are ample references to sūpaśāstra or the science of cooking. In fact people took meals with curry and rice; flat cakes of flour, the modern chapati, were eaten and water, milk and curd were drunk.[62] The epics show that wheat and barley were the main staples, rice being very popular. Rich people ate rice mixed with flesh.[63] The *Udyog Parva* states that the food of the rich consisted of flesh; that of the middle class, of milk; and its products; and that of the poor, of oil preparations.[64] Quite a large number of dainties, delicacies and sweetmeats were known. Milk and its products formed part of the daily diet and ghee was particularly valued as very substantial and nourishing.[65] Indian cookery did not differ much from that of the present day. Meat and vegetables alike were seasoned in curries and eaten with rice boiled or fried.[66] The Tāmil classics refer to feasts arranged by the patron of the poets in which meat and drink formed chief items of pleasure. Flesh of animals cooked whole such as pork from a pig which has been kept away from its female for many days and fattened for the occasion, the flesh of tortoises and particular kind of fish are mentioned as delicacies served at such feasts'.[67]

The Vinaya Texts enumerate a number of articles of food such as rice, beans, tila, fresh honey, rice-milk, honey-lumps congey, curries, salt, molasses, oil, pot-herbs, fruits, fish, meat and the five products of cow, viz. milk, curds, ghee, butter-milk and butter.[68] Megasthenes observes that Indians "eat always alone and have no fixed hours when meals are to be taken by all in common.[69]

Among the drinks in general use were grape-juice, honey, syrups made from various fruits (such as mango, Jambu, plantain) and edible roots (water-lily) and the juice of fruits.[70] Drinks were also prepared from various kinds of pot-herbs and flowers. The Tāmil classics refer to "foreign liquor in green bottle" and "toddy well-matured by being buried underground for a long time in bamboo barels."[71]

Drinking of liquor seems to be a very common practice in ancient India. The Vedic Aryans not only consumed *Soma* but offered it even to their gods. The Great Epic *Mahābhārata* condemns drinking as a *Mahāpataka* but Arjuna and Kṛishna took wine when exhausted and Jādavas were notorious addicts to wine.[72] But Manu condemns consumption of spirituous liquor as a *mahāpataka* and enjoins to king to banish the persons who sell such liquor.[73] Megasthenes also writes that the Indian do not drink except on festive occasions."[74] Later the Chinese traveller Fa-Hien also writes, "The people of the Madhyadesa except the Chandālas do not eat meat or drink liquor." Kautilya provides for state monopoly of manufacture of liquor assuming that drinking was an evil which could not be forbidden wholly, directed that wine should be sold to persons of well known character only in small quantities,[75] It should be noted that though Aśoka discouraged meat eating, he did not speak anything about drinking. Inspite of all injunctions of the Brahmanical class and the Buddhists and Jains consumption of alcohol was quite common among the people. In the south fermented sap of palmyra and coconut was the staple liquor, and is frequently mentioned in early Tāmil literature.[76]

**Festival and Pastimes**

The most popular festival in early times was the festival of spring in honour of Kāma,[77] the love-god. At this festival people forgot their caste or social distinction and paraded the streets scattering red-powder over their neighbour, squirting them with coloured water and playing all kinds of jokes. This festival still survives under the name *Holi*, though the love-god had been replaced by Kṛisna.

Social life in ancient India was vivacious and comprehensive in outlook and range of activities. The sculpture and literature are full of representation of such enjoyment and bustle and activity of life. Numerous festivals, participated by the rich and poor alike, divided the year and were marked by merrymaking and various kinds of games both indoor and outdoor were restored to.[78] The former include dice-trapball, guessing other peoples thought, etc. while the latter were hunting, chariot races, archery matches, wrestling, boxing, shooting marbles with the fingers and ploughing with mimia ploughs.[79] Festive assemblies known as *utsava*, *samāja* and *vihāra* provided not only entertainment but also dainty dishes and intoxicating drinks provided by the kings for the amusement and entertainment of the people.[80] Kāmasutra mentions literary parties as chief source of pleasure of the educated citizens.[81]

Organised outdoor games were not common, except among children and the young women, who sometimes are referred to as playing ball, like Nausicaa in the Odyssey.[82] Charriot racing was popular in later period and archery contest referred to in the Epics was much loved amusement of the warrior class.[83] Boxing and wrestling were a preserve of low-caste professional pugilists.[84]

Gambling was popular at all times among all classes of people, though the *smṛties* reprobated it. "Gamester's Lament" in the *Rig Veda* testifies its existence among the Vedic Aryans.[85] In the beginning of *akṣas* of gambling were hard nuts called *bibhiṣaka* which were drawn from a bowl. If the drawer scored a multiple of four he was supposed to win the game. Later oblong dice with four scoring sides were used. A special terminology for the throw at dice, viz. *Kṛta* (cater, four) *tretā* (trey), *dvāpara* (duce), and *Kāli* (ace) were used.[86] Gambling formed a part in the royal consecration ceremony as well.[87] The plot of the *Mahābhārata* hinges round a gambling tournament and a similar episode is seen in the story of Nala.[88] The *Arthaśāstra* recommends a strict control of gambling and fixes a five per cent tax at the stakes and a charge for the hire of dice to the gamblers, who were forbidden to use their own dice.[89]

With the dice were played board games which involved a combination of chance and skill. In the early centuries of Christian era this was played on a board of sixty-four squares (*astapada*) with a king, on elephant, a horse, a chariot, or ship, and four footmen representing the contingent of Indian army known as *Çaturanga*. The game needed four player and their moves were controlled by the throw of the dice. In the sixth century the Persians learnt the game and after the Arabs conquered Persia it became polular in the Middle East under the name Shatranj. It developed into a game of two persons and the use of dice for the moves was given up.[90] It is not known for certain whether these developments took place in India or Persia.

Classical sources refer to gladiatorial display at the court of Chandragupta Maurya. Despite the growth of the doctrine of the *Ahiṁsa*, animal fights were always very popular. Favourite animals to be pitted against each other were the fierce little Indian quail (*tavaka*), the cock and the ram; we also read of fights between bulls, buffaloes and elephants. The early Tāmil literature speaks of bull-fight in the south. Wrestling with young steers is still a favourite pastime of some pastoral peoples of India.

But many of the amusements of ancient India was provided by professional entertainers. They travelled through town and village diverting the ordinary folk who could not appreciate the nuances of the more sophisticated art forms by drama, music and dancing.

Thus it appears that though the Indian religious literature like Smrities tried to infuse in the people a pessimistic view on life, social life was richer in content and far more comprehensive in outlook and range of activities. Kings used to go out on tours of pleasure in course of which there were chases and other diversions. Worships of gods and goddesses, different sacrifices and sacraments associated with birth, marriage and sicknesses etc. provided mirth and merryments and diversions from daily round of duties. People in general were not averse to worldly enjoyments and material welfare. And yet the people had deep sense of morality. Megasthenes observes, "Truth and virtue they hold alike in esteem". The ideal of truthfulness permeates the whole life. Religious literature holds that *Dharma* should be pursued at all cost, for *Dharma* sustains the world—"*Dharma* increases us why then *Dharma* should not be pursued? In fact the Indian people struck a balance between, *Dharma*, *Artha*, *Kāma* and *Mokṣa* in which the world was given its due recognition and its portance.

We may, therefore, conclude that ancient society always contained diverse elements, both rich, ease-loving, and luxurious, as well as simple plain-folks. On the whole piety and morality were highly valued and people had a high degree of intellectual culture and refined artistic sensibilities.

REFERENCES


1. R.C. Majumdar *et al* (ed). *The Age of Imperial Unity*, pp. 83-85.
2. A.L. Basham — *The Wonder that was India*, pp. 200-05
3. *Ibid.*
4. *Ibid.*
5. *The Age of Imperial Unity*, pp. 483-85.
6. *Ibid.*
7. *Ibid.*
8. A.L. Basham, *op. cit.*, p. 201.
9. *The Age of Imperial Unity*, p. 576.
10. *Ibid.*
11. A.L.Basham, *op. cit.*, p. 208.
12. *The Age of Imperial Unity*, p. 576.
13. R.C. Majumdar — *Ancient India*, 5th edn. Reprint, Delhi, 1982, p. 207.
14. *The Age of Imperial Unity*, p. 576.
15. *Ibid.*
16. *Ibid.*
17. A.L. Basham, *op. cit.*, p. 208.

18- 22. *The Age of Imperial Unity*, pp. 576-77.

23. *Kamasutra* 1:4.
24. *The Age of Imperial Unity*, p. 577.

25-42. *Ibid.*, pp. 571-74.

43. A.L.Basham, *op. cit.* p. 213.
44. *The Age of Imperial Unity*, pp. 571-77.

45-54. *Ibid.*

55. *The Classical Age*, p. 583.

56-63. *The Age of Imperial Unity*, pp. 571-77.

64. R.C. Majumdar, *op. cit.*, p. 208.
65. *The Age of Imperial Unity*, p. 577-78.
66. R.C. Majumdar, *op. cit.*, p. 208.
67. *Ibid.*, p. 208.
68. S.K. Maity, *op. cit.*
69. *The Age of Imperial Unity*, pp. 577-78.
70. R.C. Majumdar, *op. cit.* p 208.
71. A.L. Basham, *op. cit.*, p. 209.
72. *Ibid.*
73. *Ibid.*
74. *The Age of Imperial Unity*, p. 577-78.

75-89. A.C. Basham, *op. cit*, p. 208, pp. 210-11.

90. Manu, VIII-15.

# 11

## Conclusion

Cut-off from the rest of the Asiatic Continent by the *Devatātmā* Himālaya, with its extensions to the east and the west, and surrounded by the seas on the east, south and west, the people of India had developed a culture which holds a unique place in the world. Unlike Mesopotamia, Greece and Egypt this civilisation has had a continuous development without break like the Chinese, in spite of the intermittent intrusion of foreign elements. The Indians living in comparative isolation never liked an exclusive life and carried on the torch of its civilisation to far off countries of the north, east and the west. The Indian influence over these countries, in the remote past, is still perceptible though it cannot be gain-said that modern India has enriched her culture by borrowing from the west. Therefore, a study of Indian culture is both fascinating and instructive.

Ancient Indian society and culture did not perish before the onslaught of Islam and Christianity and Hindu civilisation has remained on Indian soil as a force which still provides spiritual sustenance to teeming millions of India. Hindu society in spite of challenges from the Muslims and the British has retained its fundamental basis without break with the past because of its inherent strength to meet the challenges. Much that was useless and effete has vanished but a lot that is granite has remained. Hardly any educated Indian does not look back to the past with pride on his ancient culture.

The caste system, which has grown up in the wake of foreign influence and has replaced the old *Varṇa* system, had attained a vicious form; but its exclusiveness is vanished and a process has begun which may change the social structure considerably. Education, marriage, family and social life have undergone many necessary adjustments to cope with the demands of the time. The institutional learning of the monasteries and *āśramas* have taken the shape of schools, colleges and universities and institutions of specialised studies in technology and medicine. Marriages, though in some cases, are solemnised in courts and registrar's office put a seal on Gandharva form of marriage. Family structure has become smaller, husband, wife and children living together, but its head is still the patriarch of the bygone times. Hindu religion, spirituality and philosophy continue to hold the imagination of the Indians, nay still attract foreigners as did Buddhism and Brāhmaṇism in the remote past. Neo-Hinduism of *Purāṇa* and *Tantra* with its charm and grace still attract the masses. Not only do the Hindus enjoy the charm and grace of *Durgā pūjā, Diwālī, Sarasvatī pujā* and *Viśvakarma pujā*, people of different other faiths do enjoy and share the mirth and merit of these festivals. The people of India still love the tales of the *Ramāyaṇa* and the *Mahābhārata* the classical literature of Kalidāsa, Bhāravi, Bhartṛhari and host of other writers who shed lustre on Sanskrit literature. The Tāmil literature of the Saṅgam Age, the Thevaram and Nālāriya Prabandham still provide inspiration to the Tamilians of the present day. The universal appeal and literary beauty of these litreatures have made them international treasures of wisdom and enjoyment. The *Bhāgavat Gītā* and the *Upanishads* have been translated into all the developed languages of the world as has been the case with the Classical Sanskrit literature.

In the realm of Art Indian conrtibution in Anciant times has not been properly studied. Yet as it has been observed in chapter on Art, its influence over the world was considerable. The plastic art of India, its architectural forms and sculptural designs and colour profiles did not only impress the countries of the ancient world but still millions of people come to India to see the caves of Ajaṅtā, Ellorā, Cārle, Nāgārjunakoṇḍā and host of other temples in Orissa, Madhya Pradesh and South India and paintings in different parts of the country. Lot of Indian artefacts and images are being smuggled out of the country and much artificial and pseudo curio are sold in the international market at fabulous prices.

This society of India, its different institutions and religions and philosophies, languages and literatures and art through centuries have established certain norms and ideals which in the present century with necessary adjustments have proved sound and healthy and have made India great as a nation and civilisation. People all over the world are taking interest in things Indian and it is hoped that Indology will become more and more popular and India will emerge as the spiritual leader of the world as envisaged by Sri Aurobindo.

# Bibliography


Altekar, A.S.: *Education in Ancient India* (4th Edn.,Banaras 1951).

— : *The Position of Women in Hindu Civilisation* (Banaras, 1938).

— : *The Vakataka-Gupta Age* (London, 1546; Reprint Banaras, 1964).

Aurobindo, Sri: *Foundations of Indian Culture* (Centenary volume 14th Pondicherry, 1972).

Ayenger, P.T.S.: *Life in Ancient India.*

— : *The History of the Tamils to 600* A.D. (Madras, 1929).

Barnett, L.D.: *Hinduism* (Indian reprint,1977).

Bary, W. Th. De. (ed): *Sources of Indian Tradition* (New York, 1958).

Banerji, P.: *Dance of India* (Calcutta, 1947).

Basham, A.L.: *The Wonder that was India* (London, 1954).

— : *A Cultural History of India* (Oxford, 1975).

Beal, S. (tran): *Hiuen Tsang* (London, 1911).

Bhattacharyya, N.N: *Ancient Indian Rituals and their Social Contacts* (Calcutta, 1975).

Brown, P.: *Indian Architecture* (End Edn., Bombay, 1949).

Burraw,T.: *The Sanskrit Language* (London, 1955, 25-6-1959).

Chakravarty, S.K.: *A Study of Ancient Indian Numismatics* (Calcutta,1931).

Chanana, D.R.: *Slavery in Ancient India* (Delhi 1960).

Chaterji, S.K.: *Kamala Lectures* (Calcutta,1962).

Chaudhury, S.B: *Ethnic Settlements in Ancient India* (Calcutta, 1955).

Childe, V.G.: *The Aryans: A Study of Indo-European Origins* (London, 1966).

Choudhury, R.: *Vratya in Ancient India* (Delhi, 1964).

Clements, E: *Introduction to the Study of Indian Music* (London, 1913).

Dasgupta, K.K: *A Comprehensive History of India* (Delhi).

Davids, T.W. Rhys: *Buddhism — Its History and Literature* (London, 1926).

Gambhirananda, Swami (ed.): *The Gita-Upanishad Granthavali* (9th Edn, Vol. I, Calcutta, 1381 B.S.).

Grindle, M.(tr).: *Indica of Megasthenes* (Bonn, 1946).

Guhu, B.S.: *An Outline of the Racial Ethnology of India* (Calcutta, 1937).

Gupta, S.N.: *A History of Indian Philosophy* (5 Vols., Cambridge, 1922-55).

Havel, E.B.: *A Handbook of Indian Art* (Varanasi, 1971).

— : *Ideals of Indian Art* (London, 1920).

Hutton, J.H: *Caste in India* (3rd Edn., Calcutta, 1961).

Keith, A.B.: *History of Sanskrit Literature* (Oxford 1928).

Kane, P.V.: *History of Dharmasastra* (Poona, 1930, Reprint, 1946).

Ketkar,S.V.: *The History of Caste in India.*

Kosambi, D.D.: *The Culture and Civilisation of Ancient India in Historical Outline* (London,1908).

Kramrisch, S.: *Indian Sculpture* (Calcutta, 1933).

Krishnamurthy, K.: *Social and Cultural Life in Ancient India* (Delhi, 1982).

Law, B.C.: *Life of Mahavira* (Bombay, 1946).

Legge, J.H: *Fa-hich* (Oxford, 1888).

Majumdar, B.: *Krishna in History and Legend* (Calcutta, 1969).

Majumdar, G. Sen: *Buddhism in Ancient Bengal* (Calcutta, 1983).

Majumdar, R.C.: *Ancient India* (Varanasi, 1952, 8th Edn., 1977, Reprint, Delhi,1982).

— (ed.) : *The Age of Imperial Unity* (2nd Edn., Bombay, 1964).

— (ed.) : *The Classical Age* (3rd Edn., Bombay,1970).

Majumder, R.C.& Dasgupta,K.K.(ed). *A Comprehensive History of India* (New Delhi).

Mukherjee, R.K.: *Ancient Indian Education* (London, 1951).

Pandey, R.B.: *Hindu Samskaras*, (Banaras, 1949).

Purnalingam Pillai, M.S.: *Tamil Literature* (Tinevelly, 1929).

Radhakrishnan,S.: *Indian Philosophy* (Revised, 2 Vols., London, 1958).

Ray. N.R.: *Mauryan and Post-Mauryan Art* (Delhi).

Risley, H.H.: *The People of India* (Calcutta, 1915).

Sankhalia, H.D.: *The University of Nalanda* (Bombay, 1934).

— : *Pre-History and Pre-Pre-History in India and Pakistan* (Bombay, 1962).

Sen, S.P. (ed): *Historical Biography on Ancient India* (Calcutta, 1979).

Shankarnarayanan, S.: *Sri Chakra*, (Pondicherry, 1970).

— : *Quintessence of Sri Vidya* (Pondicherry,1970).

Sharma, R.S.: *Sudras in Ancient India* (Delhi, 1958).

Sidhanta Shastree,R.K.: *Sanism Through the Ages* (Calcutta, 1975).

Smith,V.A.: *Early History of India* (4th Edn., Reprint, 1924).

Takakusu, J.(tra.): *I-tsing* (Oxford, 1896).

Tarkaratna, P.(ed).: *Manusamhita* (Calcutta, 1320 B.S.).

Thapar, R.: *Asoka and the Decline of the Mauryans* (New Delhi, 2nd Edn., 1973).

Thomas, P.: *Hindu Religion, Customs and Manners* (Bombay).

Upadhyaya, S.C.: *The Kamasutra of Vatsyana* (Calcutta,1961).

Valavalkar, P.H.: *Hindu Social Institutions* (Madras, 1942).

# INDEX


*Abhidharma-piṭaka*, 111
*Abhiras*, 37
Āchara, 16
*Ācharya*, 54
Afghanistan, 26
Africa, 21
Agastya, 43
*Agnimitrā*, 93
*Agnishtoma*, 72
*Āgrahāyani*, 71
Agriculture, 36
Ahichchhatra, 150, 167
*Aitarya Brāhmaṇa*, 87
Ajanta, 15, 18, 163, 183,
    caves, 166
    painting, 175, 183
*Ājivikas*, 114, 115
Alberuni, 26
Alexander, 18, 26, 50
Ālvārs, 116, 148
*Ākkyānas*, 17
*Amārākośa*, 16
Amarāvati, 151, 172
*Āndāmāns*, 22
*Annaprāśana*, 80
*Antyeshti*, 79
    sanskaras, 80-81
*Anuloma*, 51
*Āpadharma*, 35
Arjuna, 106, 178
*Artha*, 69, 87
*Arthaśāstra*, 16, 44, 87
Aryan immigration, 23
Ashvattha tree, 103
*Aśitikotivibhava*, 36
Aśoka, 52, 115
Aśokan inscription, 1
*Aśramās*, 50, 56, 69, 84, 105, 182
*Āsura*, 89
*Aśvamedha*, 33, 73
*Aśvaghosha*, 137
*Atharvāveda*, 43, 70, 74, 92, 108, 117, 129
Atri, 43
Audumbaras, 15
Aurangābadcave, 166
Aurobindo, 20, 75, 107, 183
Australiods, 21
*Avantisundari*, 97
*Avatāras*, 117
Ayodhyā, 25, 138, 172

Bādāmi, 162
    cave, 166
Bagh cave, 166
Bandhuvarman, 14, 36
Banerjee, A.C., 27
Barābar hills, 163
Basham, A.L., 13, 20
Baṭṭa Nārāyana, 106, 141
Bedsā cave, 166
Besnagar Garuda pillar inscription, 26
*Bhāgvatā Gita*, 32, 34, 35, 36, 183
*Bhāgavatism*, 116, 117
Bhandarkar, R.G., 27
*Bhāradvaja*, 43
*Bharatā*, 16
Bharatavarsha, 27
Bharata war, 24
Bhārhut, 151, 152, 162, 172
*Bharṭrhari*, 183
*Bhārvi*, 183
Bhillas, 22
*Bhogi*, 93
Bhṛgu, 43
Bhubaneswar temples, 162
Bhukti-cult, 116, 117
*Bhūtayajña*, 71
*Bhūtās*, 112
Bindusara, 52, 93
Bodh Gaya, 164
    Conference, 26
*Bodhisvattas*, 51, 110
*Brhāma-yajña*, 71
*Brahāmachāri*, 65, 93, 96
*Brāhmācharin*, 82
*Brahmacharya*, 98, 105

āśrama, 54
Brāhmanas, 32, 33, 34, 35, 36, 37, 38, 39, 40, 43, 50, 51, 54, 57, 60, 68, 78, 90, 96
Bṛhaspati, 88, 97
Bridegroom, 88
Buddha, 19, 32, 93, 110, 111, 114
Buddhism, 37, 103, 109
Buddhist, 151
  education, 54
  monastries, 61
  viharas, 20
Building and houses, 172-73

Caste system, 38, 40
Cārle, 183
Ceylon, 18
Chaitya cave, 166
  halls vihāras, 151-52
Chālukya, 98, 162
*Chaṇakya*, 36, 140, 142
Chandragupta Maurya, 19, 34, 39, 113, 137, 140, 180
Chaṇḍalas, 40, 41, 60
*Charākas*, 59
Chārudatta, 34, 39, 140
*Chārvāk*, 123
Chatterjee, S.K., 23, 38
*Chaturanga*, 179
*Chaturmasya-yajñas*, 73
*Chatur-varga*, 69
*Chatur-varṇa*, 37
*Chatur-varṇa* system, 38
*Chatur-vedin*, 58
China, 19
Chola dynasty, 37, 95
Christianity, 182
*Chuḍākarana*, 80
Classical literature, 139
Classical music, 168
Classical sanskrit literature, 136, 183
Commandments, 68

*Daṇḍaniti*, 57
*Daṇḍapranitā*, 44
*Daṇḍins*, 18, 88, 96
*Daśākumāracharita*, 17, 88, 142
*Dāsas*, 44
Davis, Rhys, 47
*Dāyabhaga*, 42
Denomination, 104
*Devadāsis*, 94
*Devatātma*, 182
*Deva-yajña*, 71
Devotionalism, 116, 117
*Dharma*, 16, 69, 70, 87, 105, 180
*Dharmaśāstras*, 84, 97, 132, 133
Dhruvasena, 14, 64
*Dhvajahara*, 44
*Digambaras*, 113, 114, 143
*Dipavaṁsa*, 18
*Devyāvadāna*, 60
Dolmns, 23
Domestication, 22
Dravidians, 21, 24, 43
Dress and ornaments, 174-76
*Durga puja*, 182, 183
Duryodhana, 135
Dushyanta, 93

Education, 54, 58-59, 96
Educational system, 13
Elliot, T.S., 136
Ellora, 162, 183
Epics, 134-35
Epigraphs, 14
Ethnic composition, 21
*Ettuthokai*, 146

Fa-Hsian, 19, 151
Family life, 41-43
Festivals and pastimes, 178-80
Food and Drinks, 177-80

Gadaba, 22
Gambling, 179
Gandhara, 25
*Gandharva*, 89
  system, 97
Gaṅga, 150, 172
*Gaṅika*, 93, 94
*Garbhādhana*, 79
*Gārgi-Samhitā*, 25
*Gārhasthya*, 59, 75, 105
*Gārhasthya, āśrama*, 68, 82-84, 87, 106
*Goruḍa pūraṇa*, 107
*Gāthās*, 17
Gautama, 43, 81
*Gíta*, 105, 116
*Gomini*, 88
*Gopurā*, 161
Gorkha, 29
*Gola*, 114, 115

*Gośala*, 114, 115
*Gotras*, 42-43, 87
Greeks, 50
*Gṛhaja*, 44
*Gṛhya-Sūtras*, 16, 79
Guptas, 27
*Gurjāra-Pratihāras*, 25, 29
*Gurjaratrā*, 27
*Guru*, 54, 58, 68
*Guruparampara*, 58

Harems, 15
Harappa, 24
*Harshacharita*, 56, 66, 140, 167
Harshavardhana, 19, 27, 50
*Hāvir-yajñas*, 71, 72
Herodotus, 18
*Hīnayāna*, 110
Hindu civilisation, 182
Hinan Kush, 21
Hinduism, 103
Hiuen-Tsang, 19
*Hitopadesa*, 141
Ho, 22
Household furniture, 173-74
*Hūṇas*, 27, 50
*Hyloboi*, 39

Iksvākus, 28, 52
Indian Arts, 150-60
Indian Palace architecture, 173
*Indica*, 17, 18
Inscriptions, 14
Indonesia, 22
Inter-case marriage, 93
Iraq, 23
I-tsing, 19, 62, 65

Jain Arhats, 52
Jain Monks, 18
*Jainism*, 37, 51, 103, 112, 114, 151-52
*Jñaña*, 78, 131
*Jātakas*, 18, 52, 59, 141, 165
*Jata karma*, 80
Jāti, 38-40
Jayasena, 64
Jogimāra Cave, 165

Kabul, 25
*Kaḍambari*, 142
*Kalas*, 75

Kālidāsa, 17, 18, 20, 93, 96, 97, 131, 138, 140, 141, 183
*Kalithokāi*, 146
Kalinga war, 148
*Kalpasutra*, 54
*Kāma*, 18, 69, 87
Kāma-sūtrā, 70, 75, 76, 78, 91, 93, 166, 179
Kāñchi, 59
Kānchipuram, 162
Kānheri cave, 166
Kaṇṇda literature, 14?
Kapilāvastu, 151
*Karma*, 105, 109
*Karma-yājña*, 83
Karve, Iravati, 40
Kashmir, 26
Kashmiri Brahman, 29
Kaśyapa, 43
*Kātyayana*, 128, 142
*Kathāsaritsāgara*, 64, 139
*Katha-Upanishad*, 42, 132
Kauśāmbi, 151
Kauṭilya, 16, 35, 37, 175
*Kena Upanishad*, 102
Khājurāho temples, 162
Khaṇḍagiri cave, 161
Khāsis, 22
*Khilaas*, 65
Khybar pass, 27
*Kirātārjuniyam*, 138
*Kirāta*, 23, 28
*Kirata-Jana-Kṛiti*, 23
Kollas, 22
Konārak temples, 162
Kṛshṇa, 116, 117, 178
Kshatriyas, 28, 32, 33, 34, 35, 37-40, 43, 54, 57, 60, 78, 89, 96
*Ksatriya varna*, 52
Kumāra gupta, 14, 36, 137
Kurku, 22
*Kuṣānas*, 15, 26, 50
Kuśnagara, 151

Languages, 128-30
Learning, advanced seats of, 59-60
Levi, Sylvain, 52
Lichchhavi, 93
Literature, 128-29
*Lokāyatikas*, 66

Mādurai, 172
Magadh, 60, 61, 109
*Magi-dvijas*, 25
*Mahābhārata*, 16, 24, 44, 56, 70, 96, 116, 133, 134, 136, 138, 146, 148, 165, 175, 178, 179, 183
Māhākala temple, 17
*Mahāpātakas*, 82, 178
Maharaja Pravara Sena, 14
Mahāsthāngarh, 20
*Mahāvaṁsa*, 18
Mahāvīra, 32, 113, 114
Mahāvīra Jain, 12, 103
*Mahāyāna*, 110
Mahendra Vikrama Vaman, 141
Maity, S.K., 20
Majumdar, R.C., 13, 20, 173
*Manavatantrā*, 16
*Maṇḍalas*, 129
*Manimekhali*, 18, 114, 146
Maṅikhaliputra, 114
*Manjusri*, 110
*Mantra*, 36
Manu, 93, 94, 96, 97
Marco Polo, 60
Marriage, 87-90, 182
  forms of, 89
Mathūrā, 151, 172
*Mattavítāsa*, 141
Ma-twan-tin, 26
Mauryas, 37
Mauryan society, 14
*Medtayanana*, 80
Megasthenes, 18, 20, 34, 39, 40, 47, 151, 176, 180
*Meghadutam*, 17, 138
Mesopotamia, 23, 182
*Milindapāñho*, 18, 57, 150, 172
*Mīmāmisa*, 82
*Mitakshara*, 42
*Mlechchhas*, 25, 41
Mohanjo-Daro, 23, 24
*Moksha*, 32, 51, 69, 105
Mongoloids, 21, 22, 29
Mount Abu temples, 162
*Mṛchhakaṭika*, 34, 45, 78, 93, 140
*Mudrārākshasa*, 37, 140
*Mukti*, 105
Mundāri, 22
Munshi, K.M., 21
Music and dance, 168-69
Musical instruments, 169
Nāgās, 22, 29
Nagaraka, 78
Nāgārjuna, 115, 161
Nāgārjunakoṇḍa, 183
Nagasena, 18
Nakash-i-Rustam inscription, 25
Nālandā, 20, 62, 64
Nālandā inscription, 63
*Nāmakaraṇa*, 80
*Nārada*, 44, 98, 133
*Nātya Śāstra*, 168
Neo-Hinduism, 115
New Guinea, 22
*Nididhyāsana*, 54, 57, 58
*Nirgrantha*, 112
*Nirvāna*, 110
*Nishādas*, 22, 28, 30, 37, 40
*Nishkramaṇa*, 80
*Niyoga*, 16
Nordic Aryans, 21

Occupations, 39, 183
Odanatapuri, 20
*Odombeores*, 15
Ornaments, 175-77

Padmapāni, 110
*Padma Purāṇa*, 133
Painting, 165-168, 170-72
*Paiśacha*, 89
*Pāka-yajñas*, 71
*Palladakol*, 162
Pāli and Prakrit Literature, 143-46
*Paṇas*, 45
*Pañchāla*, 25, 150
  Parishad, 59
Pañchama, 40
*Pañcha-maha yajñas*, 71
Pāṇḍavas, 28, 139
*Pañditrupāttu*, 146
Pāṇini, 65, 128, 142
*Paraśurama Kuṇda*, 28
*Pratiloma*, 39
*Parinirvana*, 62
*Parivrājākas*, 34, 87
Parthians, 26
*Paṭachitras*, 166
Pāṭaliputra, 113, 140, 151, 172
Patañjali, 128, 142
*Patiloka*, 96

*Penance*, 81-83
*Periyapurānam*, 147
Philippines, 22
*Pinḍa*, 42
Pitalkhora cave, 166
*Pitryajna*, 71
Pole Star, 90
Polygamy, 92
Prabhavati Gupta, 14
*Prājapatya*, 89
*Prākraprakāsa*, 144
*Pratisarga*, 16
Pravara, 42-43
*Prāyascitta*, 16, 81
Prostitutes, 93, 94
Ptolomy, 19
*Pukkasas*, 37, 41
*Punarbhū*, 93, 98, 99
*Purāṇas*, 16, 17, 27, 28, 37, 133, 183
Purāṇo-Tantric religion, 115-16
*Purushartha*, 116
*Purushamedha*, 71, 73
*Puruṣha-Sūkta*, 32, 37

Radhakrishnan, 103, 107
*Raghuvaṁsa*, 138
Rajagṛaha, 151
Rajasthan, 27
*Rājasūya*, 73
*Rājataraṅgiṇi*, 16
Ramgarh cave inscription, 94
Rāmā, 136
*Rāmacharitā*, 16
*Rāmāyaṇa*, 18, 56, 134, 135, 146, 183
Ramakrishna Mission, 20
*Ratnadadhi*, 63
Ratnasāgara, 63
Rawson, P.S., 150
Remarried widow, 98
*Ṛg Veda*, 16, 20, 128, 179
*Ritusaṁhara*, 17
Rohilkhand, 25, 27
*Rishis*, 43
*Ṛta-Dharma*, 107

Sacrifices, 71
*Sahajayaña*, 111
*Saivism*, 117
Sakas, 50
Śakuntalā, 93
*Sāmaveda*, 129, 168
*Saṁhitas*, 129
*Saṁskāras*, 36, 78, 80, 81, 82, 87
categories, 79-80
Sāñchi, 151, 164, 172
*Sannyasa*, 51, 68, 84, 85, 86, 105
*Sannyāsins*, 83
Sāntali, 22
Sārnāth, 163, 165
Sanskrit Drama, 140-42
Satavahanas, 52
*Sāvitrī*, 97
Sculpture, 163-64, 170
Sex relation, 87-89
Sexual enjoyments, 95
Sexual intercourse, 91, 95
*Siddha-composition*, 65
*Śilāditya*, 14
*Silappādikāram*, 18
*Sita*, 97
Slavery, 43-44
Smith, V.A., 23, 114
*Smṛtis*, 16, 43-44, 61, 83
*Snātaka*, 68, 69, 87
Social Change, 50-83
Sompur, 20
*Soma-yajña*, 71, 72
South Indian languages, 145-46
*Spiṇḍas*, 42
Spiritual homogeneity, 88
Sri Lanka, 19, 136, 144
*Śrāddhas*, 16, 42
*Śramaṇas*, 34
*Śraūta-Sūtras*, 16
*Stridhana*, 98
Sūdras, 32, 37, 43, 50, 57, 78
*Sūdra-varṇa*, 39
*Sūpaśāstra*, 177
*Suśruta-Saṁhita*, 61
*Sūtas*, 17, 52
*Sutta-Pītaka*, 111
*Śvayaṁvara*, 35
*Śvetāmbaras*, 113, 114, 143
*Svetaśvatara Upanishad*, 102

*Taittirya Brahmaṇa*, 87
Takshasila, 59
Tamil literature, 147
*Tantra*, 183
Tantrism, 64
*Tarpaṇa*, 71
Teacher-student relation, 58-60

Terracotta, 167-68
*Tirthankaras*, 112
*Tolkāppiyam*, 145
Toramāṇa, 27
*Tri-piṭakas*, 111, 144
Triśanku, 69

Udayagiri cave, 161
Uddalaka Āruni, 59
Udambara, 56
Ujjain, 138
*Upādhyāya*, 54
*Upakhyānas*, 17
*Upānayāna*, 55
*Upanishads*, 129, 131, 183
Upaṭākas, 82
*Upāsana*, 78

Vaśistha, 98
*Vaiśhnava veda*, 116
*Vaiśyas*, 32, 33, 35, 36, 37, 38, 39-40, 43, 50, 54, 57, 60, 78, 96
Vaidyas, 39, 95
*Vaiśeśhika Sūtrē*, 70
Vaisnavism, 52
*Vajrāyana*, 111
*Vākātaka*, 14
Valabhi University, 64
Valabhipura, 64
Vālmiki, 135
*Vaṁśa*, 16
*Vāṁśāmcharita*, 17
*Vānapratha*, 68, 69, 83-84, 87, 98, 105
Varānasi, 59, 64, 151
Vardhamāna, 112
*Varṇas*, 38, 50, 105
*Varṇa-Āśrama Jati*, 13
Varṇa System, 53, 182
*Vasiṣtha*, 43
*Vātsyāyanas*, 75, 76, 90, 91, 98
*Vedas*, 16
Vedāntas, 148
Vijayāṇka, 97
*Vikramaśila*, 20, 54
*Vinaya-piṭaka*, 111
*Vishnu*, 87
Vishṇugupta, 40
*Vishnu-dharma purāṇa*, 96, 166
*Viśvakarma puja*, 183
*Viśvamitrā*, 15, 38, 43
*Vratyoshṭamas*, 35, 55, 73
*Vyavahara*, 16

Women, status of, 87-90, 95, 100

Yāavas, 116
*Yajñas*, 36
*Yajñavalkya*, 46, 52, 82, 98
*Yajnavalkya Smṛti*, 75
*Yajurveda*, 117, 128
*Yakshas*, 138, 163
*Yamapats*, 166
*Yantra*, 111
*Yati*, 84, 85, 86
*Yatishotma*, 89
*Yavana*, 41
*Yaugandharayāna*, 140
Yoga, 109
Yuan Chwang, 62, 63, 64, 65
Yudhiṣthira, 24, 135
*Yuga-pūraṇa*, 25